CALIFORNIA:

A HISTORY

OF

UPPER AND LOWER CALIFORNIA

FROM THEIR FIRST DISCOVERY TO THE PRESENT TIME,

COMPRISING

AN ACCOUNT OF

THE CLIMATE, SOIL, NATURAL PRODUCTIONS, AGRICULTURE, COMMERCE,

&c.

A FULL VIEW OF

THE MISSIONARY ESTABLISHMENTS AND CONDITION OF THE FREE AND DOMESTICATED INDIANS.

WITH AN APPENDIX RELATING TO

STEAM NAVIGATION IN THE PACIFIC.

ILLUSTRATED WITH A NEW MAP, PLANS OF THE HARBOURS,
AND NUMEROUS ENGRAVINGS.

BY ALEXANDER FORBES, ESQ.

LONDON:
SMITH, ELDER AND CO. CORNHILL.
1839.

FATHER ANTONE PEYRI (Ætat.)

Missionary at San Luis Rey Upper California.

from 1799 to 1832.

Published by Smith, Elder & Co. Cornhill.

TO

JOHN FORBES, M.D. F.R.S.

&c. &c. &c.

My dear Brother,

I herewith send you, such as it is, my work on California; in which I have attempted to give some account of that very remarkable and little-known country. If, on perusing my papers, you deem them worthy of publication, let them be published; but, in that case, you must not only be the Editor of my book but its foster-father : and as it usually happens with adopted children that they are more indebted to those who train them to manhood than to those who give them existence, so it may well be that my "California", if found to possess any merit by the public, shall owe more to your care than to the capability of its original author. I need not tell you how little accustomed

I am to literary labours of any kind; and you well know that my present position puts it even out of my power to take advantage of those emendations or improvements which are apt to suggest themselves during the progress of a work through the press. In all these things, then, I claim the help of your more experienced hand, and trust implicitly to your judgment and kindness.

Should you decide on publishing my history of California, I request that you will place this letter at its head, as a DEDICATION to yourself; as, whatever be its fate as a book, I am most desirous that it should, at least, bear witness to all those of its readers who know either you or me, with what sincere esteem and regard

I always am, my dear Brother,

Yours faithfully and affectionately,

ALEXANDER FORBES.

Tepic, 22nd. October, 1835.

PREFACE.

THE chief part of the following work was transmitted from Mexico to the editor three years ago. Circumstances, which it is unnecessary here to mention, deferred its publication to the present time. This delay, although in some respects to be regretted, has been attended with several advantages. It has enabled the author to forward to the editor some additional matter of importance, particularly the account of the recent declaration of independence by California. This and other additions have been inserted in their proper places.

In another respect, also, the delay in the publication has perhaps been rather fortunate than otherwise. The changed relations of California with Mexico, and the new relations with other states thence likely to accrue;—the existing position of Mexico in regard both to France and England;—and, above all, the great interest just now excited in the commercial world by the projected improvement between the different Spanish-American states and between Great Britain and them, by means of Steam Navigation ;—all these will, probably, render the work more attractive to many readers at the present moment, than it would have been three years ago.

The greater part of the contents of the volume, however, the editor believes, stands in no need of any adventitious help to make it interesting to most readers.   The ample details which it contains of the *Spiritual conquest* (as it has been called) of California,—that is, of the entire subjection of the native inhabitants by the Spanish missionary priests ; and the striking view which it presents of the singular system of civil polity and ecclesiastical slavery which has been the result of this conquest, and still exists in full activity—are matters which cannot fail to engage the attention of all who delight to view man in novel and strange aspects, and under the influence of circumstances calculated to try the good and the evil parts of his nature.   The editor believes that the present volume contains a much fuller account of all these things than is to be found in any other work.

An interest of a very different kind will attach

to that portion of the volume—a large portion—which relates to the natural character and productions of the country, the actual state of its agriculture and commerce, and its capabilities as a field for European colonization. In this respect the present work seems calculated to give rise to much speculation, if not to important enterprises of a practical kind. Respecting the suggestion thrown out by the author, of the chance now offered to the people of Great Britain of getting a footing in Upper California, either by the voluntary cession of the country to the state, or to a company, as a consideration for debts not likely to be otherwise discharged, the editor offers no opinion : it seems, however, to be one not unworthy the attention of the parties involved in the public loan to Mexico, or even of the British government itself.

In preparing the MS. for the press, the editor has, in accordance with the author's wish, added in the body of the volume, various brief extracts, here and there, from the works of travellers who have visited California, and which he thought would render the original account more interesting, by giving some additional details. His

authorities are here, chiefly, La Pérouse, Vancouver, Langsdorff and Beechey,—all of whose works
contain very interesting, and, no doubt, very accurate accounts of the state of the country at the
time they visited it. These additions, and the
arrangement of the original materials in a somewhat more book-like shape, are all the share that
the editor can claim in the present work. The
author wishes to be considered responsible for
everything else whether matter of fact or matter of
opinion.

For the matter in the Appendix, however, the
editor is solely responsible ; but he trusts the
author will not hesitate to sanction an addition
which must prove both useful and interesting to
his readers.

The first document in the appendix—the account
of the ports of California by Capt. Hall—is so intimately connected with the subject of the work, that
it cannot fail to be regarded as an important addition to its contents ; and the editor regrets that he
neglected to apply for the information at an earlier
period, in order that it might have been incorporated with the topographical details in the third
chapter of the second part of the volume.

The remaining documents in the appendix—those relating to the projected plan of Steam Navigation in the Pacific, and a more speedy communication between the western coasts of the American continent and England,—likewise appear to the editor of too much importance in themselves and too intimately connected with the interests of the countries described in the work, to be withheld from the reader. Whatever tends to facilitate and improve the navigation and commerce of the more southern states, must exert a powerful influence on the condition of California, a country which will be found to be pre-eminently calculated to be the granary of South America, and whose present emancipated condition will, doubtless, greatly augment its commerce generally. It cannot be for a moment doubted that if the projected line of navigation were established between Valparaiso and Panama, it would speedily be prolonged northward, to Guatemala, Acapulco and San Blas on the Mexican coast; and from thence to Upper California, either by the Pacific coast to San Diego, Santa Barbara, Monterey, and San Francisco, or along the Gulf northward to the Rio Colorado. The editor has learned from a gentleman acquainted with the

navigation of those seas, that not only the Gulf
of California is perfectly navigable by steam vessels
to its upper extremity, but that the Rio Colorado is
so also, up to its junction with the Gila. As to the
probability of the speedy accomplishment of the
designs of the projected company, the editor is not
in a situation to pronounce an opinion; but when
we consider with what gigantic steps STEAM has
proceeded since its birth, the wonders it has already
wrought in its mere infancy, and the wealth and
enterprize of British merchants,—there certainly
seems no more reason for doubting that the splendid
scheme will be realized at no distant date, than
there can be any question as to the vast benefits
its accomplishment must confer upon the countries
to which it refers.

By the message of the President of the United
States to the two Houses of Congress, of the 4th
instant, it is clear that by the convention between
Russia and the United States, made in April, 1824,
no settlements on the N.W. coast were to be formed
by Russian subjects, or under the authority of Russia, southward of North latitude, 50° 40'. Nevertheless, long before that convention and ever since,
Russia has held her settlement of La Bodega, in

North lat.38° 19′, as shown by the map. It is not in accordance with the usual spirit of the United States, in enforcing the due fulfilment of all treaties affecting their boundaries, to have acquiesced so long in this flagrant infraction; but, perhaps, as the Russian intrusion was not upon their territories, but upon those of Mexico, they did not think it worth their while to complain. However, by the refusal of Russia to renew the above convention, it appears that the Emperor does not wish that his subjects settled southward of 50° 40′ North latitude, should be subject to any molestation, or that they should be prevented from making fresh settlements in other places.

The editor does not think that the attention of the governments of Mexico, the United States, and Great Britain, has been sufficiently drawn to Russian policy on the N.W. coast of America.

The editor cannot close this prefatory notice without expressing, in the author's name and his own, the obligations they owe to their friends Capt. Smyth, R.N., R. C. Wyllie, Esq. and John Hall, Esq. for their kind assistance in rendering the work more worthy of the reader's attention. For nearly all the pictorial illustrations the author is indebted to the elegant pencil of Capt. Smyth, which has never failed to perpetuate the more remarkable scenes of the numerous countries visited by him. The plans of all the harbours delineated on the map (with the exception of San Francisco, copied from Capt. Beechey's excellent chart in the Admiralty,) have been furnished by Capt. Hall from his own original surveys. To Mr. Wyllie, whose former residence in Mexico rendered his opinion important on many points, the editor is indebted for several valuable suggestions and much active assistance during the progress of the work through the press.

J. F.

Chichester, Dec. 24, 1838.

CONTENTS.

CHAPTER IV.

PART II.

UPPER CALIFORNIA.

CHAPTER I.

CHAPTER II.

CHAPTER III.

CHAPTER IV.

CHAPTER V.

CHAPTER VI.

CHAPTER VII.

CHAPTER VIII.

APPENDIX.

ILLUSTRATIONS.

N.B. In the wood-cut of the Californian Plough, p. 248, the small wedge-shaped figure is intended to represent a section of the *sole* or main piece of the Plough.

CALIFORNIA.

THE extensive tract of country comprised under
the general name of CALIFORNIA, or the CALI-
FORNIAS, constitutes, at present, part of the Mexican Republic, and was formerly included in the
Vice-royalty of New Spain. It extends along the
border of the great Pacific Ocean, which bounds it
on the west. The northern limit of the country
actually settled by the Spaniards, is the Bay of San
Francisco, the entrance of which lies in 37° 48′ N.
lat.; but right of territory is claimed by the Mexican
government much further north; indeed, far beyond
the Russian settlement of Bodega which lies in lat.
38° 19′. The southern boundary is Cape San Lucas, the extremity of the Peninsula of Lower California, and lies in N. lat. 22° 48′. The longitude
of Cape San Lucas is 109° 47′ W. and that of San
Francisco 122° 27″ W.; consequently the direction
of the coast is towards the north-west. This extensive country is bounded on the east by the Gulph of

California, the Rio Colorado or Red River, and the Indian territory, which also limits it on the north.

. Since the division of the Mexican republic into federal states, the whole of California has been erected into what is termed a " territory," which differs from a state in this, that it has not an elective governor or legislature, but is under the immediate control of the general government of Mexico, which appoints its governor, under the name of Commandant-general, and all the subordinate officers, civil and military.

Although now constituting only one territory or province, in a political sense, this extensive region has always been considered as two distinct countries; and indeed they are well entitled to be so considered, both from their natural differences and their civil history. The name of CALIFORNIA was for nearly two hundred years exclusively applied to the great Peninsula which is now termed Old or Lower California, and which is arbitrarily bounded on the north by a line drawn from the top of the Gulf of California to the shore of the Pacific, considerably to the southward of the port of San Diego. After the discovery and settlement by the Spaniards of the country to the north of this peninsula, and which was also named California, as being part of the same tract of coast and inhabited by the same race of people, the distinctive appellations of Upper and Lower, or New and Old California became necessary, and have since been universally applied;—the peninsula being termed *Lower*, as being in a lower degree of latitude, and, of course, *Old*, from its earlier settlement. When spoken of conjointly, the two countries have been and are still frequently designated THE CALIFORNIAS, more especially by English navigators.

The principal object of the present work is to give an account of the Upper Province, this being the only one which is of much importance: it seems, however, necessary to take some notice of the Lower also, not merely from the intimate geographical and political relations which exist between the two countries, but because the history of both is closely connected, and that of the one throws light on the the settlement and actual condition of the other. On account of its earlier settlement I shall commence with the Lower province; and shall endeavour to compress into as small a space as possible what seems necessary to be said respecting it.

PART I.

LOWER CALIFORNIA.

PORTRAIT OF A NATIVE INDIAN.

Pub.d by Smith Elder & C.o Cornhill

CHAP. I.

Old or Lower California was discovered in the year 1534 by a squadron fitted out for purposes of discovery by the great Cortez, and commanded by Grijalva. This expedition sailed from the coast of Guatemala and soon reached the shores of California. The adventurers put into a harbour in the Gulf, in what they supposed to be an island and which they named Santa Cruz. This supposed island, however, is part of the peninsula of California, and the harbour is that now known by the name of La Paz; but there is an island lying off this harbour which is still called Santa Cruz. The companion of Grijalva, on this occasion, was Mendoza, who commanded the other ship; and Ximenes was pilot. Both of these perished during the expedition, the former in a mutiny of his men headed it is said by Ximenes, and Ximenes himself by the Natives in the bay of La Paz, together with twenty other Spaniards. The issue of this voyage was altogether so unsatisfactory that Cortez resolved to pursue the discovery himself; and, in the following year fitted out three ships at the same part of Guatemala, called Tehuantepec, which he himself joined when they reached the port of Chiametla, having marched over land from Mexico with a large retinue of soldiers, negro slaves, settlers and priests. He soon reached Santa Cruz (La Paz) and sent back some of the ships for the people and the provisions which he had left behind. The country was found so barren as to afford no sustenance to his armament; and the imperfect navigation of that day rendered the transport difficult and dangerous, even from so short a distance as the opposite coast. Only one vessel is said to have returned and with a very imperfect supply of stores. But in the mean time Cortez explored the gulph to the northward, visiting both shores: and it is believed that he ascertained that California was neither an island nor an Archipelago, as had been supposed. For some time after this the Gulph of California was named the *Sea of Cortez :* it was also called the *Red Sea* (El mar Rojo) either from resembling the Red Sea of the old world in its shape, or from the discoloration of its waters in its northern part by the Rio Colorado or Red River. After many labors and dangers Cortez returned to the port of Acapulco recalled by the machinations of his rivals and enemies in Mexico; but he continued to prosecute the

discovery of the new countries by means of ships
at his own cost, and commanded by his own officers.
The principal of these was Francisco de Ulloa. This
officer in 1537 sailed with three ships and continued nearly for the space of two years exploring the
different shores of the gulf up to almost its northern
point. The expedition of Ulloa confirmed the previous report of the extreme barenness of California
and the rudeness and poverty of the natives, who
were found quite naked. He saw the indigenous
goat (Argali) and observed some vessels of clay in
the possession of the Indians, a circumstance which
escaped the notice of several future travellers.

Many subsequent attempts to explore and settle
California, were made by the Viceroys of new Spain
and also by private adventurers, but with little or no
results of consequence for nearly a century. In
1562-3 Juan Rodriguez Cabrillo explored the western
coast of the peninsula, reaching as high as lat. 63°.
In 1596, in the Vice-royalty of Don Gaspar de
Zunniga, Count of Monte Rey, Don Sebastian Viscayno commanded an expedition to the gulf, and
made some effort to settle the country permanently
by establishing a garrison at the old station of Santa
Cruz, which he named La Paz from the peaceable
deportment of the inhabitants. General Viscayno
surveyed the coast a hundred leagues to the north
of this and found the inhabitants less peaceable,

having had some of his people killed by them. Owing to the want of provisions and the extreme barrenness of the coast, the attempt was abandoned, and Viscayno returned to New Spain at the end of the same year. A still more extensive expedition sailed, under the same Commander in 1602, to explore the west coast of the peninsula, and proved very successful, as far as related to the examination of the coast. Viscayno, in this voyage not only examined the port of Magdalena and other places on the west coast of the peninsula; but sailing nothwards beyond the limits of this, discovered in Upper California, the harbour of San Diego, and Monterey (so called after the Viceroy) and San Francisco, which last, as we have seen, is still the northern limit of the Spanish settlements. The coast was explored but imperfectly, as far north as the latitude of 43°.

This part of the coast was visited about twenty-four years previously by Sir Francis Drake, who remained some time in the harbour of San Francisco, and explored the interior to some distance. He named the country New Albion, and took possession of it for England, not being aware that it had been previously visited by the Spaniards under Cabrillo. Both Viscayno and Drake recognised the fertility of this country, and noticed some of the principal productions both of the vegetable and animal kingdom.

The Indians were found to be mild and friendly, resembling those in the lower province. Sir Francis Drake mistook the common head dress of some of them, which is worn around the head, somewhat in the manner of a crown, as the emblem of royalty, and considered the gift made of this to him, by one of the chiefs, as the abdication of the sovereignty of the country in favor of Queen Elizabeth!

There still prevailing among the inhabitants of New Spain, a strong belief of the great riches of California, both in gold and pearls, but particularly the latter, successive expeditions visited the coasts of the gulf, after brief intervals, through the whole of this century. Many also were set on foot not so much for the purpose of acquiring wealth, as with the view of converting the Indians; the most anxious desire for effecting this being prevalent not only among the religious orders of Mexico, but at the court of the successive monarchs in Old Spain. In 1615 Captain Juan Iturbi made a voyage to the Gulf at his own expence, and on his return to Mexico inflamed the existing desire for the conquest of California, by the display of a great quantity of valuable pearls which he brought with him. Father Venegas states, that for one of these pearls Iturbi paid 900 crowns as the King's fifth alone, making its value at least £1000. In the course of three successive years, viz. 1632, 1633, and 1634, Captain Francisco de Ortega made three voyages to the same ports; and two years later Carboneli, his pilot, followed his example. In 1648, Admiral Cassanate again made an attempt at settlement, under the authority and at the expence of government, taking with him priests for the conversion of the Indians : but like all his predecessors he was repulsed not by the natives but by the insuperable barrenness of the country. The early histories of California narrate many other attempts equally unsuccessful, as that of Pinadero in 1664, of Luzenilla in 1668, and of Admiral Otondo in 1683. The expedition of this officer was more considerable than most that had preceded it, and was distinguished by the company of the Jesuit missionary, Father Kühn, formerly a professor in a German University, and afterwards famous for his exploits in the conversion of the Indians, under the Spanish name of Kino. Otondo staid some considerable time in the country, and traversed a considerable portion of the interior, the zealous Fathers exerting all their powers in converting and baptizing the natives, but with such indifferent success that he also finally abandoned it, with the whole of his establishment, within a period of three years. This expedition, fruitless as it was, cost the Mexican government no less a sum than 225,400 dollars*. The last of these attempts made under the

* Venegas, Vol. 1 p. 224.

direction of the military and civil powers, was that of Itamarra who made a fresh descent at his own expence in the year 1694, and with the same fruitless results as all his predecessors.

Some years before this on the return of Admiral Otondo, the Viceroy and Council of Mexico had come to the resolution that the settlement of this country was impracticable by the means hitherto adopted, and that it should be no more attempted at the public expence : it was, however, decided at the same time, that the reduction of the peninsula should be recommended to the Society of Jesuits, and that a fixed sum should be paid to them for this purpose out of the King's treasury. This recommendation was most cordially received by this zealous Society, and Father Kino and the other missionaries, who had accompanied Otondo, kindled yet higher among their brethren their desire for the spiritual conquest of California, which was destined, in fact, to take place under their indefatigable zeal and courage. In contemplating what was thus effected, it is no wonder that the historian of California, himself a member of this holy order, should regard the cause as hallowed and the agents as under the protection of heaven. " The great conqueror, Hernando Cortez (he says) several times employed in the conquest of California, the whole force he could raise. His example stimulated many private per-

sons : even governors, admirals, and viceroys made
the attempt. At last the kings of Spain themselves
took the scheme into their own hands; yet the result
of all such vast expences, such powerful efforts was,
that the reduction of California was given over
as impracticable. And so indeed it was by the
means made use of by men ; but not by those which
God had chosen. Arms and power were the means
on which man relied for the success of this enterprize; but it was the will of heaven that this triumph
should be owing to the meekness and courtesy of
his ministers, to the humiliation of the cross and the
power of his word. God seemed only to wait till
human nature acknowledged its weakness, to display the strength of his Almighty arm, confound-
ing the pride of the world by means of the weakest
instruments."*

In the intended reduction of California under the
new system, Father Kino was the presiding genius
as he had been the originator of the plan. This
excellent and extraordinary man had been professor
of mathematics at Ingoldstadt where he was in high
favour with the electoral house of Bavaria. In
consequence of a vow made to Saint Francis Xavier
at a time when he was not expected to live, he left

---

* Noticia de la California y de su Conquista temporal y espiritual
hasta el tiempo presente. Por el Padre Miguel Venegas. Madrid,
1575.

his professorship and came to America full of zeal
for the conversion of the heathen. "Proposing to
himself (says Father Venegas) this holy apostle as
his model, he imitated his virtues and all the other
qualities of his seraphic mind." The new Missionary was certainly a man of extraordinary talents as
well as virtues, and his whole life proved how well
he fulfilled the vow which had transported him from
the lecture-room of Ingoldstadt to the savage wilds
of America. But in the conquest of California he
fortunately met with associates no less able and
willing than himself among the learned men of his
own order, and particularly in the Fathers Salvatierra, Ugarte and Piccolo, afterwards so distinguished for their labours and success in this undertaking. To Salvatierra the direction of the first
attempt was confided, Kino remaining on the opposite coast of Cinaloa and Ugarte in Mexico, all
equally active, in their respective stations, in promoting the great design. The spirit being once
kindled, the rich among the laity as well as the religious orders in New Spain, contributed largely to
the outfit of the expedition, and settled sums for
the endowment of the new missions expected to be
established. The government took no part in the
enterprise, further than granting the Fathers permission to enter the country, to enlist soldiers on
their own account, and to have sole authority over

all concerned in the expedition and in the intended missions—requiring only, in return, that the country should be taken possession of in the name of the king of Spain, and that the expedition should be in no way burthensome to the government.

On the 10th. October 1697, Father Salvatierra sailed from the port of Yaqui on the eastern side of the gulph, with his small band of five soldiers only and their commander, and on the third day reached California. For some days they were employed in looking out for a convenient station, and at length fixed on the bay of San Dionisio, ten leagues north of San Bruno where Admiral Otondo had pitched his camp. There on the 19th. October they landed, and finding a convenient spot near a spring of water about a league and half from the shore, they pitched their tents and transported from the ships their stores of cattle and provisions, the good father being the most active labourer of the party. "Here (says Father Venegas) the barracks of the little garrison was built and a line of circumvallation thrown up. In the centre a tent was pitched for a temporary chapel; before it was erected a crucifix with a garland of flowers, and every thing being disposed in the best manner possible, the image of our Lady of Loreto, the Patroness of the Conquest, was brought in procession from the ship and placed with proper solemnity. On the 25th. formal possession was taken of the country in the name of the king of Spain and the Indies.

Before proceeding further with the history of these true soldiers of the cross, and the minute but not uninteresting warfare which they maintained for so many years against the rude natives of California and its still ruder soil, until at length they triumphed effectually over the former and as much over the latter as was possible,—it may be well to notice briefly the nature and extent of the obstacles they had to contend against.

In all the numerous attempts that had been made to make a settlement in this peninsula, it was invariably to the rugged and unproductive nature of the country, not to the opposition of the natives that the failures were attributable. Like all the aboriginal tribes encountered by the Spaniards in America, the Californians were a feeble and weak-hearted people; and although when irritated or oppressed, they not seldom turned on their tyrants; and, when revenge could be safely indulged, did not hesitate to cut off openly or by stratagem such as fell into their power; still they never offered any effectual resistance to the invaders, hundreds or even thousands of them being often kept in awe by a mere handful of armed Europeans. These poor people had good reason both to fear and hate the Spaniards, as they were often greatly maltreated by the mili-

c

tary and commercial adventurers who visited their
country before the Jesuits ; and more especially by
the traffickers for pearls, by whom the Indians were
frequently kidnapped and forcibly compelled to act
as divers.   Yet it was remarkable that, from the
beginning, they showed little unwillingness to be
present at or even to share in the ceremonies of the
Catholic religion, (which were seldom lost sight of by
the adventurers of those days, however stained with
crimes) or to benefit from the supplies of food which
they derived from their visiters.   At the period
of the landing of the Jesuits, the natives seem to
have been in precisely the same condition as to civilization, as when first visited by Grijalva one hundred and sixty years before.   They were little
advanced from the rudest state of barbarism.   Properly speaking, they had neither houses nor clothes,
although they made use of temporary huts formed
of boughs of trees and covered with reeds, and the
women wore girdles or imperfect petticoats formed
also of reeds : the men were entirely naked except
that they wore ornaments for the head composed of
feathers, shells or seeds.   They lived by hunting
and fishing and on the spontaneous produce of the
soil.   They cultivated no species of grain or esculent
vegetable, and they seemed to possess no other arts
than what were necessary for the manufacture of
nets and bows and arrows for catching prey by sea

and land, and for the construction of their imperfect clothing and ornaments. Some of the tribes had a few vessels of clay, but their chief articles for containing both solids and liquids were constructed of reeds. Even their means of transport on the water, were rude rafts formed of bulrushes, no boats or canoes of wood or hides being found among them. They seem scarcely to have had any fixed forms of government or religion; although the different villages and tribes submitted, on important occasions, to the direction and rule of some one or more who were distinguished by their age, strength or other natural gifts; and there were also a class of persons among them, who were the ministers of some superstitious observances, and the pretenders to preternatural powers in the prediction or production of future events and in the infliction or cure of diseases. These people were termed Sorcerers (Hechiceros) by the Missionaries; although Father Venegas has the boldness to assert that " it cannot be thought that these poor creatures had any commerce or entered into a compact with apostate spirits, or that they received any instructions from them." It is, however, very true, that whether deluded or deluding, these sorcerers or priests exerted a powerful influence over the minds of their countrymen. This influence was greatly heightened by their being the exclusive professors

and practisers of the important art of healing.
" What greatly strengthened their authority (says
Venegas) was their being the only physicians from
whom they could hope to be relieved in their pains
and distempers : and whatever was the medicine, it
was always administered with great ostentation and
solemnity.   One remedy (he continues) was very
remarkable; and the good effect sometimes produced
by it, greatly heightened the reputation of the
operator.   They applied to the suffering part of the
patient's body the Chacuaco, which is a tube formed
out of a very hard black stone, and through this
they sometimes sucked and at other times blew, but
both as hard as they were able, supposing that thus
the disease was either exhaled or dispersed.   Sometimes the tube was filled with cimarron or wild
tobacco lighted, and the smoke was either blown
out or sucked in according to the doctor's direction.
This powerful caustic (adds the historian) sometimes,
without any other remedy, has been known entirely
to remove the disorder."   Of this fact such of our
modern surgeons, as are in the habit of prescribing
local irritation or scarification, by inflammable sub-
stances termed moxas, will entertain no doubt.

At the time California was visited by the Jesuits,
the whole of the country explored by them from
cape San Lucas as far north as the 28th degree
of north latitude, was thinly and irregularly peopled

by numerous tribes more or less stationary in their
rude villages or encampments, differing very little in
their general habits and condition, yet sufficiently
marked to be distinguished by fixed names, and
speaking different languages or different dialects of
the same. The best informed among the fathers,
particularly Father Taraval, of whom we shall
hereafter have occasion to speak, believed that although there were many varieties of dialect, there
were only three languages, decidedly differing from
one another so as to constitute natural distinctions.
These in their respective spheres, extended, as might
be supposed, from sea to sea, dividing the peninsula
lengthwise into three nations; the Pericues occu-
pying the southern division as far north as the bay
of La Paz, about the 25th degree of latitude; the
Monquis the middle space extending a little to the
north of Loreto in about the 26th degree; and the
Cochimis, to the nothward of this, as far as the
country was explored. As would naturally happen,
in such a rude state of society, the limits of these
countries were not at all definite, and even the different people had quite different names given them
by their own or other tribes. In particular, it would
seem that the people of the south were as commonly termed Edues as Pericues, or those of the
north as often Laymones as Cochimis. Each of
these great divisions contained clans or tribes who

professed to be distinct from their neighbours, calling themselves by different names, using a somewhat different speech and demonstrating their na-
tionality by incessant feuds and petty wars with
their neighbours ; but it would be worse then useless to follow our authorities in taking any notice of
these, as this could only tend to confuse the reader.

The country inhabited by these people was and is
one of the most barren and unattractive to be found
in the temperate or hotter regions of the earth.
The peninsula of California is seven or eight hundred miles in length, and varies in breadth from
thirty to one hundred miles, the medium breadth
being from fifty to sixty.   It consists of an irregular
chain or broken groups of bare rocks, and hills interspersed with tracts of a sandy soil nearly as unproductive.   The greatest height of this mountain
ridge is rather less than 5000 feet.   In some sheltered spots where the soil has been left safe from
the torrents, there is a fertile mould ; but such spots
are very rare and of small extent.   Water is also
very scarce.   There are only two or three small
streams in the whole country, and springs of good
water are extremely infrequent. ...It would seem as
if the action of the heavy rains from the central
ridge of rocky hills and the encroachments of the
ocean on both its shores, had gradually washed away
the mould and soil from its surface, except where it

was of such a ponderous quality as sand, or where it was penned up by a barrier of rocks on all sides. In some places of this last kind, the soil was found remarkably fertile, and when they chanced to be in the vicinity of water, which was but seldom the case, the produce extracted from them by the industry of the new comers was sometimes marvellously great. Such oases were of no especial use to the natives, except in as far as they furnished the chief localities for the growth of the trees and plants which supplied them with nuts and berries. The extreme barrenness of the soil prevented the growth of trees of any magnitude, except in a very few spots of insignificant extent, insomuch that the missionaries were obliged, as we shall see hereafter, to send to the opposite coast of Cinaloa for the materials for constructing houses.

In this region, however, the fertility of the sea seemed to make amends for the barrenness of the land. The shores of California abound in the greatest variety of excellent fish, although from ignorance or stupidity the natives derived much less benefit from this exhaustless storehouse, than it was capable of affording. In one respect, indeed, this storehouse was too productive for their happiness; since it was the fame of its pearls which, ever since its first discovery, had attracted so many adventurers to its shores, bent on enriching themselves and alto-

gether regardless of the welfare or even lives of the
natives. " Great numbers (says Father Venegas)
resort to this fishery from the continent of New
Spain, New Galicia, Culiacan, Cinaloa and Sonora;
and the many violences committed by the adventurers, to satiate if possible their covetous temper,
have occasioned reciprocal complaints ; nor will they
ever cease (adds the good Father) while the desire
of riches, that bane of society, predominates in the
human breast.*"   And nothing can show more
strongly the pure and disinterested motives of the
Jesuits than the law which they obtained, after
much trouble, from the Mexican government, viz.
that all the inhabitants of California, including the
soldiers, sailors, and others under their command,
should be prohibited not only from diving for pearls
but from trafficking in them.   This law was the
cause of great and frequent discontent among the
military servants of the Fathers, and even threatened the loss of their conquest ; but it was nevertheless rigidly enforced by them during the whole
period of their rule. Fishing for pearls was not,
indeed, prohibited in the Gulf and along the shores
of California, but it was carried on by divers brought
from the opposite shores by the adventurers engaged in it.

Before returning to the history of Father Salva-

* Vol. i. p. 50.

tierra and his little band, I must be permitted to
make one remark. If the reader should be disposed to smile at the minuteness with which, now
or hereafter, we may dwell on the humble proceedings of the Fathers, and their children the Indians,
or may detail the puny wars of their Lilliputian
armies, we can only offer the excuse preferred by
the good Father Venegas in similar circumstances.
" These particulars (he says) may possibly appear
trifles not worth mentioning; but let me entreat the
reader to try their value in the balance of reason.
Let him reflect what an agreeable sight it must be,
even in the eyes of the divine Being himself, to see
men who might have acquired a large fortune by
secular employments, or lived in quiet and esteem
within the Order they had chosen, voluntarily banish
themselves from their country and relations, to visit
America; and when there, resign employments and
leave a tranquil life for disappointments and fatigues;
to live among savages, amidst distress and continual
danger of death, without any other motive, than the
conversion of the Indians. At least let every one
ask himself, whether any worldly interest whatever
could induce him to employ himself in such low and
obscure actions and amid such privations and dangers, and he will be convinced of the importance
and dignity which actions, contemptible in the eyes
of men, receive from the sublimity of the motives

which inspire them."*   It is, indeed, impossible to read the accounts of the settlement of the two Californias by the Spanish Missionaries without feeling the greatest admiration and reverence for the bold and pious men who undertook and accomplished the most arduous task of civilizing and christianizing these savage countries.   It may be true that the means they adopted to effect their ends were not always the wisest; that the Christianity they planted was often more of form than substance, and the civilization, in some respects, an equivocal good: still it cannot be denied that the motives of these excellent men were most pure, their benevolence unquestionable, their industry, zeal, and courage indefatigable and invincible.   Not only did they suffer every hardship without repining, but they shrunk not from death itself, which more than once thinned their ranks; and it is the crowning glory of their benevolent justice that they were as zealous in protecting the poor Indians from the oppression and cruelties of the Spanish soldiers, as they were in endeavouring to subject them to their own spiritual domination :

And Charity on works of love would dwell
In California's dolorous regions drear.†

* Vol. i. p. 230.   † Southey.

CHAP. II.

No sooner was the little settlement, described in the last chapter, made, than Father Salvatierra set about his office of converting the Indians. He began by endeavouring to learn their language and sought to gain their good will by all sorts of kindness and unsuspicious familiarity; rewarding all such as would consent to be catechised and to repeat prayers, with daily largesses of boiled maize, or pozzoli, of which the Indians were very fond. Indeed the pozzoli was more attractive than the Latin prayers, and they soon began to seek for the one without the other; and this being refused, they set about considering whether they might not obtain their ends by force. Accordingly, after some smaller attempts, such as stealing the good Father's horse and his goats, both for food, they made a regular attack on the camp on the 13th November. On this occasion it was thought that no less than 500 of the Indians assaulted their little entrenchments which were defended only by ten men; and

although Father Salvatierra would not allow the
soldiers to fire on the enemy until things came to
extremities, and although the great hope of safety
of the besieged, the paderero, burst in pieces on the
first discharge, still a few wounds and deaths among
the Indians inspired such terror among them that
they soon retreated, and speedily sent messengers
to sue for peace. This victory naturally raised to a
high pitch the courage and enthusiasm of the Spaniards. " At night," says Father Venegas, " solemn
thanks were returned to God, his most holy Mother,
and St. Stanislaus (whose festival it was) for his manifold favours. They adored the holy cross as the
standard of faith; they sang *ave* to our lady as
their captain, and unanimously determined to remain in that country." Nor did they fail to see in
all this affair manifest signs of divine protection.—
To say nothing of the defeat of 500 men by ten,
" it was observed (continues our authority) that
most of the arrows stuck in the *pedestal* of the
Cross, whilst both it and the tent which served for
the chapel, were untouched."

Shortly afterwards Father Francisco Maria Piccolo arrived from the opposite coast with fresh
supplies, and the resolution to continue with his
brethren in California. He was a worthy fellow
labourer of Salvatierra who was greatly comforted
by his arrival. The small garrison now set about

erecting some works of defence and buildings of a
more permanent character, viz. "a chapel for placing
our Lady in," and houses for the Fathers and Captain; the walls of stone and clay and the roofs of
thatch. The Fathers returned to their daily labors
of catechising and maize-distributing, and all went
on favourably for a few months; but the Indians at
length perceiving that the object of the Spaniards
was neither to fish for pearls nor to obtain them in
barter, but to introduce a new religion, they were
once more excited,—on this occasion by their
priests, whose power and revenues were manifestly
in jeopardy,—to try to drive their new teachers
from the country. They were, however, immediately dispersed by the muskets of the soldiers; and
peace being restored, the Fathers once more proceeded with their zealous labours. The first step
was to learn the language of the natives, (a step,
by the bye, which seems disregarded by the present
race of Californian missionaries) for the greater
conveniency of doing which, as well as a means of
security, " Father Piccolo (we are told) took upon
him to instruct the boys and girls, whom he caused
to come within the encampment; whilst, without it,
Father Salvatierra instructed the adults, and by this
mild measure, says Venegas, they had their sons as
so many hostages." In the month of June, a new
bark arrived with fresh stores of all sorts, and a

reinforcement of seven soldiers sent by Father Ugarte; and the Fathers having now pretty well learned the language, and being moreover provided with horses, began to carry their operations into the neighbouring country both north and south. In examining the country they crossed the peninsula to the shore of the Pacific, and established the mission of San Xavier under Father Piccolo, who took up his abode there in October, 1699. Early in the following year we are told that the number of settlers already in California, including the civilized Indians and Mestizos from the Mexican coast, amounted to no less than 600; but this great number was the source rather of weakness than strength, as the country as yet afforded scarcely any means of support to the new comers. They were consequently in the greatest straits; but could obtain no relief or assistance from the government. In the month of August of this year it is stated in an official document that " they had reduced the Indians for the space of of 50 leagues, to a settled obedience and founded four towns, with above six hundred christians, most of them young, and no less than two thousand adult catechumens." But these magnificent statements had a very unsubstantial foundation; as we find that, shortly after, some of the new missions were given up, the baptisms suspended, and the garrison, with the captain at its head, muti-

nying partly from want of pay and provisions, and
partly from impatience at the restraints put upon
them by the Fathers for oppressing and ill-using the
Indians. The Fathers, however, adhered firmly to
their principles, and discharged the refractory soldiers, retaining only a few of such as were faithful
to them. The dismissal of the whole military force
was, however, contemplated, should they not speedily
receive some pecuniary aid from Mexico. The discharge of the heavy debts already incurred was
confided to a bank which we fear is hardly solvent
in these degenerate times. " After the total reduction of the soldiers," says Father Salvatierra, in a
letter to his friend the solicitor of Guadalaxara,
" we shall consult on liquidating all arrears ; and if,
for want of a military force, our Californian sons
should send us to give an account to God, there
will still remain our Lady of Loreto, who unquestionably will pay the whole."

A great relief was afforded to the mission by a
supply of stores sent by Father Ugarte in the following spring, and still greater by the arrival of the
Father himself, on the 19th of March, who had at
length determined to unite his labours to those of
his brethren in California. This worthy man seems
to have had a more enlarged mind as well as a more
robust physical constitution than his brethren. On
being appointed to the new mission of San Xavier

de Viaundo, planted a short time previously by Father Piccolo, some distance from Loreto to the south-west in the midst of the Vigge mountains, he for the first time seems to have adopted the only principle on which colonies of any kind can be settled—making them support themselves. Although from the extreme barrenness of the country and the insufficiency of the protection afforded by the soldiers, this task had hitherto been deemed hopeless, Ugarte determined to make the trial; and as he knew that it could only succeed by a more systematic attempt at civilizing the natives, he lost no time in setting about this. In one respect his position at San Xavier was favourable, as the neighbourhood contained a much larger share of soil capable of cultivation than that of Loreto or other parts yet examined. With these views Father Ugarte began at once to learn the language and study the character of the natives, preparatory to his greater schemes; and to shew his confidence in them, he speedily dismissed the few soldiers he had with him, on account of their ill conduct; and remained alone among the Indians. The following account of the good Father's diurnal labours and general mode of proceeding with the Indians, and also the speedy results, is taken from Venegas and is at once picturesque and affecting.

" In the morning after saying mass, and at which

he obliged them to attend with order and respect, he gave a breakfast of pozoli to those who were to work, set them about building the church and houses for himself and his Indians, clearing the ground for cultivation, making trenches for the conveyance of water, holes for planting trees, or digging and preparing the ground for sowing. In the building part, father Ugarte was master, over-seer, carpenter, bricklayer, and labourer. For the Indians, though animated by his example, could neither by gifts or kind speeches be prevailed upon to shake off their innate sloth; and were sure to slacken if they did not see the Father work harder than any of them : so that he was the first in fetch-ing stones, treading the clay, mixing the sand, cutting, carrying and barking the timber, removing the earth and fixing materials. He was equally laborious in the other tasks, sometimes felling trees with his axe, sometimes with his spade in his hand digging up the earth, sometimes with an iron crow splitting rocks, sometimes disposing the water trenches, sometimes leading the beasts and cattle which he had procured for his mission to pasture and water ; thus by his own example, teaching the several kinds of labour. The Indians, whose narrow ideas and dullness could not at first enter into the utility of these fatigues, which at the same time deprived them of their customary freedom of roving among the forests, on a thousand occasions sufficiently tried his patience, coming late, not caring to stir, running away, jeering him, and sometimes even forming combinations, and threatening death and destruction : all this was to be borne with unwearied patience, he having no other resource than affability and kindness, sometimes intermixed with gravity to strike respect ; also taking care not to tire them, and suit himself to their weakness.

In the evening the father led them a second time to their devotions ; in which the rosary was prayed over, and the catechism explained ; and the service was followed by the distribution of some provisions. At first they were very troublesome all the time of the sermon, jesting and sneering at what he said. This the father bore with for a while, and then proceeded to reprove them : but finding they were not to be kept in order, he made a very dangerous experiment of what could be done by fear. Near him stood an Indian in high reputation for strength : and who presuming on this advantage, the only quality esteemed among them, took upon himself to be more rude than the others. Father Ugarte who was a large man, and of uncommon strength, observing the Indian to be in the height of his laughter, and making signs of mockery to the others, seized him by the hair and lifting him up, swang him to and fro : at this the rest ran away in the utmost terror: they soon returned one after another, and the father so far succeeded to intimidate them, that they behaved more regularly for the future.

In the succeeding years father Ugarte saw the happy fruits of his patience, having not only brought the Indians to the knowledge of the christian doctrine, and a decent attendance at divine worship, but likewise to a suitable life without any of the disorders of their savage state. He inured their indocile sloth to labour, and he had plentiful harvests of wheat, maize, and other grain: he may be said to have surmounted impossibilities in watering, and cultivating craggy and rugged grounds. He even made a considerable quantity of generous wine; of which, after supplying the missions in California, some was sent to New Spain in exchange for other goods. He likewise bred horses and sheep, and was indeed, the purveyor general of the garrisons and missions, who without the assistance of father Ugarte's fortitude and industry, could not have subsisted: but no difficulty deterred him; and at last he brought his labours to the intended issue, and under a long course of obstructions and impediments, he saw his wishes happily accomplished.

To give a full idea of the industry and zeal of this religious man, we shall add what he did in the following years, for clothing his naked Indians.

His sheep, brought originally from the other coast, being sufficiently encreased, that his Indians might make the best use of their wool, he determined to teach them the method of preparing, spinning, and weaving it for clothes. Accordingly he himself made the distaffs, spinning wheels, and looms. Though to forward and improve so beneficial a scheme he sent Tepic for one Antonio Moran, a master weaver, and allowed him a salary of five hundred dollars. Moran staid several years in California, till he had sufficiently instructed the Indians in their trade and some other handicrafts. By these new manufactures, he saved the vast expenses of sail cloth and baize, a measure both political and pious.

It was not without reason that the venerable father Salvatierra used always to call father Ugarte the apostle: for sublime as the title was, his labours were not unworthy of it. Always in action and indefatigable; present every where, and doing every thing; he attempted every thing, and he accomplished every thing: but his activity never so signally appeared as in those beginnings where the difficulties seemed unsurmountable: sometimes he was preaching, assisting, admonishing, and attending the soldiers: at other times he was searching for new spots of ground for villages and fields; sometimes baptizing the children; and sometimes instructing the adults ; sometimes administering the sacraments to the sick, and performing the last offices to the dying. Sometimes he worked in the buildings; sometimes in the field making water-trenches, plantations, and fields ; sometimes he was mending the roads ; sometimes helping to get ready the barks for sea. In fine, he was continually labouring in every kind of employment, and the greatest fatigue he took upon himself."

A striking proof of the good father's exertions was seen a few years after, in 1707, when all New Spain including the province of Cinaloa and Sonora, on the opposite side of the gulf, suffered extremely for want of rain. California had also been without rain, yet we find Ugarte says in a letter to a friend : " It is now two months since the seamen and lands-men ate here good bread of our own harvests, while the poor in the other coast, in Cinaloa and Sonora are perishing." Previously to this period, however, much distress was suffered and many reverses un-dergone. Repeatedly, there were risings among the Indians both under father Ugarte and at the other missions ; and more than once the cattle and even the harvests were destroyed by them : but nothing could defeat the perseverance of the missionaries.

In 1702 Father Piccolo, after a long absence returned with a slight supply of money to pay the troops still remaining, and brought with him some

more soldiers as well as handicraftsmen and two
new missionaries, the fathers Bassaldua and Minu-
tili. In the following year, Ugarte brought from
the opposite side of the gulf a large supply of cattle
and provisions, while Salvatierra made progresses
to extend his knowledge of the country. About
the same time a great disaster befel the mission of
of San Xavier, now under the charge of Bassaldua;
the neighbouring Indians unexpectedly attacking it
and killing all the adult catechumens, or converted
Indians, with the exception of some who escaped
to the garrison. To punish this crime an expedition was sent into the country of the Indians which
speedily defeated them: the chief promoter of the
attack was taken, publicly tried, and finally executed,
by the captain, notwithstanding the entreaties of the
fathers.

This example of severity seemed to be productive of good effects, as the Indians remained long
afterwards quiet and tractable ; and the opportunity
was not lost of extending the spiritual as well as
military conquest of the country. But the distress
for want of provisions was still often extreme ; and
more than once it was proposed by the soldiers and
others that the county should be abandoned. In
this extremity Father Salvatierra was appointed
Provincial of the order in Mexico, (in 1705) an
appointment which proved of the greatest benefit

to the missions. His first step was to address a memorial to the Viceroy, detailing at great length the state and prospects of the missions, and the general condition of the country and its inhabitants. In this paper he states that although the country is so barren that it can never be made fit for the residence of Spaniards, yet that the Father Jesuits had managed to reduce a portion of it, one hundred leagues in circuit. He says that the whole of this part is in such profound peace, that the fathers can go over it alone, without any guard of soldiers; the natives willingly conforming themselves to whatever the fathers require of them, being ready, together with 1200 christians, catechumens and gentiles, to take arms in their behalf. He states also that 1,225,000 dollars had already been expended in the settling of the country.

In 1705 Father Salvatierra once more visited California with fresh supplies of money and recruits. He found a new mission established at San Juan, *Londo ;* and he recommended the immediate formation of two others, in places formerly fixed on, one about fourteen leagues south of Loreto and the other forty leagues north on the river Mulege; the former being named San Juan Baptista and the latter Santa Rosalia. The former of these enterprizes was entrusted to Father Pedro Ugarte, who seems to have possessed the same happy tempera-

ment and strong good sense as his brother Juan.
The following is Venegas's account of his mode of
proceeding on his first arrival at his mission :—

"Father Pedro Ugarte found his Indians perfectly
quiet, peaceable, and without any apprehension,
though the only shelter he had for some time among
them, was the shade of the mesquites; and afterwards of a hut made with branches of trees, whilst
the chapel and a little dwelling of adobes, or raw
bricks, was building. He endeavoured by little
presents and caresses, to gain the affections of his
Indians, not so much that they should assist him in
the building, as that they might take a liking to the
catechism, which he explained to them as well as he
could, by the help of some Indians of Loreto, while
he was perfecting himself in their language. But
his kindness was lost on the adults, who, from their
invincible sloth, could not be brought to help him
in any one thing, though they partook of, and used
to be very urgent with him for the pozoli and other
eatables. He was now obliged to have recourse to
the assistance of the boys, who being allured by the
father with sweatmeats and presents, accompanied
him wherever he would have them : and to habi-
tuate these to any work it was necessary to make
use of artifice : sometimes he laid a wager with
them who should soonest pluck up the mesquites
and small trees; sometimes he offered rewards to

those who took away most earth; and it suffices to
say, that in forming the bricks, he made himself a
boy with boys, challenged them to play with the
earth, and dance upon the clay. The father used
to take off his sandals and tread it, in which he was
followed by the boys skipping and dancing on the
clay, and the father with them; the boys sung and
were highly delighted; the father also sung; and
thus they continued dancing and treading the clay
in different parts, till meal time. This enabled him
to erect his poor dwelling, and the church. Thus,
with invincible patience and firmness under excessive labours, he went on humanizing the savages
who lived on the spot, those of the neighbouring
rancherias and others whom he sought among
woods, brakes, and caverns; going about every-
where, until at length he administered baptism to
many adults, and brought this new settlement into
some form."

In 1707, Salvatierra having voluntarily resigned
his dignity of Provincial that he might prosecute
his objects in California, returned thither with four
of the natives whom he had taken with him to
Mexico and were brought back sufficiently instructed to instruct their own countrymen. Shortly
afterwards, in the beginning of 1708, the mission of
San Josef was founded in the centre of mountains
about twenty leagues N.W. of Loreto and almost at

equal distance from both seas. In 1710, the small-
pox broke out among the Indians and carried off a
great many, particularly children; and other fevers
shewed themselves as well among the soldiers as the
Indians.   The superseded priests or sorcerers took
advantage of these misfortunes to promote discontent, persuading the Indians that the small pox was
owing to the Fathers, who introduced the disease
with the water of baptism purposely to destroy the
children.   It is probable, that independently of the
accidental source of disease and death from this
dreadful malady, the half-civilized natives began
already to exhibit that tendency to sickness and decay which has always prevailed and still prevails
among the domesticated Indians, and which forms
so striking a contrast with their comparative immu-
nity from epidemic and slow maladies in their wild
condition.

The year 1710 was distinguished in the history of
California by the death of Father Kino, a man whose
name is worthy of grateful remembrance not only
by his own order but by all good men.   Although,
as we have seen, the great promoter of the Californian missions, Kino was so engaged in his own labours of the same kind among the Indians on the
opposite coast, that he could take no other share in
the new enterprize than that of exciting the zeal of
others to the conquest, and using his utmost exer-

tions in supplying the new settlers with provisions
or other necessary supplies. This he continued to
do, in the most effective manner, until his death;
and it is certain that much of the success of the
missions of the peninsula, perhaps their very per-
manency, was owing to his exertions. In his own
particular sphere and among his own people, his
labours were incessant, most exemplary and successful. "He laboured," says Father Venegas, "in
the reduction of the Indians, with a zeal truly worthy of admiration; went undauntedly alone among
them, formed them into villages, prevailed on them
to sow their lands and take care of their cattle, as
the means of keeping them together, and employ-
ing subordinate agents for their civil polity. He
had the patience to learn the different languages,
translated the catechism and prayers, which without
being disgusted by their indocility and dullness, he
taught them verbally. He likewise composed voca-
bularies and observations for the use of his assistants and successors: and such were the happy
effects of his wonderful mildness and condescen-
sion, that they all loved him and confided in him
as their general father. He built houses and cha-
pels, formed villages and towns; reconciled nations
who were at enmity; and had he according to his
repeated request, been seconded by other missionaries, the conversion of all the nations, betwixt

Sonora and the rivers Gila and Colorado, might
have been easily accomplished, *and the missions of
New Spain and California have carried on an intercourse by land ;* a design which always appeared
extremely difficult. But the hardships which this
worthy man suffered from the Indians were the
least, or rather not to be compared to those he met
with from some Spaniards, against whose violences
he was as a wall of brass, in favour of his converts.
They obstructed his enterprises and prevented his
being assisted by others, it being their interest, that
the poor Pimas should be branded with the name of
rebels and enemies, that they might commit depre-
dations among them, and force the Indians to serve
them as slaves."

Amid all his domestic labours as a Missionary,
Father Kino could not quite forget the tastes of the
professor, and entertained an anxious desire to explore the country to the north, and more particularly
to solve the problem, at that time still doubted, as
to the insular or peninsular character of California.
It is but justice to the worthy missionary to state that
in wishing to extend his geographical researches he
was much more influenced by the desire to benefit
the cause of christianity than that of science, as he
believed it would be most important for the welfare
of the new missions in California if they could be
made accessible by land.   With the view of settling

the question he made several journies to the northward, and although he did not actually penetrate
into California by land he satisfactorily ascertained
its connection with the main land of new Spain.
He made no less than five journies in the years 1700,
1701, and 1702 and 1706, in all of which he reached
the rivers of Gila or Colorado, and on one occasion
he crossed the latter, but was prevented by an accident, from passing on to Monterey, in upper California, as he intended ; but he pointed out the way
which was followed by his successors many years
afterwards.

CHAP. III.

DURING the succeeding years the fathers, more particularly the indefatigable Ugarte, made many progresses, through the peninsula in search of more favourable localities for missions, and also with the benevolent object of composing the feuds and petty wars between the different tribes, which had always been found a great obstacle to their civilization. In the year 1716 Father Salvatierra succeeded in getting recognised and established a general system of government of a better and more definite kind than had hitherto prevailed, including the missionaries, the soldiers, divers and natives; and as this was observed not only during the whole period of the dominion of the Jesuits but also, in a great measure, during the rule of their successors and even still exists, it is necessary to give a brief notice of it here; but we shall first complete the sketch of the history of the missions.

In the year 1717, California was visited with a

tremendous hurricane accompanied with violent rains, which is deserving of notice in this place not only because it destroyed the house and church of Father Ugarte, but because' the effects then witnessed help to account for the singular bareness and barrenness of the country. Both at San Xavier and Mulege all the cultivated land was utterly destroyed, the soil being carried away by the torrents and nothing left but the bare rocks and stones. Modern travellers give similar accounts of the country and justify the obvious remark of Venegas that "if in former ages these hurricanes were frequent in California, it is not surprising that all its mould should have been swept away, its bare rocks alone remaining, and its plains and vallies covered with heaps of stones."

In 1719 a great feat was performed by the indefatigable Ugarte in the construction of a vessel of considerable size in California, with native timber, which he discovered of sufficient size—and there only—amid the mountains, full thirty leagues from the river Mulege where the vessel was built. In 1720 two new missions were founded, that of La Paz near the bay of that name, eighty leagues south of Loreto; and that of Guadalupe nearly at the same distance to the N. W. amid the mountains but much nearer the shore of the Pacific than the Gulf. This part of the country is so extremely barren that no grain can be produced in it, and the inhabitants are therefore supported either by such cattle as it will support, or by maize brought from other missions. Such however was the zeal of Father Helen, the founder, that in six years from its first settlement no less than 1700 Indians were converted and settled in five villages, each with its church. In the follow- ing year Ugarte sailed on a voyage of discovery to the north of the gulf, surveyed the coast and reached the river Colorado, confirming all the previous state- ments of Kino. In the survey several harbours and watering-places were discovered, on the Califor- nian shore, but the same barrenness prevailed over all. " There's something ails the spot, the place is cursed."—In this year also the Mission of Dolores Del Sur was founded midway between Loreto and La Paz, in a place described as the most barren of all California, there being no spot whatever fit for the growth of maize. Father Guillem, the founder, remained here however, upwards of thirty years, during which time, by his single exertions, he con- verted to christianity the whole of the natives over a tract of forty leagues extending from sea to sea, settling them in villages and destroying all feuds among the different clans. This mission, in sub- sequent years, proved valuable to the fathers as an asylum when other districts fell from their allegiance. In 1723 the mission of Santiago was founded to the south of La Paz; and in 1728 that of San Ignacio in the extreme north in latitude 28°, about seventy leagues from Loreto. This last was founded by father Luyando a wealthy Mexican Jesuit at his own expense; and as the account of its foundation and early progress gives a good picture of the general mode of proceeding of the Jesuits in establishing their settlements, at the period at which we are now arrived, I shall here give, in an abridged form, from Venegas, the simple and humble history of the establishment of this little community.

It had been a long time a great object with the fathers to found a mission to the north of Guada-lupe, as well for the great general purpose of ex-tending Christianity among the natives, as because the country possessed some local advantages. So early as 1706 this country of the Cochimis had been visited by Father Piccolo, and the Indians had shewn very favourable dispositions, which continued to be cherished by the occasional visits of the fathers from the southern missions. The spot selected for the mission of San Ignacio, which lies in about the 28th degree of north latitude and one third nearer the Gulf than the Ocean, was preferred for its extraor-dinary fertility compared with most of the other stations. It possessed both water and a soil fit for the growth of corn. In January, 1728, Father Lu-yando set out on his expedition to Loreto, accom-

E

panied by nine soldiers, the Cochini Indians of San
Ignacio having been previously prepared to receive
him favorably by father Sistiaga of Santa Rosalia.
He entered on his office of civilizing the Indians
(which was little else than that of teaching them to
repeat the prayers of the church and baptising such
as believed) and of cultivating the soil at the same
time.   As a preliminary to baptism he insisted on
the abjuration of faith in the native jugglers or
priests, and demanded the breaking and burning of
their smoking tubes and other instruments and
tokens of superstition, as a proof of this.   As usual,
the feeding of the Indians went hand in hand with
the conversion, and by his largesses and zeal, father
Luyando in a few months' time could number five
hundred catechumens at his distributions of pottage
and of holy water.   Aided by the converts the soldiers set about constructing a church, and with
such zeal that it was finished and consecrated
within the year.   The year before Sistiaga had
planted some maize and wheat; this was now har-
vested and the agricultural operations much extended.   Father Helen, also, at a former visitation,
had introduced some foreign vegetables, and father
Luyando now laid out a spot for a garden, "where
(as father Venegas says) exotic plants in that barren land throve well, and others which were natives
of it throve under his culture."   He likewise

planted vines, olive trees, fig-trees, and sugar canes, all of which seem to have succeeded and proved of of great service to the mission. The Indians in this mission proved, on the whole, more intelligent than in the others, and readily joined in the good father's husbandry, so that at the fourth harvest we are told that he garnered no less than a thousand bushels of grain of all sorts. Their new lord also endeavoured to prevail on them to live in huts, which he taught them to build of unburnt bricks and the boughs of trees; but he found it very difficult to reconcile them to live in them. Into the parts fit for pastures he likewise introduced cattle, both large and small, with the view to breeding. In short, every thing seemed prospering and likely to prosper, " when (as Father Venegas expresses it) the great enemy to the peace and happiness of mankind, instigated the neighbouring Indians to disturb the tranquillity of the mission and render all the pains of the father abortive." Previously to this greater disturbance, however, it was evident that things did not proceed quite smoothly in the little state. From the beginning it was found, here as elsewhere, that the elders of the tribes were slow to embrace the new faith, even when almost all the young and the women had done so; and it is not to be wondered (as father Venegas says) " that having been the respected teachers of the nation, they could not prevail on themselves to be scholars to strangers, or stand among boys, or even be ridiculed by them." It shewed, indeed, a marvellous ignorance of human nature in the fathers to place the seniors in such degrading relationship to their children and women. However, the actual aggressors in the attack on the new christians of the mission, came from the north, or rather had their haunts on the northern borders of the converted Indians. Some of the villages of those people they attacked, and killed a few of the inhabitants. The rest fled to the mission for protection; a great alarm was excited and war was declared. All the converts were mustered, and were proved to amount to 350 men fit for war. To these were joined the garrison of the mission, consisting of *two soldiers*; and after due preparation of arming and disciplining, they boldly marched in pursuit of the enemy. These proved to be very inferior in numbers and not very vigilant, since they allowed themselves to be surrounded while asleep during the night. Two only escaped; all the rest to the number of thirty-four, were taken prisoners and marched in triumph to San Ignacio. Great was the glory and great the rejoicings, which father Venegas records with all the solemnity of history. "The fathers, he says, led the victorious army to the church, where thanks were returned for this victory gained without shedding any blood, or even discharging a single arrow. Next day all the people were assembled; and the soldiers and governors sitting as judges, the prisoners were brought to trial, and being convicted of rebellion, robbery, and murder, they were sentenced to be removed to Loreto as guilty of capital crimes. At this the new christians danced for joy, thinking they should now have the pleasure of killing their enemies and revenging themselves." But the good fathers were too tender-hearted to indulge either the converts or the soldier-judges, and the whole affair ended by the " principal murderer" being whipped! However, the lenity as well as the victory, had good effects on the natives, as most of the conquered afterwards became converts, and the tribes to the north were at once checked by the demonstration of power and the mild exercise of it.

In 1730 the mission of San Josef close to Cape San Lucas was founded, and, soon after, that of Santa Rosa near the same extremity of the peninsula; and although they seemed to be attended at first with the usual success, this was shortly put an end to by a general rising of all the natives in this district. There being only two or three soldiers among all the missions, no effectual resistance could be afforded to the " rebels," as the Fathers termed them, and accordingly they soon had every thing their own way. In 1734 the two fathers Carranco and Tamaral were murdered, as well as one of the soldiers; the other fathers and the soldiers fled, and the whole of the southern missions were consequently lost. Apprehensive of similar disasters in other parts, the fathers were recalled from the northern missions, and at one time in the following year, not a Spaniard remained in the country except at Loreto. In this disastrous state of affairs they were relieved by a reinforcement of troops from Cinaloa headed by the Governor, who attacked the Indians in different places, and finally reduced the country to tranquillity. After some time the missions were gradually restored, and the fathers proceeded in their works of conversion and civilization. Accordingly we find, from an official report drawn up by the missionaries in 1745, that not only all the old stations were re-occupied but several new ones planted. They amounted in all to fourteen, besides two then in progress.—viz.

    1 Loreto

    2 San Xavier

    3 De los Dolores del Sur

    4 San Luis Gonsaga

    5 San Josef de Commondu

    6 Santa Rosalia de Mulege

    7 La Conception

    8 Guadalupe

    9 San Ignacio

10 De los Dolores del Norte
11 San Iago del Sur
12 La Paz
13 San Josef del Cabo de S. Lucas
14 Santa Rosa.

No very great progress, however, could be made in so unpromising a field, from which the whole race of missionaries were removed in 1767 on the general expulsion of the Jesuits from the Spanish dominions. At this time the number of missions were sixteen. The exiled Fathers were superseded in their missions by a body of Franciscans from Mexico; but they were soon displaced by the Dominican monks who still keep possession of the country.

In 1786, as Pérouse informs us, the missions were fifteen in number: ten of them being still possessed by the Franciscans, the others by the Dominicans. The whole number of converted Indians at that time was reckoned at about four thousand. The garrison of Loreto consisted of fifty-four soldiers, and this and a few soldiers furnished to the other missions was the whole military force of the country.

CHAP. IV.

CHARACTER OF THE MISSIONARY GOVERNMENT.—PRESENT
STATE OF THE COUNTRY.—PRODUCE.—PEARL FISHERY.

During the rule of Father Salvatierra, the whole
regulations relating to the property and conduct of
the missions and the treatment of the natives, were,
as already stated, reduced to a regular system; and
this has been acted on ever since, with but slight
deviation, even by the enemies of the order of
Jesuits, who succeeded them. As affording the
best security for the funds belonging to the missions, farms in Mexico were purchased by them.
At the same time the payment of the royal salaries allowed to the missionaries was put on a better
footing. These salaries were paid to the directors
of the missions in Mexico, the missionaries having
the equivalent value transmitted to them in the
form of clothes, furniture, utensils, provisions, medicines, mules, &c. The garrisons and soldiers
were paid by government, but they still continued
under the authority of the fathers, except as regarded their internal discipline, and when they were
engaged in matters of a purely military character.
The following extracts from Father Venegas give a

tolerably clear view of the general economy of the missionaries both religious and civil: but it is necessary to recollect, in reading them, that the narrator is himself one of the order which he eulogises.

"At first the fathers subsisted all the Indians, who came to settle in villages, on condition that they should no longer wander among the woods and mountains, but be instructed in the faith: and in these charities, great part of the contributions of the benefactors, has been expended. And after they were thus brought together, it being impossible to subsist all, and equally so to make fields for sowing in many parts, either from the nature of the soil, want of water, or the innate indolence and sloth of the people, the following method was taken.— First, the missionaries supported all the Indians who attended divine service. Every morning and night they have an allowance of Atole, the name they give to their pottage, made of maize, boiled and afterwards bruised, macerated in water, and put a second time over the fire; at noon they are served with pozoli, or boiled maize, with fresh or salt meat, and fruits or vegetables, according as the mission is provided. In the same manner the Indian governor of the village, the sick, the aged, and the children of all the rancherias, male and female, from six to twelve years, are provided with food. Besides this, every week the same allowance is given to all the Indians of two rancherias, male and female, in consideration that they all come in their order, two by two, to the head village of the mission, in order to renew their instructions. Lastly, every Sunday, all who attend divine service have a portion of victuals, and in passion week, the like is sent to all the rancherias.

The missionary priest likewise cloathes all his parishioners with serges, baize, and palmillas, a sort of coarse cloth woven in Old Spain; he also provides them with cloaks and blankets, which he procures from Mexico on his stipend. Those who can work are instructed by the fathers in the management of the fields, and watering the ground; the product of which is entirely for their own advantage; and the consequence is, that they gather it, and immediately waste the whole, unless the fathers take care to save it up, in order to make a proper distribution, or to send relief to another mission in necessity. Wine is the only product withheld from them, and this in order to prevent drunkenness; and it is for this reason, that though the vintages are but inconsiderable, some quantities of it, there being but few consumers in California, have been exported to New Spain, in exchange for other commodities. What wine the father has is chiefly given to the sick, whom he likewise supplies with medicines; so that a missionary and priest of

California, is not only charged with the care of their souls, but likewise with all the several duties of a father of a family; together with the several mechanical occupations from a labourer to a cook. He is likewise a tutor, apothecary, surgeon and physician to all: and this without the least profit, advantage or reward, spending his own substance, abridging himself of conveniencies, even necessaries, to supply their wants.

In every mission newly founded, the father is attended by a soldier, who within certain bounds has the power of the captain of the garrison. When the father has assembled any rancherias, he appoints the person, whom he thinks most proper, as governor of the village: another Indian to take care of the church, and out of each rancheria, a person of the most promising morals, and particularly instructed, is appointed catechist. The governor's office is to keep peace and good order; and if any thing happens that he cannot remedy, he is to acquaint the father and soldier with it. The churchwarden is to take care of the church and keep it clean; he is also to take notice of those that fail coming to mass, and other exercises of devotion; those that do not behave with proper respect; and those who either return to their former superstitions, or betray any ill-will against the fathers, or disgust at the instructions. The catechist of the rancheria summons them every morning before they go to the woods to repeat their prayers and catechism ; and if any thing deserving animadversion happens in the rancheria, he acquaints the father of it.

During the absence of the father, either to visit villages and rancherias, attend the sick, or terminate quarrels, the soldier acts as his vicegerent, and has an eye to every thing. He is at the father's order to go wherever it is necessary ; he can seize delinquents and mildly punish them, unless in capital cases, when he is to lay the case before the captain of the garrison, who is invested with the judicial power. Lesser faults are punished with whipping, and the greater with imprisonment or the stocks.

The first care is of the children, as the whole depends on their education. Some from all the missions are brought up at Loreto, which has a reading, writing, and singing school, with proper masters who come from the opposite coast. They become gradually polished by conversation ; they are taught the Spanish, and afterwards are promoted to be churchwardens or catechists in their rancherias, where they are greatly respected. At the head villages every morning, the churchwarden assembles all the inhabitants in the church, whither the rancherias come by turns, and there the Te

Deum is sung. This is followed by the mass, and afterwards by the catechism, which is translated into their languages; and several times a week the whole concludes with an explication, or sermon; instructing and animating them in every part of the christian life. The adult christians then undertake some employment, or go among the woods in quest of sustenance. At night they all meet again in the church, and perform their devotions. Every Sunday they walk in procession round the village singing; they then return to the church, where a sermon is preached to them. The like is done at Loreto every Saturday, in Spanish, for the garrison.

No one is compelled by force to receive the faith; all who are baptized, desire it not only freely, and without the least compulsion, but all possible assurances are given of their sincerity and perseverance. The garrison and soldiers check the insults of the savages: but if the orders and intentions of his majesty, and the Spanish government be complied with, they never offer them the least injury, never so much as pursuing them unless provoked: the chief end of their service is no more than as a just and prudent safeguard for the lives of the missionaries."

What with the insuperable barrenness of the country and the injurious influence of the system of civilization—or more properly speaking *domesti-*

cation—so rigidly persevered in by the missionaries, the indigenous population of Lower California has greatly diminished, while the defect has not been in any degree supplied by the influx of strangers. Indeed the nature of the soil and the institutions of the Fathers conspire in forbidding all immigration. Humboldt states the total amount of the national population not to exceed nine thousand, rather more than half of which are the tributary converts of the Fathers. This estimate is perhaps too small. I can, however, state with confidence that, even at the present time, the population including all classes, does not exceed fourteen or fifteen thousand. Most of the misssions are in a wretched condition, and the Indians poor and helpless, slaves both in body and mind, have no knowledge and no will but those of the Friars.

We shall defer all particular notice of their peculiar character and position until we come to give an account of Upper California.

The capital Loreto has less than three hundred inhabitants. The only town of any importance, as to size, is La Paz, which, together with San Antonio, contains perhaps a population of two thousand—most of them the mixed progeny of European seamen, Spanish creoles and Indians. The vicinity of a tolerable harbour (Pichilingo) renders this place of more importance.

The indomitable barrenness of Lower California, the more remakable as contrasted with the fertility of the upper province, has not only necessarily kept at an extremely low ebb her agriculture and commerce, but has given the country so bad a character that its resources have fallen far below their intrinsic value. If the country is capable of producing little, the antiquated monastic institutions by which it is throughout possessed, are ill calculated to improve this little. The natural productions are nearly the same as those in Upper California. There are said to be many mines of gold and silver in the peninsula, but none are now worked, unless, indeed, we may except those of San Antonio near La Paz which still afford a trifling supply. Besides Indian corn, the sheltered vallies near the different missions produce a variety of fruit such as grapes, dates, figs, quinces, peaches, pears, olives. The dates, figs, &c. are dried and preserved, and exported ; and wine is made from the grapes and also exported, as well as a kind of spirit distilled from the mescal. These articles, with pearls, tortoiseshell, a few bullock's hides, some dried beef, cheese, soap, &c. constitute all the exports which are, for the most part, sent to San Blas and Mazatlan in small coasting vessels. The imports are chiefly provisions and clothing, agricultural and domestic utensils, supplies for the ceremonies of the church and a small share of the ordinary luxuries of life.

For one branch of Commerce, the Pearl Fishery, California has been famed from its first discovery. The glory and the riches derived from this source are, however, almost traditional; at least, the actual amount of the trade is insignificant. Nevertheless it is by no means certain that the sources of a beneficial commerce in this respect do not yet exist, provided proper means were taken for pursuing it with effect!

Long before the discovery of America by the Europeans, the natives of many of the maritime parts of it were acquainted with the art of diving for pearls, as these were found by the first discoverers to be held in great estimation as ornaments.* Hernando de Soto found them in great quantity in Florida where the tombs of the native princes were ornamented with them; and among the presents made to Cortez by Montezuma before his entry into Mexico, necklaces of precious stones and of pearls are mentioned by Gomara: these Cortez sent to the Emperor Charles V. The Incas of Peru, also, we are told by Garcillasso, set a great value on pearls, but the laws of Manco-capac prohibited the natives from exercising the trade of diver, as being dangerous to the individual and not very profitable

* It was not indeed necessary that they should be divers in order to possess pearls, as we find from the voyage of Father Consag (Venegas, vol. ii, p. 310,) that in certain places (as at Cape San Miguel in lat. 29 deg.) the sea throws up on the shore great quantities of them.

to the state.* After the discovery of America the traffic in pearls became considerable. They were found chiefly near the island of Cubagua, in the mouth of the Rio de la Hacha and in the gulf of Panama near the Islas de las Perlas (whose inhabitants still pursue the fishery), on the shore to the north of Acapulco, and on the east Coast of California, in the gulf. We are told by Acosta that in 1587, 697lbs of pearls were imported into Seville from America, upwards of 11lbs. of which were of the greatest beauty and destined for the king, Philip II. The pearl fisheries of Cabagua and Rio de la Hacha seem to have been of short duration; and their exhaustion turned the traders more eagerly towards that of California, which had already supplied the crown of Spain with its richest pearls, found in the expeditions of Yturbi and Pinadero. In those times the trade in pearls was certainly very considerable; and this continued to be carried on, without any restriction, up to the period of the settling of the country by the Jesuits. It is stated by Torquemada that previously to the arrival of the strangers, the Californians hardly put any value on the pearls, as they were in the habit of throwing the oyster into the fire, in order to obtain the flesh for food; the pearls being destroyed by the same process. " But the avidity of others" he adds " has

* Humbolt's New Spain.

F

communicated its flame even to this simple people; who are now eager to get, and careful to keep, what they have seen highly valued by foreigners." The conduct of the Jesuits in regard to this fishery has been already stated : it was strictly forbidden on account of the oppression and cruelty to the natives to which it led.

The rude and savage adventurers of those days little regarded the welfare or even lives of the Indians when put in competition with their own selfish interests ; and it was customary to kidnap and employ by force as divers in the pearl fishery all they could lay their hands on, on the coasts and islands of the gulf. Many of the natives, no doubt, voluntarily lent themselves to this employment, under certain terms of remuneration ; but this was rather the habit of the few regular traders than of the many casual adventurers who sought the peninsula in search of its boasted treasures. A characteristic illustration of this fact is mentioned by Father Consag in his voyage for surveying the coast of California in 1746, and which we believe to be no less just as indicative of the character of the Fathers than it is of the practices of the pearl-fishers. On reaching a part of the coast near the top of the gulf, he says, " The people on seeing the canoes took us for *divers* and fled up the country ; the outrages and brutality of these men having ren-

dered them equally dreaded and detested by all the
natives of California; but on being made acquainted by some of their countrymen, who were
with me, that *A Father* was come in the canoes,
they immediately returned*." It is, indeed, true,
that after the establishment of the Jesuits, the pearl
fishery, which had been previously greatly inter-
rupted by the opposition of the natives originating
in these cruelties, began to be prosecuted with
greater vigour and success than ever, now that the
divers were left in a considerable degree unmolested; but the divers and traders did not belong
to California but came from the opposite shores of
the gulf, whose inhabitants to this day are the principal fishers. The Jesuits had the influence to obtain
authority from the government not only for excluding all vessels from fishing in the gulf except
such as had the Viceroy's license, but also that the
military commandant in California (who, be it re-
membered, was under the authority of the Fathers)
should have the power to examine and verify these
licences and to prevent the approach of all vessels
not provided with them. It was expressly forbidden to every one, whether soldiers or seamen, belonging to the missions to have any thing to do with
the fishery; a regulation which excited extreme
discontent at the time, but which the Fathers had

* Venegas.

the power to get fully carried into effect. Their reason for debarring their people from this trade, was their conviction, founded on experience, that, if permitted, it would not only seduce them from their proper duties in the missions, but would inevitably lead to the oppression of their children the Indians—as they termed them.

At the period of these regulations, at the very commencement of the seventeenth century, the revenue to the crown was not inconsiderable, as the king's share (a fifth) amounted to no less than 12,000 dollars per annum for every bark employed. After the expulsion of the Jesuits the trade seems to have declined greatly, partly no doubt from the exhaustion of the oyster-beds, but partly also from the mismanagement of the whole system adopted in its prosecution.

When the pearl fishery was prosecuted to its greatest extent, from six to eight hundred Indian divers called " Busos" were employed; it was carried on by small vessels of from fifteen to thirty tons burden, which were fitted out by private adventurers, and carried each from thirty to fifty divers. The owners accompanied the vessels, and carried with them provisions for the people, and a little money to advance them in the course of the season. The place of fitting out was at the port of Guaymas on the opposite coast, and when ready they had to procure a license from the Commandant-general of the province of Sonora in which that port is situated; being so provided they made sail for the coast of California, and cast anchor on such banks as contained pearl oysters, which banks are called " Placeres." The whole fishery, however, was not anciently carried on by vessels of the size above mentioned; and, perhaps, decked vessels were not at all then employed. The armadores went in launches, and the divers used canoes, bringing the oysters on shore for the purpose of opening them. This is evident from the large heaps of shells yet remaining in many spots. Numerous canoes are still attached to the larger vessels employed at the present time.

The manner of carrying on the fishery was as follows :—The vessel being anchored, and every thing ready, the divers plunged down in all directions, and dug up with a sharp-pointed stick as many oysters as possible while they could remain under water ; they then came up, took breath, and at the same time deposited the oysters in bags hung over the vessel's sides. Having done this, they again plunged under water, repeating the same operation till the bags were full, or the usual time for working expired; they then all came on deck with the bags, and placed themselves in a circle round the owner, or as he was called the " armador," who took the contents of the whole bags and made a division as follows :—two oysters for the armador, two for the busos, and one for the king; proceeding in this way till the whole of the oysters were disposed of. When this operation was concluded, they all began to open the oysters, beginning with those which fell to the lot of the armador, but without moving from the circle which they had formed round him; and he had then to watch with the utmost vigilance, for they had a dexterous knack of swallowing the most valuable pearls along with the live oyster, which they threw into their mouths by a kind of slight of hand, which it was almost impossible to detect. The king's fifth was then opened under the same precautions, and the pearls deposited in the presence of all. Lastly, the divers opened their own oysters, and the pearls were equally divided amongst them, and generally sold on the instant to the armador, to whom they were always indebted for their outfit, and for previous advances. They however never failed to reserve some which they sold to the dealers on shore who always accompanied the busos, and who often made more money than the armadores. Those dealers carried with them spirituous liquors, chocolate, sugar, cigars, and other cheap articles of which the Indians are passionately fond; and for which they often exchanged pearls of great value.

The season for carrying on the fishery is from the beginning of July till the beginning of October. The exact value of pearls produced while this business was prosperous cannot be now easily ascertained. It has been variously estimated. From documents supplied to Mr. Hardy in 1825 and published in his Travels in Mexico, it is stated on the authority of Don Jose Maria Retes, that the number of vessels employed annually on the fishery of Loreto was from six to eight, and the quantity of pearls from four to five pounds weight, worth from 8 to 10,000 dollars. Captain John Hall, an experienced navigator and trader in these seas, gives us some valuable information on this subject about the same date. A letter of his is published in Mr. Hardy's travels; but we have obtained much further information from him on this and other matters touching California. He gives a somewhat different version of the mode of proceeding in the distribution of the oysters in the year 1825. He says "every time the diver comes up, the largest oysters which he may bring with him are placed on one side for the Virgin. All the rest are then thrown into a large pile, and in the evening they are divided thus : eight shells are put on one side for the owners, eight on the other for the divers, and two in a third heap for the government." It would thus appear that the present ruling powers are contented with one-half the share of their predecessors. It is, however, somewhat curious, in these times, that the Virgin should retain her full privileges, if not an augmentation of them. Mr. Hardy says that about sixteen or eighteen small vessels are annually employed in the fishery, and obtain when the weather has been favorable and the divers fortunate about 500 dollars' worth of pearls each,—sometimes as much as 1000 dollars. He adds, however, that the expence of the fitting out and other contingencies, reduce the net profits to the proprietors very considerably.* The following statement, kindly furnished me by a friend who resides on the spot, will shew the extent and value of this fishery in the year 1831.

This year two vessels sailed on the Pearl Fishery from the Port of Guaymas, and other two from the River Yaqui in its vicinity, as also two boats: the whole carried two hundred Busos; the largest vessel had seventy; the next fifty; the third thirty; the fourth also thirty; and the boats ten each. One vessel brought forty ounces of Pearls, great and small, which were valued at 6500 dollars; another twenty-one ounces, valued at 3000 dollars; another fifteen ounces valued at 1800 dollars, and the fourth twelve ounces valued at 2000 dollars; making the value, exclusive of the two boats,

* Travels in Mexico, p. 238

amount to 13,300 dollars, or about two thousand six hundred and sixty pounds sterling.

It has always been the popular opinion among the Spaniards, that there were immensely rich banks of Pearl Oysters on the shores of an island near the head of the Gulf called Tiburon; but that its inhabitants, who use poisoned arrows, were of such a savage disposition, that no one could approach it without being sacrificed: this originated in or at least was confirmed by the circumstance of some people being killed near it, and in consequence the king of Spain, whose laws seemed always to be made on the supposition that none of his subjects had the power to risk his own life, or the common sense to judge when it was in danger, decreed, that no one should hereafter approach that island for any purpose, or on any pretext whatever. This interdict has been to the present time strictly obeyed, and although the Mexican Republicans have thrown off the Spanish dominion, yet the dominion of early prejudice is not so easily got rid of, and consequently the island of Tiburon is still considered by the Mexican Spaniards as equally rich and perilous as heretofore; although recent visitors, and among others Mr. Hardy, have proved the risk and the riches to be equally apocryphal.

The most remarkable incident in the recent history of the Pearl Fishery of California is the fact

of an Association having been formed in London in
the year 1824 or 1825 for the express purpose of
prosecuting it, under a new and improved system.
The new company was termed the " Pearl and Coral
Fishery Association," and great expectations were
entertained from the activity of the Director, Lieut.
Hardy, R.N. and the use of a diving bell with which
he was furnished. The employment of the diving
bell certainly at first sight seems to hold out a great
prospect of success; and we learn from Humboldt
that long before the formation of this Association
the same idea was entertained by the Mexicans
themselves; and a project of this kind was started
in 1803 by an ecclesiastic residing at the City of
Mexico. He conceived that as the *busos* (divers)
lose much time and also injure their health in their
repeated descents and ascents, there would be immense benefits derived from taking advantage of
the facilities afforded by the diving bell for exploring the depths of the ocean. Furnished with a
mask and a flexible tube the diver, he conceived,
would be enabled to explore not merely the space
immediately below the bell, but all around it as far
as the length of the tube would permit. This tube
was connected with the body of the bell which not
only acted as a reservoir for the supply of air, but
also as a place of refuge or resort when the diver
was exhausted. Humboldt says that he saw a

a number of experiments made with this apparatus in a small lake or pond near the castle of Chopoltepec; and remarks that it was no doubt the first time a diving bell was constructed at a height of upwards of 7000 feet above the level of the sea.

It would appear that subsequently the priest, the maker of this diving bell (which was made of wood), proceeded to California and was reported to have realized, by means of it, a large fortune in a short period. We have, however, no authentic accounts of the expedition. The diving bell of the London Association, was, we believe, not a whit more advantageous to the progress of pearl-fishing or to the shareholders in London, than was that of the good Padre, even if it had never left its native pond at Chopoltepec. Some very ineffectual attempts seem to have been made, but not at all of a kind to decide the impracticability of such a plan of fishing: and we believe we may safely say that this problem remain still to be solved.

PART II.

UPPER CALIFORNIA.

CHAP. I.

FIRST SETTLEMENT OF UPPER CALIFORNIA BY THE FRANCIS-
CANS.—HISTORY OF THE MISSIONS TO THE DEATH OF
FATHER SERRA.

NEW or Upper California was discovered about the
year 1542, by Juan Rodrigues Cobrillo, a Spanish
navigator, and the coast explored by him (or by his
pilot, after his death,) as far north as 43° or 44° N.
lat. Part of the same coast, as formerly stated, was
visited by Sir Francis Drake in 1578. He did not,
however, touch so far to the southward as the country now called California; although the whole of
this coast has generally been called New Albion,
the name given to it by Sir Francis. In 1582 the
same coast was visited by Francisco Gali: and was,
as we have already seen, more fully explored in
1603 by Sebastian Viscayna. Captain Cook's discoveries did not reach so far to the southward as even
Drake's; but the whole of the coast has been since
visited and fully explored by other European navigators, besides Spaniards. The most distinguished
of these and who have published accounts of the

country, are Pérouse in 1786; Vancouver in 1792; Langsdorff in 1805; and Beechey in 1826. All of these found the country completely settled by the Spaniards; and it is the object of the present chapter to give an account of how this settlement was first effected. On this occasion, as in the case of Old California, I shall also avail myself of the information supplied by an old Spanish or rather Mexican chronicler; and here my authority is Father Francisco Palou, one of the original missionaries, and subsequently Principal of the Convent of San Fernando in Mexico. The work of Father Palou was published in Mexico in 1787. It gives a most minute account of the settlement under the name of " A Life of the Chief Missionary Father Junipero Serra."

The expulsion of the Jesuits from Lower California in 1767, seems to have attracted public attention more strongly to the countries of which it forms a part, and led to the determination of settling and civilizing the upper province. In the year following, this settlement was finally resolved on by the Viceroy of Mexico, the Marquis de Croix; and, as on former occasions, the enterprize was committed to the care of the priesthood. Accordingly, in 1768, Father Junipero Serra, a Franciscan Friar, was nominated Missionary President of Upper California, with a staff of sixteen brothers of his own

order all taken from the convent of San Fernando.
Some of these friars were destined to replace the
Jesuits in Lower California; and the remainder,
together with their chief, to proceed to the "spiritual conquest" of the Upper Province. Before
proceeding with the detail of the humble proceedings of these good men, I would warn the
reader here, as in the case of Lower California, that
if he is prepared to estimate the importance of the
history only according to the magnitude of the
events or the dignity of the actors, he had better
pass over the following narrative. To those, however, who look below the surface of things, and
who, in the pages of history, regard more the springs
of action, the motives and conduct of the agents,
than the grandeur of the results, and who study the
influence of progressive events, however small, on
the happiness of communities, " the short and simple annals" which I am about to trace will not be
devoid of interest.

The Father President having arrived at San Blas
in the month of February, 1768, with his sixteen
missionaries, they there met an equal number of
Jesuits who had arrived from Lower California,
whom they were to replace; and on the 12th March
they sailed for Loreto in the same vessel which
brought the Jesuits.   " This seraphic and apostolic

squadron (as Father Palou calls it) headed by the venerable Father Junipero Serra" arrived at their destination all well on the first of April, and dispersed themselves each to his respective mission to wait the arrival of the " Visitador General," Don Joseph Galvez, who was soon to follow them. He arrived, and embarked at San Blas on the 24th of May following, but experienced such a bad voyage that he did not arrive at La Paz till the sixth of July, having been unable to make Loreto. Galvez not only brought orders to visit the missions of Lower California, but also a royal order to superintend the expeditions to be dispatched for Monterey and San Diego in Upper California. Accordingly, after examining the situation of the different missions in Lower California, and particularly those on its northern frontier, the Visitador thought the best mode of putting the orders of the king into execution would be, to add to the projected expedition by sea, another by land; which setting off at the same time, might join at San Diego, and there make the first establishment. This plan he communicated to the Father President, who fully approved of it, and offered to hold himself and a competent number of his brother missionaries ready when required. It was subsequently determined that three missions should be formed in Upper California, viz. one at the port of Monterey, another at the port of San Diego, and a third between those two ports to be called San Buenaventura.

Soon afterwards two of the three packet boats destined for this expedition arrived from San Blas; one called the San Carlos, and the other the San Antonio. The former vessel having been put in a state fit for sea, the provisions and stores which had been brought from San Blas were put on board, as well as those collected in La Paz. There were also put on board agricultural implements, various seeds, both of Old and New Spain, and such other necessaries as could be procured, and which they thought would be useful in the new country. It was at the same time resolved, that the land expedition should take two hundred head of black cattle from the most northerly of the missions of Lower California, in order to stock the new establishments with that useful animal, and to enable them to cultivate the soil.

The San Carlos being ready, the Visitador General fixed the day of her departure, and ordered that all should prepare themselves by means of the holy Sacrament. This was accordingly done; and the Rev. Father President, after saying the Mass " de rogativa" to the most holy Patriarch, San Joseph, (whom they named patron of all the expeditions by sea and land), blessed the vessel and colours, and

gave his benediction to all the people. The Visitador then pronounced a long discourse, and every
thing being embarked, they set sail on the 9th day
of January, 1769.

There were embarked in this vessel her commander Don Vincente Vilal, twenty-five soldiers of
the Catalonion volunteers, with the Lieutenant Don
Pedro Prat, surgeon in the royal navy, with a sufficient crew and corresponding number of officers;
accompanied, for their spiritual consolation, by the
Father Friar Fernando Parron. The San Antonio
not having got higher up than Cape San Lucas, the
Visitador proceeded there on the sailing of the San
Carlos; and having examined and repaired her also,
every thing was embarked, and she made sail on
15th of February of the same year. Her commander was Don Juan Perez, an able navigator,
brought up in the Phillipine trade; in her also went
two father missionaries, Friar Juan Biscayno, and
Friar Francisco Gomez. The third vessel was called
the San Joseph, and was despatched from Loreto
on the 16th of June the same year; her commander's name is not known, and the Friar that was to
have proceeded with her fell sick, so that none of
the missionaries were on board.

The fate of these vessels proves the deplorable
state of navigation among the Spaniards in those
seas at this period. The San Carlos arrived at San

Diego on the first of May, and lost the whole of the people by the scurvy, thirst and hunger, except the officers, the cook, and one seaman. The San Antonio, although she sailed five weeks later, arrived on the eleventh of April, but lost eight of her crew by scurvy. The San Joseph was never heard of after her leaving Loreto.

The land expedition was set about with all possible activity; and it appears that those worthy Fathers and Visitadores, not only took their divinity from the bible, but their military tactics also; for Father Palou relates, " that considering the land expedition not less arduous and dangerous than that by sea, owing to the many savage and depraved tribes through which they had to pass, it was resolved, in imitation of the patriarch Jacob, to divide it into two companies, in order that if one was unfortunate, the other might be saved."

Don Gaspar de Portala captain of dragoons was appointed Governor of California, and Commander of the land expeditions, captain Fernando Rivera y Moncada was nominated his second, and appointed to proceed with the first division. The Governor was to follow with the second. Capt. Rivera y Moncada and his people left Santa Anna in Lower California in the month of September 1768; and after a short time arrived at the village of Nuestra Senora de los Angelos, which is on the Indian frontier, and where they met part of the baggage which had been sent in launches to the bay of San Luis. Having examined the country, and found it incapable of maintaining even the cattle from its entire want of pasture, they proceeded farther into the Indian territory ; and at the distance of eighteen leagues, in the direction of San Diego, they found a place suited to their wants. The whole caravan was accordingly conducted thither. From this place the Commander gave notice to the Visitador, who was then in the South fitting out the vessels, that in the month of March he expected to be ready to continue his route. Accordingly they left this place, called by the natives Villacata, and proceeded on their destination on the twenty-fourth of March, 1769. This division consisted of its commander Rivera y Moncada; Father Crespi ; a midshipman ; twenty-five soldiers; three muleteers ; and a number of converted Indians as servants or assistants to the muleteers and for other purposes : they were armed with bows and arrows. After having passed fifty-four days on their march without experiencing any thing remarkable, they arrived at the Port of San Diego on the fourteenth day of May, when they found at anchor the San Carlos and San Antonio.

The mules, horses, black cattle, muleteers, and baggage, which were to accompany the second

THE PYRAMIDS and QUARRIES of MOKATTAM, near CAIRO.

Day & Haghe Lith\`rs to the Queen.

division, being collected at Villacata, the Governor and the Father President arrived there on the thirteenth of May. Being detained some time waiting the arrival of troops and necessaries, they took the opportunity to examine the neighbourhood, and finding it superior to that of another mission not very distant called San Francisco de Borja, and considering that it would be well calculated for a point of communication between Upper and Lower California, they resolved on removing the mission to that place.

Father Palou thus describes the ceremony of taking possession : " this being determined on, and the day following being the fourteenth of May the first of the Pascua of the Holy Ghost, they immediately set about taking possession of the soil in the name of our catholic monarch; and thus laid the foundation of the Mission. The soldiers, muleteers and servants set about clearing away a place which was to serve as a temporary church, hanging the bells and forming a grand cross. On the day following they commenced the foundation; the venerable Father President being invested with the *Capa* and *Alba Pluvial* blessed the holy water, and with this the site of the church, and then the holy cross: which, being adorned as usual, was planted in front of the church. The patron named for this church, and of the whole mission, was Saint Fer-

nando, the same name as that of our college in
Mexico. Having chaunted the first mass, the venerable President pronounced a most fervent Discourse on the coming of the Holy Spirit, and the
establishment of the mission. The sacrifice of the
mass being concluded the *Veni Creator* was then
sung; the want of an organ and other musical
instruments being (says Father Palou) supplied by
the continual discharge of the fire-arms during the
ceremony, and the want of incense, of which they
had none, by the smoke of the muskets!"

The second division commanded by the Governor
Portala, and accompanied by the President, commenced its march from Villacata on the fifteenth of
May, 1769. They followed the track of the Jesuit
Winceslaus Link who went, three years before, towards the Rio Colorado, to a place which he called
Cieneguilla, distant from the new mission of San
Fernando Villacata twenty-five leagues northward.
From this place they pursued the same direction
with the view of finding the mouth of the Rio Colorado; but they were unable to arrive at it, on
account of a rocky and steep mountain, which they
reached after a few days, over which their cattle
could not pass. This obliged them to return to the
frontier mission of San Borja, from which the expedition of Link had set out. They now changed their
route to the North West, and approximating the

coast of the Pacific, were soon enabled to find the
port of which they were in search, and where they
arrived on the first day of July, having spent forty-
six days on their journey.

The following letter written by the President to
his future biographer, Father Palou, will serve to
explain their situation and views after they reached
San Diego :—

" My dear Friend and Sir,—Thank God, I arrived
the day before yesterday, the first of the month, at
this port of San Diego, truly a fine one, and with
reason called famous. Here I found those who had
set off before me both by sea and land, except those
who have died. The brethren Fathers Crespi, Biscayno, Parron, Gomez, are here, and, with myself,
all well, thanks be to God. Here are also the two
vessels, but the San Carlos without sailors, all having died of the scurvy except two. The San Antonio, although she sailed a month and a half later,
arrived twenty days before the San Carlos, losing on
the voyage eight sailors. In consequence of this
loss it has been resolved, that the San Antonio shall
return to San Blas to fetch sailors for her and for
the San Carlos. The causes of the delay of the San
Carlos were, first, lack of water, owing to the casks
being bad, which, together with bad water obtained
on the coast, occasioned sickness among the crew;
and secondly, the error which all were in respect-

ing the situation of this port. They supposed it to
be in thirty-three or thirty-four degrees of N. latitude; some authors saying one, some the other; and
strict orders were given to Captain Vila and the
rest to keep out in the open sea till they should arrive in thirty-four degrees, and then make the shore
in search of the port. As, however, the port, in
reality, lies in 32° 34', according to the observations
which have now been made, they went much beyond the port, thus making the voyage much longer
than was necessary. The people got daily worse
from the cold and the bad water, and they must all
have perished if they had not discovered the port
about the time they did; for they were quite unable to launch the boat to procure more water, or to
do any thing whatever for their preservation. The
Father Fernando did every thing in his power to
assist the sick, and although he arrived much reduced in flesh, he had not the disorder, and is now
well. We have not suffered hunger nor other privations, neither have the Indians who came with
us; all have arrived fat and healthy. The track
through which we have passed is generally very
good land, with plenty of water, and there, as well
as here, the country is neither rocky nor overcome
with brushwood. There are however many hills,
but they are composed of earth. The road has
been in some places good, but the greater part bad.

About half way, the vallies and banks of rivulets began to be delightful. We found vines of a large size, and in some cases quite loaded with grapes; we also found abundance of roses, which appeared to be like the same as those of Castile. In fine, it is a good country, and very different from that of Old California. We have seen Indians in immense numbers; and all those on this coast of the Pacific contrive to make a good subsistence on various seeds and by fishing; this they carry on by means of rafts or canoes made of Tule (bulrush) with with which they go a great way to sea. They are very civil. All the males, old and young, go naked; the women, however, and even the female children, are decently covered from their breasts downwards. We found in our journey, as well as in the places where we stopped, that they treated us with as much confidence and peace as if they had known us all their lives, but when we offered them any of our victuals, they always refused them. All they cared for was cloth; and only for something of this sort would they exchange their fish or whatever else they had. During the whole march we found hares, rabbits, some deer, and a multitude of Berendos (a kind of wild goat). I pray God may preserve your health and life many years.

" From this port and intended mission of San

Diego in Northern California, 3rd July, 1769. I kiss the hands of your Reverence and am your affectionate brother and servant,

FRANCIS JUNIPERO SERRA."

In consequence of what had before been determined on, the San Antonio was dispatched on the 9th July to San Blas, under the command of Perez, with what was reckoned a sufficient crew; but she arrived at that port with very few people, nine having died in the course of the voyage. It was now resolved that the principal part of the united expedition commanded by the Governor should proceed over land from San Diego to the northward, to discover and settle the port of Monterey, and that the Father President should remain with two of the missionaries and eight soldiers. The Fathers Juan Crespi and Francisco Gomez were named by him to accompany the expedition. The fourteenth day of July was fixed on for the departure of this expedition, and the following persons nominated for the same; Don Gaspar Portala commander-in-chief, with one servant; the two fathers before-named with two converted Indians of Lower California for their service; Don Fernando Rivera y Moncada, second in command, with a sergeant and twenty-six soldiers of his company; Don Pedro Foxes Lieutenant of the Catalonia company, with seven of his soldiers who remained fit for the march;

Don Miguel Constanzo, engineer, and seven muleteers, and fifteen Indians of Lower California, to
assist in conducting the mules with the provisions
and baggage.

This expedition, after having been absent six
months, returned to San Diego without finding the
port of Monterey; or at least what they considered
to be such, judging from the description given of it
by Sebastian Viscayno; although, in fact, they had
visited this bay, but considered that it was either a
different place, or that the port had been filled up
with sand. They proceeded on to the northward
till they discovered the fine harbour now called San
Francisco, to which they were induced to give that
name from the following circumstances :—When
the President left Lower California, he took his orders from the Visitador-general respecting the
names of the new missions, and the patrons to be
assigned them; but observing that he did not point
out any one which was to be that of the founder of
the order, he exclaimed, " And is our Father San
Francisco to have no mission assigned to him ?"
The Visitador replied, " If San Francisco wishes to
have a mission, let him shew you a good port, and
then let it bear his name." The Friars who accompanied the Monterey expedition as well as its commander, on seeing the fine bay at which they had
arrived exclaimed, " This is the port to which the

Visitador referred, and to which the saint has led us," and immediately called it the bay of San Francisco. They then set up a cross, took possession, and proceeded on their return to San Diego, where they arrived on the 24th Jannuary, 1770.

Whilst the Governor and his companions were absent on the discovery of Monterey, the President was not idle at San Diego. His proceedings are thus described by his historian, Father Palou :— " The zeal which burned in the breast of our venerable Father Junipero, did not permit him to forget the principal object of his coming, and on the 16th day of July he commenced the foundation of the mission, by chaunting a mass, and performing the other ceremonies which are expressed in the treaty of foundation of that of San Fernando. On this day the Spaniards are accustomed to celebrate the triumph of the Holy Cross ; and it was hoped that as by that sacred signal, they obtained on this same day in the year 1212, the famous victory over the barbarous Mahometans, they might obtain, by erecting the same standard, the discomfiture of the infernal army, and be enabled to subject to the easy yoke of our holy faith, the barbarous Gentiles who inhabit this California.

Having dedicated one of the huts which they had erected as a church, they endeavoured by presents and affectionate expressions, to bring the natives

towards it, who came within sight; but they paid
no attention to any thing except to receive whatever was offered them, except provisions; but on
no account would they touch any of our victuals;
and on a bit of meat being forced into a child's
mouth, it spit it out as if it had been poison. This
circumstance was considered as a miracle from heaven; for if they had been as desirous of provisions
as they were of cloth, they would have left the
strangers to have starved of hunger. Their desire
for all sort of cloth was extreme, so much so, that
the sails of the vessel in the bay were not safe, they
having gone one night in their rush canoes and cut
a large piece out of one of them. At length precautions were taken to prevent like acts; yet as no
punishment was inflicted, they proceeded to still
greater lengths and stole openly, confiding in their
numbers, and being armed with bows and arrows,
wooden swords which cut like steel, and clubs which
are very formidable. And now finding that they
were opposed, they resolved to try their fortune,
and by taking our lives possess themselves of all
our spoils. This they attempted to do on the
twelfth and thirteenth of August, but were obliged
to retire. On the fifteenth of this month, after the
Father Fernando had gone on board to say mass,
with two soldiers, four only remaining on shore, and
our venerable President and Father Biscayno hav-

ing finished mass at the mission, there fell upon
them a great number of Indians, all armed for
war, who began to rob every thing they could
find, taking away from the sick even their sheets.
The corporal immediately called out to arms, and
when they saw the soldiers putting on their lea-
ther armour, and taking their muskets, they retired
a little and began to shoot their arrows. The
four soldiers, the carpenter, and the blacksmith, also
commenced firing with much valour; but particularly the blacksmith, who although he had not armour to defend him, advanced, calling out, " Long
live the faith of Jesus Christ, and die the dogs his
enemies." Whilst this was going on, the Father
President with his companion went inside the house,
recommending all to God, and praying that there
should not result any deaths, either among his own
people, or among the Gentiles; and that the souls
of the latter might not be lost which otherwise
would be saved by future baptism.

The war, however, still continued, accompanied
by the terrible yells of the Indians, when a boy
called Joseph came running in great haste, and pros-
trated himself at the feet of our venerable President, saying, " Father, give me absolution, for the
Indians have killed me." The good Father absolved
him, and he died immediately, an arrow having
passed through his throat, but his death was kept

secret. Of the Indians many fell; and the rest seeing the destructive effect of the fire-arms, retired, carrying with them the whole of their dead and wounded, in order to prevent us from knowing their loss. They were enabled to conceal the deaths, but the number of wounded was soon known, because in a few days they returned in peace, requesting to be cured, which was done by our good surgeon. This charitable conduct on our part, caused them to be somewhat grateful, and the sorrowful experience of their unsuccessful attack created fear and respect, which made them deport themselves differently from what they had hitherto done, and they still continued to resist the mission, but without arms. Of the christians four were wounded, viz. the Friar Biscayno, one soldier, an Indian of California, and the valiant blacksmith; but none of them dangerously, so that in a short time all were well, and the death of the boy was concealed."

The following narrative, given by Father Palou, will shew the importance the missionaries attached to the baptizing of the Indians, and the inconsolable disappointment which the good Father Junipero suffered by the caprice of the parents of one of the children. This was the first of the inhabitants of Upper California who had submitted to this ceremony:—

Of those who came oftenest amongst them was an

Indian of about fifteen years of age, who seldom let a day pass without coming, and he at last was induced to eat whatever was given him without any fear. Our Father Junipero had a great desire to encourage him, and to teach him something of the Spanish language, to see if by this means he could accomplish the baptism of any of the youths. After some time, and when the Indian understood a little of the language, the venerable Father desired him to try if he could bring a little one with consent of its parents to become a christian, and told him to inform them, that by allowing a little water to be put upon its head, it would become a son of God, and of the Father Junipero, and also be of the kindred of the soldiers; that it would be clothed, and, in short, be equal to the Spaniards. The young man seemed to understand what was said to him, and after going amongst the Indians, returned, accompanied by a great many; one of whom brought a child in his arms, and made them understand by signs, that he wished it to be baptized. Full of joy our venerable Father gave some clothes to cover the child, asked the corporal to be its godfather, desired the soldiers to attend the celebration of this first baptism, and also ordered that all the Indians should be present. When the President had finished the previous ceremonies, and was about to pour the water, the Indians suddenly snatched away the

child, and immediately made off in great haste for
their huts, leaving the good Father in amazement,
with the water in his hands. Here (says the Father
Palou) all his prudence was necessary to enable him
to hold his peace under such a gross action; and
he was obliged to employ all his influence over the
soldiers, to prevent them from taking vengeance for
the affront; but on considering the barbarism and
ignorance of those miserable beings, it was deemed
necessary to dissemble their chagrin." Father Palou adds, " that the feeling of the venerable Father
was such, seeing the baptism of this child so frustrated, that for many days the sorrow and pain
which he suffered might be discovered in his countenance; his Reverence attributing the conduct of
the Indians to his own sins; and many years afterwards, when he related this circumstance, he had to
wipe the tears from his eyes."

The country at this time did not furnish them
sufficient provision for their subsistence, so that
they had to depend on supplies from San Blas; to
which place the San Antonio had been sent; but as
she had not yet made her appearance, and it being
apprehended that she was lost, the Governor ordered
an account of the provisions on hand to be taken,
and found that they could not hold out longer than
to the month of March following. He in consequence gave notice to the Father President, that

unless the vessel arrived with provisions by St. Joseph's day (the twentieth day of March), the whole
expedition would set out on their return by land for
Old California, and abandon entirely the enterprize
of settling the new country. This notice afflicted
the good Father Junipero in the most sensible manner, who, according to his biographer, " finding no
other resource but in God, had recourse to prayer;
asking in the most earnest manner, that he would
have compassion on so many Gentiles whom
they had discovered, and not allow their labours to
be in vain, seeing that if they were to abandon the
present enterprize, the conversion of those Indians
would be left to an indefinite time, and perhaps
abandoned for ever. At the same time the Father
fully resolved not to accompany the expedition back,
but to remain with some of his companions, and
sacrifice himself for the love of God, and for the
advancement of his glory." The eventful day at
last arrived, and was celebrated by the chaunting
of the mass, and by every other mode of solemnizing
it which their circumstances permitted. The Father President preached a sermon, and every preparation was made for the departure of the expedition the following morning; but on this very day
(says Palou), " God was pleased to satisfy the ardent
desires of his servant through the intercessions of
the most holy Patriarch, and gave every one the

consolation to perceive clearly and distinctly a vessel," which however disappeared next day. This sight of the vessel was sufficient to delay the departure of the expedition, every one viewing it as a miracle of the Patriarch Saint, and which animated them to remain some time longer, not doubting that this was, if not the San Antonio herself, at least a sure presage of her speedy arrival. This, in effect, happened four days after; it being the identical San Antonio which was seen on the day of San Joseph, and which was prevented from entering the harbour from those casualties so common in sea voyages. The Father President made a vow to celebrate this miracle by an annual mass on the day of San Joseph, which he religiously performed to the end of his life.

On the arrival of the San Antonio which brought a supply of provisions, it was determined to make another effort to discover Monterey; for which purpose Father Junipero proceeded by sea in the San Antonio and the Governor by land, accompanied by Father Crespi. Both left San Diego about the middle of April, 1770, and after forty-six days' navigation, the San Antonio anchored in the bay of Monterey; the land expedition having arrived some days before. Nothing can show more strikingly the backwardness of nautical science at this time among the Spanish navigators than the fact that this coasting voyage of a few degrees took up forty-six days;

in the present day it would be no miracle for a vessel to sail between San Diego and China in the same space of time.

The following is the letter of the President to Father Palou on taking possession of the future capital of the dominions over which he was to preside:

" My Dearest Friend and Sir,—On the 31st day of May, by the favour of God, after rather a painful voyage of a month and a half, this Packet San Antonio, commanded by Don Juan Perez, arrived and anchored in this horrible port of Monterey, which is unaltered in any degree from what it was when visited by the expedition of Don Sebastian Viscayno in the year 1603. It gave me great consolation to find that the land expedition had arrived eight days before us, and that Father Crespi and all others were in good health. On the third of June, being the holy day of Pentecost, the whole of the officers of sea and land, and all the people, assembled on a bank at the foot of an oak, where we caused an altar to be erected, and the bells to be rung; we then chaunted the *Veni Creator*, blessed the water; erected and blessed a grand cross, hoisted the royal standard, and chaunted the first mass that was ever performed in this place; we afterwards sung the *Salve* to our Lady before an image of the most illustrious Virgin which occupied the altar; and at the same time I preached a sermon, concluding the whole with a *Te Deum.* After this the officers took possession of the country in the name of the King our Lord, (whom God preserve). We then all dined together in a shady place on the beach; the whole ceremony being accompanied by many vollies and salutes by the troops and vessels."

The concluding part of this epistle may not be thought the least interesting, as it will show, that while men of an ordinary education would only have thought of their own personal situation and present difficulties, and of asking for assistance to help them out of them; the pious Franciscan only meditated on Popes, Saints, and Calenders. He continues :—" As in last May it is a whole year since I have received any letter from a Christian country, your Reverence may suppose in what want we are of news; but for all that, I only ask you, when you can get an opportunity, to inform me what our most holy Father, the reigning Pope is called, that I may put his name in the canon of the mass: also to say if the canonization of the beatified Joseph Cupertino, and Serafino Asculi has taken place; and if there is any other beatified one, or saint, in order that I may put them in the calender, and pray to them ; we having, it would appear, taken our leave of all printed calenders. Tell me also if it is true, that the Indians have killed Father Joseph Soler in

Sonora, and how it happened; and if there are, any other friends defunct, in order that I may commend them to God, with any thing else that your Reverence may think fit to communicate to a few poor hermits separated from human society. We proceed to-morrow to celebrate the feast, and make the procession of Corpus Christi (although in a very poor manner), in order to scare away whatever little devils (Diablillos) there possibly may be in this land. I kiss the hands, &c.

FR. JUNIPERO SERRA."

They then proceeded to found the mission of Monterey, and to construct a chapel; but the Indians were so terrified by the noise made at the celebration of the first mass, and by the firing of the artillery and muskets, that it was a considerable time before they ventured again to approach the strangers. It was not till the 26th of December that the first baptism of the Indians was celebrated at Monterey, which however turned out better than the first essay at St. Diego, and filled the pious mind of Father Junipero with inexpressible pleasure. He afterwards boasts, that in three years this mission had 175 baptized Indians; which is a proof of how slowly savages admit of civilization, or receive a new religion, however fervently practised or perseveringly advocated.

It was soon found that the first place selected for

Capt. Smyth R.N. &c.

THE BAY OF MONTEREY. UPPER CALIFORNIA.

by King sculp^t to the Queen

the mission was inconvenient; they therefore moved it to the borders of the river Carmelo, its present situation. The San Antonio being detained for some time, the Father President was enabled to examine the adjoining country; and finding many Indians, and good situations for establishing more missions, he wrote to the Chief of the College of San Fernando in Mexico, that although a hundred missionaries more were sent, there would be employment for them all.

In consequence of this favourable report of the promising appearances of the new country, the Viceroy, in concert with the College of San Fernando, ordered thirty missionaries to proceed from Mexico to San Blas; ten for Upper and twenty for Lower California; and provided them with sacred vessels and ornaments for the churches, and also with ten thousand dollars in money, to enable the Father President to form the other missions which he had projected. Orders were given to have two vessels ready at San Blas for the conveyance of the missionaries and their effects, viz. the San Antonio with the ten missionaries destined for Upper California, and the San Carlos with the twenty for Lower California. The San Antonio left San Blas on the second of January, 1771, and arrived at San Diego on the twelfth of March; all on board affected with the scurvy. The missionaries then

proceeded over land to Monterey. The missionaries who embarked for Loreto, had much worse
fortune than their brethren; for although Loreto is but a few days voyage from San Blas,
within the gulf, and the transit subject to no
peril whatever; yet it so happened, that the unlucky
San Carlos, instead of proceeding up the gulf of
California northerly, was driven, as they reported,
by winds and currents southerly, to Acapulco. Nor
was this all: the captain of this vessel, after having
allowed himself, at the best season of the year, and
on a sea the most placid in the world, to be carried
—one can hardly suppose how—so far south, put
into a port on the coast called Mansanillo now well
known as a good one, got his vessel on shore, and
gave notice to the viceroy of Mexico that he could
not proceed on his voyage! The poor friars being
now left to shift for themselves, resolved to proceed
overland; a distance of not less than twelve hundred miles, and along a coast without roads, without inhabitants, and abounding in all manner of
hardships and dangers, as well as being remarkable
for its insalubrity. This journey they actually performed, and marched along the shore of the Pacific,
and the gulf of California, till they arrived opposite
to Loreto, and then passed over to that place.

The captain in the mean time got positive orders
from Mexico to repair his vessel, and proceed on his

voyage. He at length sailed from Mansanillo, and after many difficulties arrived at Loreto on the thirteenth of August, extending the voyage to eight months, which is now usually made in five or six days!

By the arrival of the new missionaries in Upper California, the Father President was enabled to extend his operations, and proceeded to found the mission of San Antonio de Padua in the hills of Santa Lucia, distant from the coast of the pacific about eight leagues, and about twenty from Monterey. Some time after the establishment of this mission, we are told by our authority that so severe a frost took place on the first day of the Pascua of the resurrection, in the year 1780, that a field of wheat, which was shot, and in flower, became as dry and withered as if it had been stubble left in the field in the month of August. This was regarded as a great misfortune by the Indians, and still more by the Fathers, they knowing better the great loss to the mission from the want of food. It became necessary to send the converts to the woods to collect seeds and fruits for their subsistence, in the manner they had been accustomed to do before their conversion. The Fathers however (says Palou) encouraging their faith, and confiding in the patronage of San Antonio, invited the new christians to celebrate the Novena of this saint. At the same time they ordered the frosted field to be artificially irrigated with water; and in a few days the fresh blades were seen springing from the roots of the former stalks, so that at the end of the Novena the field was perfectly green. The watering was continued, and the wheat grew so rapidly, that in fifty days, the new wheat was as high as the former had been, and in full bloom; it filled well, and was ripe at the same time as in former years, giving such an abundant harvest, and such fine grain, as was never before experienced. "The Fathers (continues Palou) as well as the Indians, acknowledged this to be a special miracle which the Lord deigned to work in their favour by the interposition of the holy patron San Antonio, and rendered him their most affectionate thanks accordingly." Some less faithful than our good Fathers and their humble converts may doubt, whether San Antonio, or the water with the rays of a summer's sun had the greatest merit in this miracle; but it may be granted on all hands, that the prodigy had the excellent effects which the friars deduced from it, viz., that it encouraged new converts to come to them, and saved them from the threatened famine.

Soon after the settlement of San Antonio, the establishment of San Gabriel was determined on, and missionaries with soldiers were dispatched from San Diego for that purpose. The following is the

miraculous accounts given of this expedition by'
Father Palou.

" On the tenth of August the Father Friar Pedro
Cambon, and Father Angel Somera, guarded by ten
soldiers with the muleteers and beasts requisite to
carry the necessaries, set out from San Diego, and
travelled northerly by the same route as the former
expedition for Monterey had gone. After proceeding about forty leagues they arrived at the river
called Temblores; and while they were in the act
of examining the ground in order to fix a proper
place for the mission, a multitude of Indians, all
armed and headed by two captains, presented themselves, setting up horrid yells, and seeming determined to oppose the establishment of the mission.
The Fathers fearing that war would ensue, took out
a piece of cloth with the image of our Lady de los
Dolores, and held it up to the view of the barbarians.
This was no sooner done than the whole were quiet,
being subdued by the sight of this most precious
image; and throwing on the ground their bows and
arrows, the two captains came running with great
haste to lay the beads which they brought about their
necks at the feet of the sovereign queen, as a proof
of their entire regard; manifesting at the same time
that they wished to be at peace with us. They
then informed the whole of the neighbourhood of
what had taken place; and the people in large

numbers, men, women and children, soon came to see the holy virgin; bringing food which they put before her, thinking she required to eat as others. In this manner (continues our historian), the gentiles of the mission of San Gabriel were so entirely changed, that they frequented the establishment without reserve, and hardly knew how much to manifest their pleasure that the Spaniards had come to settle in their country. Under those favourable auspices the Fathers proceeded to found the mission with the accustomed ceremonies; and celebrated the first mass under a tree on the nativity of the virgin, the eighth of September, 1771."

After the settlement of San Gabriel, which was the fourth, and is now one of the richest missions of California, the missionaries found that neither their numbers nor their means enabled them to commence others; and they continued doing all in their power to improve those they had already established. The following letter from Father Junipero, dated so late as the eighth of August, 1772, shews that their situation was not the most comfortable, nor their progress very much advanced; although they had been more than three years in the country:—

"My Dear Friend and Sir,—Thanks be to God, I am in good health; and hunger, which in this country mortifies and has mortified many poor people, has not been felt, either by me or the Fathers, my fellows. There is no fear of being under the necessity of abandoning any of the missions now established. The people are chiefly maintained by the Indians, and they live God knows how. The milk of the cows and the vegetables of the garden have been two great sources of subsistence for these establishments; both begin however now to get scarce, but it is not for this I feel mortified; it is because we have not been able to go on with other missions. All of us feel the vexatious troubles and obstacles which we have to encounter, but no one thinks of leaving his mission, or desires to do so. The consolation is, that, troubles or no troubles, there are various souls in heaven from Monterey, San Antonio, and San Diego; from San Gabriel there are none as yet, but there are among those Indians many who praise God, and whose holy name is in their mouths more frequently than in that of many old christians; yet some think, that from mild lambs which they are at present, they will return one day to be lions and tigers. This may be so if God permits; but we have three years of experience with those of Monterey, and with those of San Antonio two years, and they appear better every day. If all are not already christians, it is in my opinion only owing to our want of understanding the language. This is a trouble which is not new to me;

and I have always imagined that my sins have not permitted me to possess this faculty of learning strange tongues, which is a great misfortune in a country such as this, where no interpreter or master of languages can be had until some of the natives learn Spanish, which requires a long time. At San Diego they have already overcome this difficulty. They now baptize adults and celebrate marriages, and we are here approximating the same point; we have begun to explain to the youth in Spanish, and if they could return us a little assistance in another way we should in a short time care little about the arrival of the vessels as far as respects provisions; but as affairs stand at present, the missions cannot much advance : upon the whole I confide in God who must remedy all."

After begging of his friend to procure more missionaries to be sent, he proceeds—

"Let those who come here come well provided with patience and charity, and let them pass on in good humour for they may become rich; I mean in troubles : but where will the labouring ox go, where he must not draw the plough? and if he do not draw the plough how can there be an harvest?"

Having now formed four missions the Father President resolved on returning to Mexico; and for that purpose set out for San Diego, where he intended to embark. On his way to that place he founded another mission, which he called San Luis Obispo de Tolozo: and having visited that of San Gabriel, being the only one he had not seen, he proceeded to San Diego, where he embarked in the packet boat San Carlos, on the twentieth of October, and arrived at San Blas on the fourth of November, 1772.

On his arrival in Mexico, which was on the sixth of February following, he found that the viceroy Bucareli had determined to withdraw the marine establishment from San Blas, and to abandon that port: but Father Junipero represented to him, that this was the only place from which a communication could be kept up with California, and so fully impressed him with the importance of the new missions, that he not only consented to continue the establishment at San Blas, but also ordered a frigate which had been begun to be built there to be finished for the purpose of exploring the coast of Upper California: and in the mean time gave orders for one of the packet boats to be dispatched to Monterey with provisions. This packet boat, with the usual mishap attending all their sea voyages, in place of making Monterey, was driven up the gulf, and reached Loreto with the loss of her rudder, and otherwise so much damaged that she could not again proceed on her voyage; by which accident the missions were nearly all starved, and the whole

Fathers, soldiers, and converts, were obliged to subsist chiefly on milk for eight months.

Having obtained all his demands the Father President left the city of Mexico in September 1773, with various missionaries, officers, and soldiers, as also a grant of necessaries, consisting of maize, beans, flour and clothing, to the value of above twelve thousand dollars : and by his recommendation an expedition was ordered to proceed by the rivers Gila and Colorado, and to discover a passage by that route for the purpose of keeping up a communication by land, and thus avoid the misfortunes which had always befallen their expeditions by sea. Captain Juan Bautista Anza, commandant of Tubac in the province of Sonora, was appointed to this land expedition, and eventually arrived safe at Monterey. Father Junipero proceeded to San Blas in January. He divided the supplies between the packet boat San Antonio, and the new frigate ; and embarked in the latter himself. She was called the Santiago of New Galicia, and commanded by his friend Don Juan Perez. Although they were bound direct to Monterey, yet from some of those fatalities which never ceased to attend them, they were obliged to put into San Diego, where they arrived on the thirteenth of March, after a passage of forty-nine days. The frigate afterwards pursued her voyage to Monterey, but Father Junipero chose to go overland for the purpose of visiting the other missions, and on his way met captain Anza, who had, as before stated, passed overland from Sonora, and who informed him, that it was practicable to open a communication by the route he had come, and that according to his orders from the viceroy, he was about to take measures for establishing this communication.

Aranza here also informed the President of the deplorable state in which Monterey was from the want of Provisions, that " there was not so much as a cup of chocolate to enable them to break their fast"—a privation of all others the most insufferable to a Mexican Spaniard, to whom chocolate is one of the most indispensable necessaries of life. The captain added, that they were reduced to live entirely on milk and herbs, without bread or any other thing whatever. This relation made the good Father shed tears, and he made all possible haste to arrive with the succours he had with him. He arrived on the eleventh of May, and found that the frigate had been there two days before him. The Father President was received at Monterey with the greatest demonstration of joy, and plenty once more appeared amongst them.

The frigate after remaining at Monterey till the eleventh of June, sailed, in conformity with the instructions of the viceroy, in order to make discoveries on the north-west coast. She proceeded as far as fifty-five degrees north, when she discovered

an inlet which they named Santa Margarita, and
without seeming to have done anything else, they
returned to Monterey, where they arrived on the
twenty-seventh of August of the same year.   A
second voyage was afterwards made from San Blas
by the same frigate, under the command of Don
Bruno de Ezeta a captain in the royal navy, who
took with him as his second in command, the same
Don Juan Perez who commanded the previous expedition. The frigate was accompanied by a schooner commanded by Don Juan Francisco de la Bodega the future friend of Vancouver and who was
so well known on this coast. This expedition sailed
from San Blas in the middle of March, 1775. They
proceeded to the northward, surveying the coast
to forty-seven degrees of north latitude, when they
lost sight of the schooner in a gale of wind on the
thirtieth of July: the frigate however continued to
coast northward till they arrived about the same
latitude as in the last voyage, and having again returned to the forty-ninth degree they held a consul-
tation of officers on the eleventh of August, and it
was resolved in consequence of the greater part of
the crew being ill of the scurvy, and the advanced
state of the season, to return along shore, and to
look out for the schooner. This plan was adopted,
and they arrived at Monterey on the twenty-ninth of
August, with almost all the sailors ill of the scurvy.

They here found the schooner which had safely arrived some time before them.

After receiving the account of this expedition, the Viceroy Bucareli determined to set on foot a third; and for that purpose ordered a frigate to be built at San Blas; and also sent a Lieutenant of the Navy to Peru to purchase a vessel to accompany the frigate. The new frigate was named the Princesa, and the ship purchased in Peru the Favorita; they were ordered to be got ready with all haste, and the Viceroy gave directions to put on board every thing necessary for a voyage of one year, with a sufficient crew, and complement of marines. Don Ignatio Artiago was appointed to command the squadron, and two missionaries from the Convent of San Fernando accompanied him. These two vessels sailed from San Blas on the twelfth of February, 1779; and as Don Juan Perez had died at sea on the former voyage, they took another pilot in his stead. The chief object of the expedition was said to be, to discover a passage to the North Atlantic. Nothing worthy of notice happened till they arrived at fifty-five degrees of north latitude on the third of June, when they entered a strait which they called the Strait of Bucareli; here they occupied themselves in looking for a passage to the eastward till the first of July, when they proceeded to the northward, and were in about sixty degrees of north latitude on the first of August; and here they say they found a large port quite secure, and well provided with wood and water, as well as abundance of fish. This they took possession of and named Santiago. It is supposed to be what is now called Cook's Inlet. Finding an arm branching off to the northward, and appearing to run far inland, the commander dispatched an armed launch with an officer and a pilot to examine it, but after passing up this creek for some days, the launch returned without seeing any appearance of its termination; the crew, however, bringing with them some natives from the interior of the bay. The commander did not proceed farther in this survey, but as there were many sick, resolved, as the season was far advanced, and the equinox near, not to make any more surveys, but to consider his labours as concluded. He accordingly desired the pilots to make for some of the new settlements in California where he might cure the sick, and pass the equinox. Thereupon they stood for the port of San Fernando, which they reached on the fifteenth of September, 1779, when the usual masses and other religious ceremonies were performed to celebrate the happy issue of this adventurous voyage.

I have gone before the order of time for the purpose of giving a connected account of these voyages to the north-west; but I wish only to notice them in as far as they relate to the establishments of California. It is sufficient to look at the dates, and the time employed on those voyages to show, that little could be added by them to nautical science or discovery. Modern voyagers know, that the summer weather continues in those latitudes long after the time the Spaniards considered it as concluded, and it would not now-a-days be thought very enterprizing, if any of our commanders gave up his discoveries in the northern regions at the end of August! But the President and Commandant, Artiago, whose apprehensions of the equinox overcame his faith in the protection of our Lady of the Regla, thought it best to return in time, and found himself safely anchored in San Francisco on the fifteenth of September, seven days before the justly dreaded time of the sun's passing the line.

With the supply of provisions and other necessaries which the President brought from Mexico, the missionaries recommenced their labours with much vigour, and had a corresponding success in the conversion of the natives and the establishment of new missions; but in the following year an occurrence took place which was considered of great importance, being no less than the attack of San Diego, and the assassination of one of the missionaries by the natives. This affair is related by Father Palou with great unction and becoming gra-

vity. " In proportion (says he) as the Fathers and
the new christians were full of joy and peace, the
discontent of the great enemy of souls was increased; his infernal fury could not suffer him to
see that in the neighbourhood of San Diego his
party of Gentiles was coming to a close, so many
being brought over to our true religion by means
of the ardent zeal of the ministers; and the more
particularly, as they were about to plant another
mission between San Gabriel and San Diego, which
would effect the same with the Indians in that district, over which he still had the power, and which
would of course diminish his party. He therefore
bethought himself of some means, not only of preventing this new establishment, but of destroying
that of San Diego, which was the oldest of the
whole, and so revenge himself on the missionaries,
his opponents. In order to accomplish these diabo-
lical intentions, he availed himself of two converts
from among those who had been sometime baptized,
who after the feast of San Francisco, went amongst
the Indians, publishing, that the fathers intended to
put an end to the Gentiles, and to make them become christians by force; and in proof of this, desired them to consider how many had already been
baptized. Although many doubted, yet the greater
part believed the story of those apostates; and the
Devil having so disposed them, he engendered in

their breast the passion of anger against the fathers; and with this disposition they formed the cruel intention of taking away their lives ; as also to kill the soldiers, set fire to the mission, and so destroy the whole. Nothing of this was known at San Diego, nor was any such plot in the least apprehended ; for although a serjeant and some soldiers were sent in search of the two converts who went away without leave, yet the only account they received was, that they had gone a long way inland towards the river Colorado, and nothing was observed among the Indians which indicated war : but what soon happened shows their intentions, which however they concealed with great art. More than a thousand Indians collected from different places, and divided themselves in two parties ; one to attack the mission, and the other the Presidio where the soldiers were quartered. They intended to set fire to both at the same time, and to kill all the people ; on which wicked design they set out armed with bows and arrows, spears and clubs.

They arrived at the bed of the river on the night of the fourth of November, whence the two divisions took their respective routes ; the one for the Presidio, and the other for the mission. The party destined for the latter arrived at the huts of the converts without being observed ; putting some Indians as guards to prevent the inmates from

going out or giving any alarm, and threatening them
with death if they attempted to do so.   Some then
proceeded to the church and sacristy, for the purpose of robbing the ornaments, vestments, and whatever else they might find; while others laid hold
of lights, and endeavoured to set the quarters
of the soldiers on fire.   These, who consisted only
of a corporal and three men, were soon awakened
by the horrid yells of the Indians, and immediately armed themselves; the Indians having
already begun to..discharge their arrows.   The
Father Vincente joined the soldiers, together with
two boys.   The Father Lewis who slept in a separate apartment, on hearing the noise went towards
the Indians, and on approaching them made use
of the usual salution, " Amar a Dios, Hijos," (Love
God, my children) when observing it was the Father
they laid hold of him as a wolf would lay hold of
a lamb, and carried him to the side of the rivulet.
There they tore off his holy habit, commenced
giving him blows with their clubs, and discharged
innumerable arrows at him.   Not contented with
taking away his life with so much fury, they beat
and cut to pieces his face, head, and the whole of
his body, so that from head to foot nothing remained whole except his consecrated hands, which were
found entire, in the place where he was mudered.

" Meanwhile others of the Indians proceeded to

the place where two carpenters and the blacksmith
were sleeping, and who were awakened by the noise.
The blacksmith ran out with his sword in hand,
but was immediately shot dead with an arrow ; one
of the carpenters followed with a loaded musket,
and shot some of the Indians, who were so much
intimidated, that he was allowed to join the soldiers ;
the other carpenter who was ill was killed in bed by
an arrow. The chief body of the Indians now engaged the soldiers, who made such good use of
their fire arms by killing some and wounding others,
that the Indians began to waver, but they at last
set fire to the quarters of the Spaniards, which was
only of wood, and who in order to avoid being
roasted alive, valiantly sallied forth and took possession of another small hut which had served for a
kitchen, and which was constructed of dried bricks.
The walls however were little more than a yard in
height, and only covered with branches of trees and
leaves to keep out the sun. They defended themselves by keeping up a continual fire upon the
multitude, who however annoyed them much with
their arrows and wooden spears, more particularly
at one side of the hut which was without a wall.
Seeing the damage that by this means they were
suffering, the soldiers resolved to take out of the
house that was on fire, some bales to fill up the
open part of the kitchen. In doing this, two of

them were wounded and disabled from giving any more assistance, but they succeeded in fetching the the bales, and filling up the breach with them. There then only remained the corporal, one soldier, the carpenter, and the Father Vincente. The corporal who was of great valour, and a good marksman, ordered that the others should load and prime the muskets, he only firing them off; by which method he killed or wounded as many as approached him. The Indians now seeing that their arrows were of no avail owing to the defence of the walls and bales, set fire to the covering of the kitchen; but as the materials were very slight, the corporal and his companions were still enabled to keep their position. They were greatly afraid lest their powder should be set on fire; and this would have been the case, if Father Vincente had not taken the precaution to cover it over with the skirt of his habit, which he did in disregard of the risk he ran of being blown up. The Indians finding that this mode of attack did not oblige their opponents to leave their fort, commenced throwing in burning faggots and stones, by which Father Vincente was wounded, but not very dangerously. The whole night passed in this manner, till on the rising of the sun the Indians gave up the contest, and retired carrying off all their killed and wounded. The whole of the defenders of the kitchen fort were wounded, the corporal concealing his injuries until the Indians had retired, in order to avoid discouraging his companions."

I have given the description of this contest at full length, and in the language of the Franciscan historian, in order to show, that a battle, when the forces on one side only consisted of three soldiers, commanded by a corporal, may be made nearly as much of on paper as when mighty armies meet. The account of the defence of the kitchen fort, is given with as much gravity and circumstantiality, as if the narrative were of one of Napoleon's victories; and it must be confessed, that the issue was as important to the individuals engaged in this Lilliputian combat, as was the result of Austerlitz or Lodi to their victor. It is also worthy of record, as being the most serious attempt to obstruct the Spanish missionaries in their *spiritual conquest* of California; and it may in some degree account for the apparently miraculous conquests of the Spaniards in Mexico and Peru in former times, by proving how superior the European with his musket and his gunpowder, is to the feeble and unskilful Indian with his bow and arrow.

On hearing of the misfortune which befel San Diego, the Father President who was then at Monterey, resolved to proceed to that mission; but was not able to accomplish his design till the month of

June. He then proceeded by sea in the Princesa, and with the assistance of the seamen of this vessel, the soldiers and others, he repaired the damages done by the Indians, and again put matters on the same footing as before the attack. Subsequently he set about forming another mission called St. John Capistran. On his way to this place he was about to be attacked by the Indians ; but was saved by one of the converts, who had the presence of mind to call out in the Indian dialect, that many soldiers, were close behind ; on which the assailants gave up their intention, and finally joined the Spaniards on their journey, receiving beads, and becoming friends.

After founding this mission, the President proceeded to Monterey, and prepared to establish that of San Francisco on the borders of the bay of that name, which had long been projected. He left Monterey on the seventeenth day of June, 1776, with some soldiers, and several families of people, who had come overland from Sonora to establish themselves in the country, carrying with them black cattle, mules, and necessaries for the new mission. One of the packet boats proceeded at the same time for the harbour of San Francisco, with the rest of the necessaries.

On the twenty-seventh of June the expedition arrived near the situation where they intended to

plant the mission, on the banks of the lake near one of the arms of the bay of San Francisco. While they there waited the arrival of the vessel to determine the exact spot for its foundation, many of the natives came to them with demonstrations of peace, and expressed pleasure at their arrival. Finding that the packet boat did not make its appearance, they commenced cutting timber for their houses, and pitched upon the most eligible situation for the Presidio near the place where they had halted. Indeed the vessel did not arrive till the eighteenth of August, having been detained by contrary winds which drove her back as far as to the latitude of thirty-three degrees.

They took solemn possesion of this Presidio on the seventeenth day of September, " this day being (says Father Palou) the festival of the impression of the sores of San Francisco the patron of the Port. After blessing, adoring, and planting the holy cross; the first mass was chaunted, and the ceremony concluded by a *Te Deum*; the act of possession in the name of our sovereign being accompanied with many discharges of artillery and musketry by sea and land."

They afterwards proceeded to survey the harbour both by land, and by a launch; and ascertained that there was no other outlet to the ocean except by the passage through which they had entered.

Previous to the vessel returning to San Blas, they performed the ceremony of taking possession of the mission, in the same manner as they had before done of the Presidio; and this they did on the day of San Francisco in the ninth of November.

It appears that about this time Father Palou joined the missionaries in Upper California, as he now begins to speak in the first person; consequently his authority is even more valuable than before. We resume our narrative in his words.

" None of the natives attended these ceremonies, as in the middle of August the whole of those who inhabited this place disappeared, going in their rush balsas, some to uninhabited islands in the bay, others to the other side of the strait. This movement was occasioned by their being surprized by a tribe or nation called the Salsonas, their great enemies, who on this occasion, killed a great number of them, and set fire to their huts. This misfortune we were unable to prevent, as the surprise and destruction took place without our knowledge, and when we endeavoured to detain the flying Indians they paid no attention to us. This flight of the Indians was the cause of our being a long time without making any converts, as we did not see any of them again till the end of March of the following year. They then began to get over the fear of their enemies and once more reposed some confidence in us. The first baptism performed in this mission was on St. John's day of this year, 1776.

I shall not further follow the progress of the President Junipero Serra and his spiritual associates in the formation of the other missions; suffice it to say, that before his death, in 1782, there were established in addition to those already mentioned, Santa Clara, Santa Barbara, and San Buena Ventura; which, together with San Diego, Monterey, San Antonio, San Gabriel and San Francisco, made in the whole eight missions, all of which he occasionally visited.

But he had at last to yield up his account, and to withdraw from the field in which he had so long and so laboriously toiled; in the hope, however, of joining in another world his prototype and master San Francisco—whom he had so assiduously made the object of his veneration, and model for his labours in this.

"We piously believed (says Father Palou) that he had slept in the Lord a little before two in the afternoon, on the day of San Augustin, in the year 1782, and that he would go and receive in heaven the reward of all his apostolical labours. He finished his labourious life at the age of seventy years, nine months, and twenty-one days: he had passed fifty-three years, eleven months, and thirteen days,

K

in holy orders; and of this time, thirty-five years, four months, and thirteen days, in the office of apostolic missionary; in which time, he performed the glorious actions which we have seen; having lived in continual activity, occupied in virtuous and holy exercises, and in singular prowesses; all directed to the greater glory of God, and the salvation of souls."

CHAP. II.

———

THE same plan of colonization and management
which has been described in the preceding chapter,
continued to be carried on with little or no variation by Father Serra's successors, until the whole of
the littoral territories of California, with all their
inhabitants, came under the temporal and spiritual
dominion of the missionaries. A description of the
settlement and progress of the individual missions,
if their history could be obtained, would possess little interest. In a subsequent chapter I shall give
an account of the actual condition of the whole;
and will now conclude this by a brief notice of the
civil history of the country up to the present time.

During the long period that had elapsed since the
first foundation of the missions, many large dona-
tions had been bestowed, and numerous estates in
land and houses left for the benefit of the missions,
which were consolidated into a fund called the

K 2

California Pious Fund.   This fund was managed
by the Convent of San Fernando and other trustees
in Mexico, and the proceeds regularly remitted
annually to California, as also the salaries assigned
to the missionaries by the king.   The government
likewise sent soldiers to protect them from the attack of the wild Indians and foreign enemies.

Under this state of things the missions greatly
prospered.   They went on augmenting their possessions, increasing their stock of domestic animals,
and the number of converted Indians, until they
had absorbed nearly the whole of the valuable lands,
to the almost total exclusion of free white settlers.
No one could possess land except by a grant from
the missionaries, who on all occasions were very re-
served in conceding such grants; and few colonists
were to be found, except the officers of the troops,
the soldiers, and their followers.   Great care was
taken, that the soldiers should not leave too many
descendants to the supposed prejudice of the missionary plan; and as no officer or soldier in his
Catholic Majesty's service can marry without his
special licence, it could easily be managed that as
many marriages were permitted as was desired, and
no more.   This fully accounts for the very scanty
number of free colonists that exists in California.

In Upper as in Lower California the missionary
establishments were acknowledged to be the great

objects for which the country was settled and maintained; and they existed in an almost complete
state of independence of the Mexican government.
Still the country belonged to Spain, and all the ordinary government establishments were kept up in
it, although to a much smaller extent than in the
other provinces of the Vice-royalty of New Spain.
The general commandant of all the troops in the
country was also governor of all places and persons not under the immediate authority of the Fathers.   He resided at Monterey, and had a salary
of four thousand dollars.   He could not interfere
with the affairs of the missions, but was obliged to
grant them assistance when they claimed it.

The antient system remained in full force until
the period of the revolution in Mexico and the separation of all the Americas from Spain.   At that
time Upper California was formed into what is called
a territory, and Lower California into another, on the
ground of their respective population not amounting
to the number entitling them to be federative states;
these being established on the basis of population.

The territories are not entitled to have governors or legislatures, but are allowed to send one
member to the general congress.   This member is
entitled to sit and take a part in discussions, but
has no vote.   The territories are, from their being
deprived of governors or legislatures, subject to the

immediate government and legislation of the general
government in Mexico. This reduced Upper California to be directed by an agent of the government,
who resided there under the denomination of commandant general. This state of things California
has not as yet had much cause to lament; for until
wiser legislation is adopted, and greater harmony
exists between the general government and the
different state legislatures, it is no great misfortune
to be deprived of the labours of a provincial popular
assembly.

The two Californias send each a member to the
general congress, elected by popular suffrage. The
first deputy elected for Upper California was a
captain of the Californian troops, and a Spaniard by
birth; but on his arrival at San Blas he found a law
had been passed excluding natives of Spain from
congress, and he was obliged to return. A lieutenant was then elected to succeed him who proceeded
to the city of Mexico where he died. A serjeant
of the same corps was next elected, who served out
his term of two years in the Mexican congress, and
then returned to his native country: this retrogres-
sion in the rank of the honorable members is rather
singular.

When an enlightened man shall govern this distant and thinly peopled country, it must be much
better regulated than if it were domineered over and

plundered by a set of ill-informed and rapacious men, united into a democratic council, and daily manufacturing absurd laws and regulations which, after a very short time, are laid aside for some fresh whim, as a child throws away its play-thing at the sight of a new one.   It is true that even in the territories there is some semblance of a local government, for they have what is called a deputation, which is a sort of privy council, more for the purpose of advising with the commandant, than of originating any thing of themselves; their powers are consequently very limited and their re-union takes place but very seldom.

When visited in 1826 and 1827 by Captain Beechey, the missions had begun to feel the effect of the recent changes in the government of Mexico. At this time there had arrived orders to liberate all the Indians " who had good characters and were supposed able to maintain themselves from having been taught the art of agriculture or some trade." They were directed to have portions of land given to them for their maintenance and the district to be divided into parishes, with curates provided for each. At the same time, the missionaries' salaries, formerly paid by government (400 dollars per annum) were suspended, the country being expected to support its own establishment.   Considering the utterly helpless and enslaved -state of the Indians, which we shall describe more fully by and bye, it is not to be supposed that a system of legislation of this sort, however philanthropic in appearance, could really answer the intended object. Accordingly when captain Beechey returned in the following year (Nov. 1827) he found that the new project had failed, and matters were in some degree restored to their former state. In consequence of the strong remonstrances of the Fathers, the governor had modified the orders received from Mexico and agreed to make the experiment on a small scale. " After a few months trial (says captain Beechey) he found that these people, who had always been accustomed to the care and discipline of school-boys, finding themselves their own masters, indulged freely in those excesses which it had been the endeavours of their tutors to repress, and that many having gambled away their clothes, implements and even their land, were compelled to beg or to plunder ; in order to support life. They at length became so obnoxious to the peaceable inhabitants, that the padres were requested to take some of them back to the missions, while others who had been guilty of misdemeanors, were loaded with shackles and put to hard work, and when we arrived were employed in transporting enormous stones to the beach to improve the landing place."* This unfor-

* Voyage to the Pacific. Vol. ii. page 320.

tunate result was taken advantage of by the Fathers,
and their remonstrances procured not only the re-
storation of their salaries but a promise of payment
of the arrears, they consenting to be submissive to
the new government.

Since this time various contradictory laws have
been passed respecting this country, and projects
for its government and improvement, equally contradictory set on foot: yet it is true that no change
of government or of system has been able materially
to alter the original Franciscan dispensation, which
may still be said to exist in all its primitive purity.
The great source of the property of the missions is,
however, now, I believe, effectually dried up: viz.
their supplies from Mexico; for although the natives of Spain and their descendants inhabiting
Mexico, retained their religious zeal for conquering
infidels and converting heathens, longer, and in
greater force, than the other European Christians,
yet the American revolutions swept this, together
with the inquisition and many other equally venerable customs, entirely away; and the modern Republicans want money too much at home to think
of sending any to so remote a place as California;
so that the *Pious Fund of California*, like most
other funds that could be made available, has been
put to less pious uses. But the value of the estates
of the missions has so much increased, as well from

the multiplication of the domestic animals and augmented agricultural produce of the soil, as from the
additional demand and consequent increase of
price which the opening of the trade to strangers has
caused, that the missionaries are not only able to
maintain themselves, but have to spare; and in
place of receiving supplies from Mexico are even
obliged to maintain the government troops. And
although it has been a general opinion in Mexico
since the Revolution that the Californian system
should be altered, yet it would appear that the
government under the presidency of Bustamante,
or rather the ministry of Alaman, thought otherwise;
for in 1833 they sent a reinforcement of eleven Franciscan Friars with a new Prefect of the same order
at their head. These Friars were some time detained at Tepic, a town near San Blas, waiting for a
vessel, where I had an opportunity of seeing them.
They were fresh from a Convent of Zacatecas, where
the rules are very strict; they all wore a habit of
the coarsest grey woollen cloth, their crowns shaven,
and sandals on their feet. They were totally ignorant of the world, and of every thing respecting the
country which they were going to govern. They
brought to one's mind, in the most lively manner,
the days of the pilgrimages of the middle ages; and
if the anomalous nature of their destination could
have been kept out of view, they would have formed

an interesting group. As it was, it was impossible not to feel respect for their character, and a degree of veneration mixed with pity on thinking on their destiny and observing their very pious, humble, and meek demeanor. It will not be here out of place to give, in a few words, the future history of these poor friars, as it will illustrate at once their character and the still very unsettled state of these countries. It will also doubtless remind the reader of the old days of Fathers Salvatierra and Junipero Serra.

General Figueroa being appointed military governor or commandant general of Upper California, chartered a vessel in Acapulco to take himself with some officers and soldiers to Monterey, and intended to call at San Blas for eleven Missionaries who were to join him there. Instead however of proceeding directly to San Blas, he thought it would be better to touch at San Lucas in Lower California, disembark there with the soldiers, and send the ship to San Blas for the friars, and then to proceed to Mazatlan for some military stores. This was accordingly done; and while the vessel was in the bay of Mazatlan, and after having the gunpowder and most of the other stores on board, she was struck with lightning, which passed along the mizen mast into the hold and set fire to some materials very near the powder. The fire was fortunately extinguished before any bad consequence ensued. The lightning passed close to the cabin of the friars who were all below, and it was remarked with what wonderful calmness they betook themselves to their only remedy, their sacred offices and rosaries; it was indeed only by force that the officers and seamen could remove them from off the hatch to get down the magazine which was immediately below them; and they were thus only saved by the prompt exertions of the seamen from being blown to atoms. This danger being over and the vessel again put to rights, she proceeded to cape San Lucas to take on board the general and troops; and as the friars were all sick,—never having before even seen salt water—they went on shore the moment the ship came to anchor. The general then gave orders for embarcation next morning, and the first division of soldiers proceeded to the beach with ammunition, arm-chests, &c. When the whole was ready for putting off in the launch, a serjeant informed his officers that he and his comrades had determined not to proceed to Upper California, declared for the party of general Santa Anna then in revolution against the government, and avowed their intention of proceeding to San Blas to join their brother patriots engaged in the same cause; at the same time arming themselves they proceeded to fire upon the quarters of the general with whom were the unfortunate friars. In this extremity the general and

his companions, who were unarmed, had to fly, and
the mutineers took possession of the ship, and
obliged the captain to carry them to San Blas,
taking along with them the military chest in which
were sixteen thousand dollars, as well as the private
property of the general and his officers. The
serjeant, however, generously, or rather piously, sent
on shore before his departure three thousand dollars
for the friars, thus verifying what is far from uncommon, that a very considerable degree of religious feeling may be manifested by those who are
guilty of the most atrocious crimes. The poor
friars were now left in an almost desert country;
and having experienced so unpromising an onset in
their sea voyage, resolved not to trust themselves
again to that element which seemed to them so
unpropitious, and which had also been so fatal to
their predecessors the first settlers of California.
They at first determined to follow the route by land
which the Father Junipero had done so many years
before them ; but reflecting upon the difficulties
which presented themselves, and receiving the coun-
sel, or perhaps commands of the general, they were
at length prevailed on to proceed to La Paz and
there wait further orders from Mexico.

In the mean time the vessel proceeded on her
voyage to San Blas, during which the serjeant
broke open the military chest, and took what money

he thought necessary to divide amongst his followers and the sailors ; he also assigned a sum for the
captain and mates, which, as they did not think it
prudent to offend him, they received, but returned
on their arrival at San Blas. On the arrival of
the vessel at this port which had also declared for
Santa Anna, the serjeant and his soldiers were received by their compatriots with open arms, and
the remainder of the money which he chose to
deliver up to the authorities, was thankfully received, leaving this worthy character to appropriate
to himself what he pleased. The ship after repairing her damages, getting some fresh stores, and
spending a long time on the coast, at last proceeded
to La Paz, where the friars once more embarked,
and finally arrived at their destination.

Notwithstanding this indication of following up
the old system, a law was soon after passed by the
general congress of Mexico for entirely removing
the missionaries, dividing the lands and cattle
amongst the Indians and settlers, and appropriating
their funds in Mexico to the use of the state. The
democratic party then in power, soon after the
passing of the law, named commissioners amongst
their own friends to carry it into execution, and
empowered them to engage emigrants in Mexico
to accompany them, and to whom the pay of half a
dollar a day was assigned till their arrival in Cali-

fornia, with a free passage and provisions during their voyage. Nearly three hundred people engaged on those terms, consisting of men, women, and children. They were of every class of persons except that which could be useful;—for there was not one agriculturist amongst them. They were chiefly from the city of Mexico, and consisted of artizans and idlers who had been made to believe that they would soon enrich themselves in idleness in this happy country. There were to be seen goldsmiths proceeding to a country where no gold or silver existed, blacksmiths to where no horses are shod or iron used, carpenters to where only huts without furniture were erected, shoemakers to where only sandals of raw hide were worn, tailors to where the inhabitants only covered themselves with a blanket, doctors to where no one gets sick; there were also engravers, printers, musicians, gamblers, and other nameless professors, all bound on this hopeful crusade, which their enthusiastic leaders assured them would procure unalloyed felicity and unbounded riches. The projectors and leaders of this colony had also formed and published a magnificent plan of a public company which they entitled " The Cosmopolite Company" (compania cosmopolitana). It embraced the three great branches of agriculture, manufactures and commerce, which were to be carried on upon a scale of great magnitude. Governors, directors, secretaries, clerks, inspectors of accounts, administrators, major-domos, and all the other multifarious officers so well understood in Spanish undertakings, and so necessary in such projects, were provided in profusion, and the most minute regulations specified for their government: none of our celebrated companies of 1825 could possibly surpass them in the extent of their views, or the exactness of their detail. To carry this scheme into execution, subscription shares were opened for the emigrants and others, and it is said that about eight thousand dollars (£1,600) were obtained. Doubtless if this colony and company had been allowed to put their plan of spoliation of the missions in execution, it might not have turned to so bad account. But immediately after their leaving San Blas, General Santa Anna assumed the government, displacing Gomez Farias, the leader of the democrats; and one of his first acts was to dispatch a messenger over land by the way of the Rio Colorado and round the head of the Gulf of California, in order to prevent the Californian Commissioners from carrying their projected plan against the missions into execution. The commissioners and emigrants having embarked at San Blas in two vessels, had a long passage, and allowed Santa Anna's messenger to arrive before them; so that General Figueroa refused to admit of their commission, but assigned them lands on which they might settle as emigrants : this was remonstrated against most violently, but they were obliged to submit, and they retired to a spot on the bay of San Francisco, where they were for a time supported on provisions from the nearest mission. They endeavoured to settle themselves among the other colonists, but being accused of views contrary to the existing state of things, they were banished from the country ; and in the month of May, 1835, the leaders of this colony, together with many of their followers, returned to Mexico, landing in a vessel at San Blas.

Thus ended the first attempt made by the Mexican republic to augment the population and to alter the state of California. Its termination has been such as was to be expected from such an ill-concerted plan. This foolish scheme cost a very large sum of money at a time when the government could ill spare it. However, had this money been applied in a proper manner, and had industrious agricultural settlers been sought for and introduced judiciously, the result both to the country and to the settlers would have been highly beneficial ; whereas it has only brought misery on the emigrants, and loss and ridicule on the government.

It is perhaps advantageous for California that it should remain a part of the Mexican republic, in as

much as it reaps the advantage of disposing of its
produce in the Mexican ports free of foreign duties.
This advantage is, however, at present, but nominal;
for, in the first place, it sends little or no produce to
that country; and, in the second place, the coasting
duty is exorbitant, being twelve per cent on the
selling price where the articles are landed.   But
when a wiser policy is adopted, and when California
becomes an exporting country, this advantage would
be of much consequence.   California, however, is
quite a distinct country from Mexico, and has nothing in common with it except that the present
inhabitants are of the same family; it is therefore
to be apprehended, that on any cause of quarrel
between the two countries, it will be apt to separate
itself from the parent state.   This from its distant
situation, and the difficulty of conveying troops
from Mexico, would be easily effected; and although
the present population is inadequate to form permanently an independent nation, yet the fashion of
splitting countries into small independent portions
has become so prevalent in the late Spanish possessions, that an attempt to realise such a project may
not be so improbable as it should now seem.   The
situation and natural resources of California are so
favourable, that a small number of inhabitants could
resist any attacks made upon it by such a nation as
Mexico, or it might even soon overawe the coast

of Mexico itself; and force the government of that country to grant it such terms as it should demand. The shores of the Mexican republic on the Pacific are ill calculated for maintaining any maritime force; it has none at present; and from its unhealthy situation, scarcity of materials, and want of sailors or maritime enterprize, it is not likely ever to have on the Pacific any formidable navy. On the contrary, California is calculated, in an eminent degree, to become a maritime power; its coasts are healthy, its harbours excellent, and its capacity to produce materials for ship-building and marine stores is almost without limits. If, therefore, there should ever exist a sufficient population to maintain a separate sovereignty, or the occupiers of the country be of a quality and character capable of taking advantage of those resources, Mexico, instead of being able to reduce California, would be obliged to succumb to it.

Any foreign power if disposed to take possession of California could easily do so; but the happy state of peace which reigns at present in the world, and the just principles which the great powers of Europe have adopted of not interfering with the possessions of others, put any fear of that kind out of the question. The settlement of the Russians at Bodega is, strickly speaking, in the Mexican territory; but it has conducted itself so quietly that no

attempt has been made to disturb it, although sus-
picions have been entertained that at some future
day the whole of Upper California would fall into
their hands.

A latent jealousy, also, exists in the minds of
some of the Mexican politicians, that if foreign
emigrants were admitted in great numbers into
California, they might set up for themselves, and
cause the loss of the country; this however is but
an imaginary contingency; and if the Mexican
government would adopt a wise system of colonization laws, and a liberal general policy, under which
their citizens could live happily, no fears on that
account, for a great length of time, need be entertained; under the present system it is of little
consequence to whom it belongs. If, indeed, a
future Cochrane should visit the shores of California, and make common cause with its inhabitants,
as our hero did with the Chilinos, the period might
not be remote when it should make the Mexican
shores tremble as Chili did those of Peru. And,
truly, there seems no alternative except to admit
foreign emigrants or to allow the country to remain
stationary; for the character of the present population leaves no probability of its rapid increase
either in number or enterprize; and nothing can
be expected of emigration from the other Mexican
states which are themselves but too thinly peopled,

and whose inhabitants are but ill fitted for such a country as California.

[The preceeding part of this chapter, as well as the whole of the present work, was finished and sent to England in the year 1835. The following additional particulars are given from a recent letter received by the editor from the author, and are too important to be suppressed.]

In the year 1836, the inhabitants of Monterey and the vicinity rose, and, declaring themselves independent, attacked the garrison and forced the commandant and troops to capitulate. At a public meeting of the inhabitants called subsequently, on the 7th November, at Monterey, the following Resolutions were passed as the basis of a provisional government:—

1st.—Upper California is declared to be independent of Mexico during the non-re-establishment of the Federal system which was adopted in the year 1824.

2nd.—The said California shall be erected into a free and governing state, establishing a Congress which shall dictate all the particular laws of the country and elect the other supreme powers necessary, declaring the actual " Most Excellent Deputation" constituent.

3rd.— The Religion shall be the Roman Catholic

Apostolic, without admitting the exercise of any other; but the government will not molest any persons for their particular religious opinions.

4th.—A Constitution shall regulate all the branches of the Administration " provisionally," in conformity, as much as possible, with the expressed declaration.

5th.—Until what is contained in the foregoing articles be put in execution, Senor Don Mariano Guadalupe Vallejo shall be called on to act as Commandant General.

6th.—The President of the " Most Excellent Deputation" shall pass the necessary communications to the municipalities of the territory.

They followed up these proceedings by expelling the whole officials of the Mexican government, and all the troops from the country, and transporting them to the Mexican territory.

On receiving notice of this revolution, the Mexican government immediately had recourse to their usual mode of warfare, fulminating furious proclamations and addresses to the citizens, appealing to their patriotism, and ordering to be prepared, without delay, a formidable expedition to proceed against such audacious and unnatural sons of the Republic, whom it was incumbent on them to put down and chastise as their treason deserved. The first patriotic ebulition however soon subsided; no expedition

was prepared, California was soon forgotten, and it
has remained for nearly two years to do as it pleases,
to have a government of its own manufacture, or to
live without a government at all. Being thus left
to the freedom of their own will, the Californians,
true to the spirit which has animated all the Spanish
American colonies since their emancipation, immediately began to divide themselves into parties; and
although there are only about five thousand Spanish
creoles in the whole country, they had their party of
the north, which declared for an entire independence
on Mexico, and the party of the south, which adhered to Mexico on certain conditions. The want
of frequent communication with Mexico renders it
quite uncertain what may at present (June, 1838)
be the state of the country; but it is, at least, evident now, if there was any doubt formerly, that
it is at this moment in a state which cannot prevent its being taken possession of by any foreign
force which may present itself. The British government seem lately to have had some suspicion that
California would be encroached upon, if not taken
entire possession of, by the Russians who are settled
so close upon its northern frontier; but by the latest
accounts no encroachment has been made, nor
has any augmentation been made either in the
number of people in the colony, or in the fortifications. The danger does not lie there. There is
another restless and enterprizing neighbour from

whom they will most probably soon have to defend themselves, or rather to submit to : for although the frontiers of North America are much more distant than the Russians, yet to such men as the Back-settlers, distance is of little moment, and they are already well acquainted with the route. The northern American tide of population must roll on southward, and overwhelm not only California, but other more important states. This latter event, however, is in the womb of time: but 'the invasion of California by American settlers is daily talked of; and if Santa Anna had prevailed against Texas, a portion of the inhabitants of that country, sufficient to over-run California, would now have been its masters.

There have been some thoughts of proposing to the Mexican government that it should endeavour to cancel the English debt—which now exceeds fifty millions of dollars—by a transfer of California to the creditors. This would be a wise measure on the part of Mexico, if the government could be brought to lay aside the vanity of retaining large possessions. The cession of such a disjointed part of the republic as California would be an advantage. In no case can it ever be profitable to the Mexican republic, nor can it possibly remain united to it for any length of time, if it should even be induced to rejoin this state, from which at present it is to all intents and purposes separated. Therefore, by

giving up this territory for the debt, would be getting rid of this last for nothing. But would the
English creditors accept of it? I think they might,
and I think they ought. They have lately displayed
an inclination to treat and to receive lands as a part
of the debt where no land exists belonging to Mexico.
In the settlement made with Lizardi and Co. as agents
for the Mexican government in London, lands are
stipulated to be delivered at a certain price per
acre, in Texas in which Mexico does not possess an
acre, in the state of New Mexico which is many
hundred leagues inland in Sonora, and God knows
where. To the good fortune however of the English creditors this contract has been disapproved
of by the Mexican government, and it is hoped that
some more rational scheme will be hit upon to give
the creditors some sort of tangible security for at
least a part of what they have been so scandalously
fleeced out of. If California was ceded for the
English debt, the creditors might be formed into a
company, with the difference that they should have
a sort of sovereignty over the territory, somewhat
in the manner of the East India company. This in
my opinion would certainly bring a revenue in time
which might be equal to the interest of the debt,
and under good management and with an English
population, would most certainly realize all that
has been predicted of this fine country.

CHAP. III.

The part of Upper California at present occupied by the missions and settlers, is about five hundred English miles in length, and the breadth from the sea to the first range of hills may be stated at an average of forty miles, which will give an area of twenty thousand square miles and about thirteen millions of English statute acres. This however is but a small part of Upper California, as the whole country extending to the Rio Colorado, and to an undefined limit northward, is included in its territory; and although the missionaries have hardly extended their settlements to the northward of the bay of San Francisco, yet the most fertile lands and those fittest for European settlers, lie to the north of and around that bay. The whole extent of Upper California properly so called presents a superficies equal to many of the most extensive and powerful kingdoms of Europe.

All this immense extent of territory, except that occupied by the missions on the coast, is possessed by scattered tribes of Indians, and has been hitherto but little known. Since, however, the Mexican country has been opened to strangers by the revolution, those plains and wilds have been traversed by adventurers from the United States of North America: parties of hunters armed with rifles and carrying a few articles for barter have travelled from the borders of the Mississipi to the shores of the Pacific, and have astonished the Californians by their sudden appearance, and still more by the fact that they had escaped the vengeance of the wild Indians. The adventures of those American hunters furnish examples of the most extraordinary daring, and present a remarkable contrast to the conduct of the indolent native creole. The latter seldom leaves his own habitation or exposes himself to the rays of the sun; whereas these men, from their being always in the open air, and from the effect of their rough pursuits, appear nearly as wild as the beasts they are in chase of. The Spanish settlers always considered the Indians on the Rio Colorado and countries adjacent, as ferociously inimical to white men, and that it was almost impossible to pass through their territory. This is, however, a great exaggeration; for although some of the tribes may not be so docile or pusillanimous as those formerly living on the shores of the Pacific and in other parts of Mexico, yet there are none of them very formidable.

The country immediately behind the high lands which bound the present possessions of the missionaries, is reckoned even superior to that on the coast, and is said to consist of plains, lakes, and hills, beautifully diversified, and of the greatest natural fertility, capable of yielding every variety of vegetable productions, and abounding with timber of great size. To the northward of these plains, are situated two large lakes said to be distant from one another about eighteen or twenty leagues, and their extent is described to be very great; but so little certain is known respecting them, that it would only lead to error to repeat the tales related by those who have never seen them; there is no doubt however of their existence, and that they possess many fine islands which are inhabited by Indians. The lakes and streams in this district abound with bulrushes called by the natives *Tulé,* and from this the whole country takes its name, being called the plains of the *Tulares.*

As bearing on the topographical character of the Indian countries, I will here introduce a short notice of some misssionary travels through a part of them, undertaken shortly after the first establishment of the missions in Upper California. The information is interesting from the earliness and authenticity of its source, and not the less so because it throws some little light on the character of the natives and the policy of the original founders of the Californian missions. For this and other valuable information on the subject of the present work, derived from some scarce books and old manuscripts, I am indebted to the great kindness of Don Manuel Najera, prior of the Carmelite convent in Guadalaxara, in the republic of Mexico, a gentleman as distinguished for his extensive learning as his excellent moral qualities. Don Manuel has in his library a collection of valuable and scarce books and MSS on the subjects of Mexican history and antiquities; and it is to be hoped that he will one day, give to the public the result of his extensive researches.

The first of these curious documents is a manuscript written by friar Francisco Garzes, giving an account, in the form of a journal, of a journey performed by him in the year 1775, from the missions on the borders of Sonora to Upper California and his return by nearly the same route. This journey was made about six years after the establishment of the Franciscan missions in Upper California. The Father Garzes naturally expected to be received by his brethren and the military authorities in the new settlements, with kindness, and admitted as a coadjutor in the work of civilizing the natives, and in establishing the true faith amongst them; more particularly as having verified by his successful journey, the facility of communicating by land with

Mexico, and of connecting in one bond, the whole
territory from the Rio Colorado to the Pacific.   But
very different was his reception.   On his arrival at
the mission of San Gabriel, he was told that it was
not at all desirable that a communication should be
opened by which the Indians on the Rio Colorado
and the intervening plains might be enabled perhaps to molest or attack the new settlments.   So
much displeasure did the governor of California
shew to the traveller, that he refused him all suc-
cour or assistance, and even denied him the necessary provisions to enable him to return.   Finding
such an unhospitable reception Father Garzes remained only a few days with his brother missionaries,
and set out on his return, traversing the country
called the Tulares and finally arriving at his own
mission in Sonora without any accident.

There is a short manuscript annexed to that
of the Father Garzes, professing to be the journal
of Father Francisco Atanacio Dominguez, and
Father Silvestre Velez de Escalante, kept during a
journey performed by them in 1776, from Santa
Fé the capital of the province of New Mexico
towards Monterey in Upper California.   Those
friars took a more northerly route than Garzes, and
were by their account at one time as far as 41° N.
But after they had arrived as far as what they considered to be 136 leagues in a direct line west of
Santa Fé, and reckoning themselves yet a great

distance from Monterey, they determined to give up the enterprize and to return.

From the accounts given by these missionaries, it appears that the borders of the Rivers Gila and Colorado were thickly peopled by Indians in a very low state of civilization. They, however, cultivated some maize and even wheat, and they had also cattle. The travellers did not encounter the slightest opposition or hostility from any of the tribes through which they passed; on the contrary, they were received with kindness and presented with a part of such food as they possessed. On leaving the vicinity of the Rio Colorado and proceeding westerly, they found the natives fewer in numbers and less civilized, the greater part being entirely naked and living on roots and seeds of trees.

Father Garzes says that his manuscript will be accompanied by a map made by Father Pedro Font, who accompanied him a part of the journey, but who separated from him and returned. This map, however, is missing; and although Garzes informs us that he carried with him a quadrant and mariner's compass, it is difficult to trace his route, as he only gives the latitude at very distant points; but he gives the number of leagues daily travelled, and the point of the compass towards which he directed his course.

The Journies of those Friars are chiefly valuable,

in as far as they prove that there is nothing in the
character of the Indian population of the country
lying between the peopled Mexican states and California which can prevent its being easily colonized,
or which could prevent a free communication over
land; neither is the distance at all formidable. It
is also proved by them that the whole of this vast
country is free from any natural obstruction to its
settlement and cultivation. There are no impene-
trable forests, and the greater part is a level country,
full of pasturage and capable of being cultivated.

The Father Garzes travelled between the thirty-
fourth and thirty-fifth degrees of latitude, having
taken his departure from the west bank of the Rio
Colorado in about 35° N., keeping in the direction
of the mission of San Gabriel in Upper California,
making the distance by his diary from this river and
the said mission only about ninety leagues, which
agrees very well with the distance as laid down upon
the maps. He makes the distance from the last of
the missionary settlements in Sonora, called " Tucsion," to the Rio Colorado, seventy-five leagues—
thus making the whole distance from those settlements to San Gabriel on the Pacific, 165 leagues.
This distance, by the usual mode of travelling in
Mexico, would only be about ten days' journey. As
these travellers, however, take no observations for
the longtitude, for which they had not the necessary

instruments, there is no great certainty as to the distances they give. They calculate the leagues by the rate at which their mules travel; and as the maps we have are formed by this mode of surveying, they cannot be much depended upon.

These missionary travels being undertaken chiefly with the intention of converting the natives and of fixing on the proper places for planting missions, every thing which is most interesting to the general reader or geographer is almost lost sight of. The Father Garzes travelled with the Virgin Mary painted on one side of a piece of canvas, and the Devil in the flames of hell on the other. To unfurl this standard was his first operation on arriving at the habitation of a tribe of Indians; and he observes, that on shewing the Virgin they generally exclaimed, " Good !" but on turning the other side, they said, " Bad !" This introduction was followed by some questions, put through interpreters, respecting their willingness to become christians, and vassals of the king of Spain; whether they knew any thing of Heaven, of God, or of the Virgin, &c. The Father, however, took some pains to ascertain the names of the different tribes on the rivers Gila and Colorado, and of their wars and numbers. He gives the following list of the nations he visited or had an account of: viz.

M

ON THE RIVER GILA.		ON THE RIVER COLORADO.	
Nations.	*Souls.*	*Nations.*	*Souls.*
Papaga, ...	4,000	Cucopa, ...	3,000
Pima, ...	2,500	Tallignamay, ..	2,000
Cocomaricopas, ..	2,500	Carjuenché, ..	3,000
		Yuma, ...	3,000
		Talchedon, ...	2,500
		Tamasabs, ...	3,000
	9,000		16,500
Total, ... 25,500			

He gives the names of eleven other nations which inhabit the country more to the northward, but does not state their numbers. This numeration is exclusive of all the tribes in the intervening country from the vicinity of the Rio Colorado to the Pacific ocean; and although the tribes which he saw there do not appear to have been so numerous as those on the rivers, yet they were very considerable. The Fathers Domenguez and Escalante found to the northward, as far as they reached, the whole country occupied by tribes, which appear to have been more civilized and better clothed than those on the rivers and plains to the southward, so that the aggregate population of these, as yet unknown countries must be great.

Since these journies which seem to have been undertaken by the missionaries with some zeal, there has been nothing done either to ascertain the real state or situation of those countries, or to civi-

lize the natives. The whole country beyond the
mission of Tucsion is, as in former days, in the possession of the Indian tribes, and the vast region
between the frontiers of Sonora and the strips of
country occupied by the descendants of the Spaniards in Upper California is a *terra incognita,* and
not merely so, but, apparently, utterly forgotten by
the inhabitants and government of Mexico.

The lakes of the Indian country abound with a
great variety of fish and aquatic birds, and have on
their borders and islands great numbers of otters
and other animals which supply valuable furs. The
Spanish missionaries had long ago an intention to
form new missions in the plains of the Tulares, but
this was never accomplished; and the revolution
has probably put an end to all such projects for a
long time.

The situation of Upper California, between the
tropical and northern zones, places it in the list of
those countries which have always been most prized
by mankind; and the nature of its soil and climate
and most of its other topographical relations, are
calculated to justify all the favourable expectations
which its happy geographical relations naturally
give rise to. " The climate (says Pérouse) differs a
little from that of the southern provinces of France;
at least the cold is never so piercing there, but the
heat of summer is much more moderate, owing to

the continual fogs which reign there, and which procure for the land, a humidity very favourable to vegetation."

This account of Pérouse is not quite correct. The southern parts of the country are not entirely exempt from the periodical rains and long droughts to which the tropical climates in their vicinity are liable. For this reason irrigation of the land sown with wheat becomes necessary there. In the northern districts, however, and particularly around the bay of San Francisco, the rains are more general and irrigation unnecessary. The periodical rains of the south, which are very heavy, begin to fall in November and continue till April; being the reverse of what takes place on the Mexican continent, where the rains commence in June and end in November. From Monterey northward, a thick fog commences on the cessation of the rains, and continues till the month of August. During this period the fog prevails almost daily in the morning; but during the rest of the year, the sky is beautifully clear and serene.

The degree of temperature in a country extending through so many degrees of latitude, and possessing such a variety of surface, must vary much in different places. I regret that I possess no accurate data to fix this. In the month of December (1826) it is stated by Capt. Beechey that the mean tempera-

ture of San Francisco was 53° 2′ the maximum
66° and the minimum 46°; and the hygrometer is
said to have indicated a dry atmosphere.

The surface of the country is considerably varied
in different districts, being in some places elevated
into ranges of low hills, in others spreading out into
extensive plains. The hills vary from one thousand
to upwards of three thousand feet in height. Some
seem chiefly composed of sandstone. The soil is in
some places of a light sandy character, yet far from
sterile; in others, of the richest loam. In some
spots the surface is marshy; but the prevailing
character of the soil is dryness. Indeed, the chief
defect of the country is the infrequency of springs
and rivers; although this infrequency is far from
amounting to a serious obstacle to agriculture or
even to extreme fertility. Water can be obtained
in most places by digging, and the plains between
the mountains and the shore are here and there
intersected by small streams, on the banks of which
most of the missions are founded. The largest
rivers are those which run into the bay of San
Francisco and arise from the north, the north-east
and the south-east. The largest of these, the Sacramento, has been traced some hundred miles upwards to the north-east where it was found still a
large river; it is supposed by some to flow out of a
large lake, but this point remains yet unascertained:

it is navigable, at least by boats, to a great distance inland. The San Joachin, also of considerable size, rises in the distant mountains in the south-east.

The Jesus Maria empties itself into the Sacramento, at some distance from its mouth; it is also navigable by boats to a considerable distance. It flows from the south and east, through a country said to be of great fertility and susceptible of irrigation by it. The other rivers are much smaller, and indeed most of them are only rivulets: most of them water different missions, and derive their names from them. They are, Rio del Ranchio (which flows into the bay of Monterey); El Pajero; San Carlos; Santa Clara; San Gabriel; Santa Anna; Los Angeles; San Juan Capistrano; Santa Cruz; Santa Ynes; San Buenaventura.

California possesses several harbours, and one, at least, of great excellence.

SAN FRANCISCO is not only the principal port in California, but the largest and safest on the whole western coast of America. It is an arm of the sea or bay which runs a considerable distance inland, and is accessible by a narrow but deep and safe entrance; it divides itself inside into various wide branches, so as to make it one of the most capacious harbours in the world.

MONTEREY is only an open bay or roadstead, but is safe from almost all winds. This station

From a Photo from a Sketch by I. Hall Kerr

Lith⁹ by J. M. Atwater

SANTA BARBARA ... UPPER CALIFORNIA.

being more centrical than San Francisco or San Diego, has been hitherto the place of chief resort for foreign vessels, and has been considered as the capital of Upper California; but if the country around the bay of San Francisco was peopled and cultivated, that port would be the most convenient for the foreign commerce of the country, it being in all respects so much superior to the others.

The Canal of SANTA BARBARA as it is called, that is, the strait between the island of Santa Cruz and the main land near the mission of Santa Barbara, is also much frequented; and although it is not considered a very safe anchorage, yet vessels often discharge and take in their cargoes there. The bay of Santa Barbara, is completely sheltered from the north-west and westerly winds, but exposed to the S. E. and S. W. The anchorage is very indifferent, being all hard sand. The best anchorage is about half a mile off the outer Head which forms the little bay where the landing place is. There is no kind of tide or current here, but there appears occasionally to be a rise and fall of two or three feet.

SAN DIEGO is a good harbour and very secure; it is quite sufficient for the reception of merchant vessels, but is of much less capacity than San Francisco. This harbour runs a considerable distance inland, and is very convenient and commodious for commerce. About one mile within the mouth, there is good anchorage in ten fathoms water. The tide here runs four times in the twenty-four hours, six hours flood and six ebb. The port extends to a considerable distance to the eastward, where there is a channel in the centre, of four or five fathoms water all along; the sand banks run off on each side about a cable's length, and are in part dry at low water. There is no water to be got here except at the Presidio; it is brought down to the beach in carts.

PORT SAN PEDRO is a very extensive bay, being sixteen miles from point to point. It is difficult for a stranger to find the best anchorage, as it is not indicated on the ordinary charts; there is no kind of mark whatever on the shore, the nearest house being four leagues off, half-way to the mission of San Gabriel. The best anchorage —and that which all vessels trading with the mission occupy— is close under the N. W. point of the bay, about half a mile from a large rock which is in-shore, and about one mile from the beach. There is good holding ground of stiff mud, in four and a half fathoms, at a place from which the point bears S. half-west, the rock N. E., and the landing place W. N. W.

SAN JUAN.—The anchorage of this bay (lat. 33° 33′, long. 117° 12′) is close under the western Head.

Care must be taken in coming to anchor in the night, to round the head (if coming from the north-westward) about a mile distant, as there are several very dangerous rocks some distance from it nearly level with the water. It is difficult landing when the wind blows from the S. E. on account of the high surf; but when the wind is westerly and N. W., it is quite smooth. The anchorage is good throughout the bay; the ground a mixture of sand and mud in five fathoms.

All travellers in this country have been struck with its fertility and beauty but especially with its fertility. In many places, however, even where the vallies and plains are fertile, the hills are bleak and bare; and on the coast, in many places, as in the neighbourhood of San Francisco, the sea-winds and fogs blast the foliage of all the trees in exposed situations. Capt. Beechey compares the effect to that produced by the same cause in Shetland; it is probably more analogous to that observed in Cornwall. More inland, nothing of the kind is seen; but a succession of scenes which are indeed most delightful to the traveller, whether he has come from the arid wilds of the south, the bleak north, or from the ocean. Such scenes were not lost on Vancouver when he visited this coast. In his account of a journey from Monterey to Santa Clara, he notices many such. "We

considered our route (he says) to be parallel to the
sea coast; between which and our path, the ridge of
mountains extended to the south-eastward; and as
we advanced, their sides and summits exhibited a
high degree of luxuriant fertility, interspersed with
copses of various forms and magnitude, and ver-
dant open spaces enriched with stately fruit trees of
of different descriptions.   About noon, we arrived
at a very pleasant and enchanting lawn, situated
amidst a grove of trees at the foot of a small hill,
by which flowed a very fine stream of excellent
water.   We had not proceeded far from this delightful spot, when we entered a country I little expected to find in these regions.   For about twenty
miles it could only be compared to a park which
had originally been planted with the true old English oak; the underwood, that had probably attained its early growth, had the appearance of
having been cleared away, and had left the stately
lords of the forest in complete possession of the
soil, which was covered with luxuriant herbage, and
beautifully diversified with pleasing eminences and
vallies; which, with the lofty range of mountains
that bounded the prospect, required only to be
adorned with the neat habitations of an industrious
people, to produce a scene not inferior to the most
studied effect of taste in the disposal of grounds*."

* Vancouver's Voyage, II. 16.

When it is considered that this was in November, the beauty of the scenery is not a little enhanced. " New California (says Humboldt) is as well watered and fertile as Old California is arid and stony. The climate is much more mild than in the same latitude on the eastern coast of the new Continent. The frequent fogs give vigour to vegetation and fertilize the soil which is covered with a black and spongy earth." This last observation is only partially true, as will appear from what is stated above.

Respecting the extreme fertility of the soil, all observers accord with La Pérouse; and also as to its singular aptitude for the growth not only of European productions, but of those of the warmer regions of the earth. In the garden at the mission of Buenaventura, Vancouver was alike struck with " the quality, quantity and variety of its excellent productions, not only indigenous to the country, but appertaining to the temperate as well as torrid zone; not one species having yet been sown or planted that had not flourished and yielded its fruit in abundance and of excellent quality." "These (he adds) have principally consisted of apples, pears, plumbs, figs, oranges, grapes, peaches, and pomegranates, together with the plaintain, banana, cocoanut, sugar-cane, indigo, and a great variety of the necessary and useful kitchen herbs, plants, and roots*." It would not be easy to match such an

* Ib. p. 494.

assemblage as this elsewhere; and yet this is only a
part of the useful fruits and vegetables now cultivated in California.   We shall defer what we have
to say of its farinaceous products until we come to
speak of the state of agriculture.   The object of the
present sketch being mainly economical, or commercial and statistical, it never was my intention to
notice matters foreign to this, however interesting.
Had it been otherwise, I should have greatly regretted my inability to give any account of the
natural history of California, which remains a rich
and almost untrodden field for future enquiries.   I
will merely put down here a few observations which
my scanty materials and imperfect knowledge enable me to make.

The country abounds with trees which grow not
only in detached groupes or clumps on the plains
and vallies, but spread out into extensive forests.
They grow to a large size and are of various kinds,
some resembling those of Europe, others peculiar to
the country.   Of the former kind are the oak, elm,
ash, beech, birch, planes, and various varieties of
pine.   These last, and the oak, of which there are
several varieties, are the most plentiful, and grow to
the greatest size.   The number and variety of shrubs
are great; but the stock of indigenous trees bearing
fruit is very small.

An indigenous variety of vine was found by the
early settlers, yielding grapes of a considerable size

but not ripening to sweetness. The Fathers introduced the true wine-grape (vitis vinifera) which had long flourished in the Old California. Indeed in many parts of California the native vine is so plentiful and its produce so abundant, that brandy is now made from them in considerable quantity. The latitude of the bay of San Francisco corresponds almost exactly with that of Lisbon, and is consequently not very much to the northward of Bourdeaux; other parts of the country correspond in latitude with Madeira, and, in the opposite hemisphere, with the Cape of Good Hope; so that this country embraces the analogues, at least, of the most celebrated wine countries in the world, and consequently offers a wide and most promising field for the cultivation of the grape in all its varieties.

The missionaries long ago, also introduced the European olive, which is successfully cultivated for its oil.

The country is singularly free from underwood, a circumstance which renders travelling through even the uncultivated parts, much easier than in many other wild countries.

No minerals of particular importance have been found in Upper California, nor any ores of metals. There are, however, a variety of rocks suited for building as well as limestone slabs fit for paving, and plenty of clay for making bricks.

The country abounds with animals, both indigenous and imported. Of the former, a few are peculiar to that part of America, but the majority are found in the countries lying to the north and south of it. Among the indigenous animals are found the American lion (Felis concolor), the American tiger (Felis onca), buffaloes, stags, roes, the wild mountain cat, foxes, bears, pole cats, jackalls, hares, rabbits, field rats, &c. &c. The great tameness of some of these animals, the facility with which some are caught, and the re-acquired wildness of others, show at once their number and how little civilization has extended in the country. " Numerous herds of horses and cattle (says Langsdorff) were running wild here, without any attention being paid to them ; the horned cattle even render the country not very safe for foot passengers. Besides the herds, we met a great number of foxes, and a large wolf, which ran away frightened ; the the foxes appeared to live upon the most friendly terms with the young calves, and followed the cows about as if they had been equally their children." " We often amused ourselves (he says in another place) with shooting the crested partridges and the rabbits which abound upon the sand-hills near the shore. One day we went, accompanied by twelve people and conducted by thirty or forty Indians, to catch hares and rabbits by a sort of snaring, when, in three hours, without firing a shot, we had taken seventy-five, and most of them alive."—Voyages and Travels, II. 179—192.

Of the indigenous quadrupeds two of the most interesting is that termed by the Spaniards *Berendo*, and a very large deer, which has been supposed by travellers to be the rein deer, but which is the elk or moose deer of North America. The animal termed Berendo is also a native of Old California, where it is termed by the natives, *Taye*. " It is (says Venegas) about the bigness of a calf a year and half old, and greatly resembles it in figure, except in its head, which is like that of a deer, and the horns very thick, resembling those of a ram; its hoof large, round and cloven, its tail short." This animal is the *Argali*, a species which seems intermediate between the goat and the sheep. The Californian species is the American Argali, *Ovis Pygargus* of Cuvier. They still abound in the plains at the foot of the mountains and are always found in large herds. This animal is probably only a variety of the Asiatic Argali, so plentiful in north and central Asia. The roe abounds. The large deer are now become scarce in California, being driven from their haunts by the herds of European cattle; but they are still hunted for the sake of their hides and tallow; the latter being of very excellent quality, much superior to that of oxen. They were very

plentiful when the country was first visited by the
Spaniards. A large herd, we are told by Father
Palou, was encountered by Father Serra on his first
journey from Monterey to Francisco, in the great
plain of San Bernardino. The Spaniards, he says,
at first took them for European cattle, and marvelled
not a little how they came there. But they soon
found out they were deer, and the soldiers of the
party contrived to shoot several of them. They
found their horns to measure no less than eleven
feet from tip to tip. Another large animal, termed
by the natives *Cibolo*, is the wild American ox, or
bison. It is also now banished to the wilds, but is
sought by the hunter for its skin, which is dressed
in a particular manner with the hair on, and is used
in many parts of Spanish America as a sort of bed
or carpet.

The otter and beaver are still to be found on all
the rivers, lakes, and bays; but their numbers have
greatly decreased since the country has become
more settled. Even during the last twenty or thirty
years the diminution of these animals is most
marked. When Langsdorff's ship was lying in the
bay of San Francisco in 1804, he says, " the valuable sea-otter was swimming about the bay in numbers, nearly unheeded;" and when Pérouse was
there he calculated the annual power of supply of
the Presidency of Monterey alone at 10,000 skins

of this animal;* and he was assured that double that quantity might be furnished by the whole country.† The Indians at that time caught the otters in snares on land, or knocked them down with sticks, their want of any other boats than balsas making them very inexpert fishermen by sea. In 1824, Capt. Beechey estimated the annual export of skins at 2000. Now, the quantity is probably less than even this; but there can be no doubt that the amount of produce might be greatly increased by a better system of hunting. Nothing can show the ignorance and folly that prevail in this country respecting all matters of commerce, more than the fact stated by this traveller, that, at the period of his visit, the inhabitants were actually buying otter skins of the Russians at twenty dollars a-piece, while the animals were swimming about unmolested in their own harbours!

We will defer any account of the domestic European animals until we come to speak of the agriculture and commerce.

The feathered tribes both of the land and water are found in very great abundance. Some few are peculiar to California, but the majority are found either in the countries that lie to the south or north of it; but, as Captain Beechey observes, "there are not many which delight either by the brilliancy or beauty of their plumage, or by the melody of their

* Voyages Vol. iii. 307.   † Voyages Vol. ii. 227.

note." This general character of the birds curiously indicates the character of the country as intermediate between the tropical regions, where the brightness and variety of the plumage of birds are so remarkable, and the colder climates of the north, which have such a delightful compensation for the soberer colours of their birds in the excellence of their song. The following list chiefly taken from La Pérouse, Vancouver, Langsdorff and Beechey, comprehends all the more common birds. I set them down without any particular order :— white headed eagle, black vulture, great and small falcon, goshawk, sparrow hawk, large horn owl, raven, magpie, crane, curlew, crow, oriole, woodpecker, goat-sucker, golden-crested wren, bee-eater, partridge, quail, jay, wood-pigeon, plover, snipe, razor-bill, humming bird, crane, goose, duck, cormorant, pelican, heron, water-hen, shag, &c.

The small tufted partridges peculiar to California are most plentiful in the plains. They keep together in large flocks of three or four hundred, and are excellent eating. Some of the species of sea-birds exist in immense abundance. Capt. Beechey says, that a species of wild-goose which came from the north in November, may be seen " covering whole acres of ground or rising in myriads with a clang that may be heard at a very considerable distance."

The inhabitants of Upper California, like those of the Lower, seem little regardful of the exhaustless stores of food contained in the waters of their shores. In the former (certainly not in the latter), Captain Beechey's explanation of the fact may be admissible, viz.,—that " fish are not much sought after in consequence of the productions of the land being so very abundant." " Several sorts, however, (he adds) are brought to the tables of the missions. In the bay of Monterey we noticed the scomber colias and another kind of mackarel, the torpedo and another species of raia, achimara, and swarms of small fish resembling the Sardinia. Muscles are found in considerable quantities upon the shores, and form a large portion of the food of the Indians bordering upon the coasts and rivers. At Monterey, two species of *haliotis* of large size are also extremely abundant, and equally sought after by the Indians. They are found on the granite rocks forming the south-east part of the bay, which appears to be their northern limit. The natives make use of these shells for ornaments, and decorate their baskets with pieces of them. Besides these shell-fish, there were noticed a few patella, limpet, turbo, cardium, and mya shells, and among other lepas, a rare species of *l. anotifera* and a *chiton (tunicatus?)**

* Vol. II. p. 83.

N 2

CHAP. IV.

UPPER California when first visited by the Spaniards was, as we have already seen, inhabited by the same race of men as the Lower Province; the natives of Upper California, however, varied somewhat both in their physical characters and customs from those of their southern brethren, but hardly more than they differed from one another in different districts. They were acknowledged by all to be a timid and feeble race, compared with the hardy red men of the north-eastern parts of North America; but remarkable variations as to their physical character, in regard to size more especially, prevails among them. Hence, although the general testimony of observers gives them the above character, such striking exceptions are noticed that some have been led to give to the whole population a different character. Thus Venegas in speaking of the natives of the southern province, says: "Of all the natives hitherto discovered, the Californians are at least equal to any in the make of their bodies." Capt. Beechey says, "The stature of the Indians which we saw in the missions was by no means diminutive. The Alchones are of good height, and the Tularaios were thought to be, generally, above the standard of Englishmen." On the contrary, La Pérouse describes them as in general small and weak. M. Rollin, his surgeon, although he says, they are taller than the Chilian Indians, yet gives the average height as five feet two and half inches. Langsdorff says, none of the men seen by him were above five feet. They are of a considerably darker colour than the natives of the provinces more to the south, and what with their filthy habits and constant exposure to the sun, they approach the hue of the negro. They resemble the negro also in their large projecting lips and broad and flat noses. Their hair, however, is very different from that of the negro, being long and straight, not crisp; if left to grow it hangs down to the hips; but they commonly cut it to the length of four or five inches, which makes it stick out like quills. The hair grows very far down towards the eyes, which makes their naturally low forehead look extremely low; the eyebrows are in general small, though in some bushy; the beard is also in general very scanty, although occasionally a full flowing beard is observed; the causes of the difference not being well known.

Our earliest authority, Father Palou, notices the difference of colour between the tribes on the two sides of the bay of San Francisco, and also the contrast between the Upper and Lower Californians in the mode of wearing their hair. He also considers this custom, as also that of sprinkling ashes on the body, as partly dependant on causes of temporary occurrence. " All the natives of Upper California (he says) both men and women, cut their hair very short, particularly when any of their relations or friends die. In these cases they also put ashes on their heads, faces, and other parts of their bodies. This practice of throwing ashes on their persons was general among all the nations which had been reduced under the dominion of the Spaniards; but those in the south never cut their hair. On the contrary they seem to have great pride in its abundance and stick beads and other ornaments into wreaths of it bound round their heads. They are also in the habit of painting themselves in party coloured stripes of red and black; and this is also an emblem of mourning for their friends for whom they seem to entertain strong affections."

La Pérouse doubts whether the scantiness of beard so generally seen is natural or the effect of art; we believe that it is partly natural but chiefly the effect of art; and they apply the same depilatory process to other parts of the body. These people also tatoo their bodies but in a much less degree than the Indians of the islands; and the practice is chiefly confined to the women. They turn their toes inwards in walking; and their timid carriage at first sight announces their pusillanimous character. Both sexes in their native state go nearly naked, having only a wrapper of greater or less extent around the waist. In the winter, however, they use a sort of outer garment of deer-skin or otter-skin, or of the feathers of water fowl. These latter are chiefly worn by the women and are rather ingeniously constructed. The feathers are twisted and tied together into a sort of ropes and these are then tied close together so as to have a feathery surface on both sides. They twist strips of otter skins in the same manner so as to have the fur on both sides.

Like all savages they are fond of ornaments for their persons. These consist of bits of carved wood worn as ear-rings; bandeaus of feathers around the head; shells rounded and strung as beads, &c. &c. Their feather-bandeaus are sometimes very beautiful; and the acquisition of the materials of some of them must be a work of great labour. Langsdorff counted in one 450 tail feathers of the golden-winged woodpecker; and as there is only two of these in each bird, that are used; half the number of birds must have been killed to make up the wreath.

The moral qualities of these people are certainly not beyond the range of their physical, although in judging of these we must neither take the estimate from the early reports of the Spaniards, nor from the reports of travellers who have seen them only in their domesticated state. The Spaniards have always been anxious to establish a low estimate of their mental powers, as a reason and excuse for their manner of treating them. Still it must be admitted that the Californians are, as formerly stated, a feeble hearted and feeble minded race. " It is not easy (says Father Venegas) for Europeans who were never out of their own country, to conceive an adequate idea of these people. For even in the least frequented corners of the globe, there is not a nation so stupid, of such contracted ideas, and weak, both in body and mind, as the unhappy Californians. Their characteristics are stupidity and insensibility; want of knowledge and reflection; inconstancy, impetuosity and blindness of appetite; an excessive sloth and abhorrence of all fatigue; an incessant love of pleasure, and amusement of every kind, however trifling or brutal; in fine, a most wretched want of everything which constitutes the real man, and renders him rational, inventive, tractable, and useful to himself and society."

In accordance with this view of the character of

the natives, the Spaniards in the missions are in the habit of applying the degrading epithet of *beasts* (bestias) to the wild or unconverted natives, while they assume to themselves, and even to their con-vertites, the term which has generally been supposed to belong to the whole human family—viz. *rational creatures* (gente de razon). Certain it is, that they at least have none of that boldness and inde-pendence of character, and very little of that acti-vity, industry and perseverance, which distinguish the Indians nearer the pole. Even the tribes only a few degrees to the north, are much more ingeni-ous and enterprising; indeed in every way more civilized.

The whole of the Indians at present inhabiting the vast plains of the Tulares as well as those on the Rio Colorado and to the north-east, are of the same race as those which formerly inhabited the coast, and whose children are now the subjects or slaves of the missionaries. They seem to have made no advances towards civilization since the first discovery of their country. Although they possess so favoured a por-tion of the earth, they almost entirely neglect tillage, and live by the chace and spontaneous productions of the fields and forest. A trifling exception must, indeed, be made in favour of those who live in the immediate vicinity of the Spanish settlements, as they now possess some cattle and horses. The wild

Indians are divided into small tribes, which wage
frequent wars with each other, chiefly, it is believed,
on account of disputes respecting the boundaries
of the districts wherein they respectively claim the
exclusive right of hunting and gathering fruits and
other means of subsistence. Their numbers, in
proportion to the extent of the country they inhabit,
are, like those of all tribes in such a stage of civilization, or rather uncivilization, very small.

Their habitations are small round huts of rushes,
of a temporary character, erected where they halt
for a season and burnt when they change their
station. There huts are well described by Captain
Beechey, as well as the wretched condition of the
inmates. " They were about thirty-five feet in circumference, constructed with pliable poles fixed in
the ground and drawn together at the top, to the
height of twelve or fifteen feet. They are then
interwoven with small twigs and covered with bulrushes, having an aperture at the side to admit the
inhabitants and another at the top to let out the
smoke. The exterior appearance of these wretched
wigwams greatly resembles a bee-hive. In each
dwelling are nine or ten Indians of both sexes and
of all ages, nearly in a state of nudity, huddled
round a fire kindled in the centre of the apartment,
a prey to vermin, and presenting a picture of
misery and wretchedness seldom beheld in even the

most savage state of society." Although this picture is taken from a tribe of Indians that had left wild life and voluntarily come in to one of the missions, Captain Beechey or his companions were given to understand that this was the state in which they live when free. It is to be believed, however, that these people, thus coming voluntarily to join the mission, had been previously *sophisticated* from their native wild. habits by the vicinity of the strangers.

" It is true (says old Venegas) that they stand in no need of large rooms for depositing their furniture, and the various articles of their wardrobe, by which the greatest part of our houses is taken up. In removing they take all their furniture on their shoulders: for they consist only of a chest, a dish, a bowl made in the shape of a high-crowned hat, a bone which serves them for an awl in making it, a little piece of touch-wood for kindling a fire, a small net in which they put their fruit and seeds, another in the shape of a purse or bag fastened to a kind of prong across their shoulders, in which they carry their children, and lastly their bow and arrows,—to which some, who affect elegancy, add a shell for drinking. Those who live near the coasts have also nets for fishing. This furniture the women carry when they remove from one place to another; the men have only the bow and arrows with their appurtenances, as flints and feathers for the arrows, and sinews for the bows. But, to secure them, and at the same time not to incommode them in their march, they make holes in their ears, where they hang a large case which holds the things they need." (I. 78.)

The following account of the mode of subsistance and of some of the habits of the natives of Upper California is particularly worthy of attention, not only as being drawn up by a resident, but as the first notice of these matters that can, in any way, be depended on. It is taken from Father Palou's work, to which we are already so largely indebted.

"The natives of this part of the country maintain themselves by the seeds and herbs of the field, to collect which, when in season, is the duty of the women. The seeds they grind, and of the flour make gruel; and sometimes a kind of pudding or dough, which they form into balls of the size of an orange. Some of this flour has an agreeable flavor and is very nutritive; that produced from a black seed has the taste of toasted almonds. To this diet they add fish which they catch on the shores of the bay, and which are exceedingly good; they have also shell-fish in abundance. In addition they have the produce of the chace and wild fowl; such as deer, rabbits, geese, ducks, quails, &c. It also sometimes happens that a whale is driven on shore, an event which they celebrate with great rejoicings, as they value its flesh and blubber above all things. They roast the flesh of this animal in holes made in the earth; and when their first voracity is appeased, they hang up the remainder on the trees, and cut pieces off as they do with the seal, which they esteem next to the whale. In the woods they also find acorns which they grind in like manner and make gruel and balls of. There are likewise nuts of the same quality as in Spain; and on the high ground and 'sand-hills, strawberries of excellent flavour, and much larger than those of Europe; which ripen in the months of May and June. There is likewise a blackberry which is found in great abundance. In the highlands there is an edible root which they call 'Amole' about the size of an onion, and which after being roasted in their ovens, has an agreeable sweetish taste.

Another variety of this amole serves all the purposes of soap; but of this the natives have no great need as their clothing is very scanty. This indeed is exclusively confined to the females; the men going without any except what nature gave them.

The other sex, however, even the young girls have always some covering which is made of the tulé or bulrush, and which consists of one piece before and one behind, in the manner of a petticoat: they have also a piece thrown over their shoulders. The men in the mornings are accustomed to plaster themselves over with mud. This they say keeps out the cold ; and accordingly when the sun grows hot they wash it off.

These people have their marriages, but they consist of no other ceremony than the consent of the parties, and they are only binding till they disagree or choose to part. They have no other mode of cancelling a marriage than by using the phrase, ' I throw you away.' It is nevertheless true that we found many couples, both young and old, who lived in great unity and peace; esteeming their children, and their children them. Parentage or relationship forms no obstacle to their intermarriages. It is very common for the wife to urge her husband to to marry her sisters, and even their mother : and the common custom is, when a man first marries that he takes the whole of the sisters for wives. These many wives of one husband live without jealousies or disputes, each looking on the whole of the children as if they were their own, and the whole living in one house. In fact the first baptisms made at this mission were of three children all born within two months, sons of an Indian man and of three sisters, to all of whom he was married : as well as to their mother." Father Palou adds, that this description of the natives found on the borders of the bay of San Francisco, may be applied, with some local differences, to the whole of the Indians of Upper California ; as, although those Indians spoke many different languages, yet their habits and customs differed but little.

The Tulé or bulrushes with which the rivers and lakes of the Indian country abound, are put by the natives to a variety of uses. One of the most important or singular of these is the structure of the rafts or boats, if they may be so called, with which they navigate their lakes and rivers and even the bays and shores of the ocean. This raft, which at the time of the arrival of the Spaniards, and even to this day, constitutes almost their sole means of transport on the river, is termed *Balsa*, and is, perhaps the rudest or most primitive mode of navigation found among any people. The balsas are entirely formed of the bulrush and are constructed by binding them together into bundles of about ten feet in length, of considerable thickness in the middle and gradually tapering to each end. These bundles or sheaves are then tied together at the ends until the whole mass is of sufficient size to buoy up two or more persons. The boat thus formed is about ten feet long, of considerable breadth in the middle, and tapering regularly to each end. They are propelled by paddles, and from their shape go equally well with either end foremost. In calm and smooth water the centre parts of the rafts may be dry, but more commonly

the rowers sit on them soaked in water, as they seldom rise above the surface. The greatest mechanical ingenuity displayed by the Indians is in the
construction of their baskets and bows and arrows.
Some of the former constructed of the barks of trees
are water-tight and used for carrying water. They
are likewise employed for roasting their grain before
it is ground. This operation is performed by the
women, over a little lighted charcoal, and is done
with so much rapidity and address that the grain is
thoroughly roasted without setting fire to the basket, although this is made of very combustible materials. Many of the baskets are ornamented with
the scarlet feathers of the *Oriolus phœniceus* or with
the black crest feathers of the Californian partridge,
and are really very handsome. The Californian
bow is of a good shape, from three feet to four feet
and a half long, neatly wrought and strengthened
with the tendons of deer. These not only support
the wood but greatly augment its elasticity. The
arrows, as well as the bows, are neatly wrought having points of obsidian or a kind of flint, which are
let into the wood and bound fast with tendons. The
Indians are extremely skilful in the use of these
weapons, killing the smallest birds with them. In
doing so, however, they exhibit fully as much cun-
ning and patience as skill, as they steal along concealed till they are very near their game, seldom

stooping until within fifteen or twenty paces. They show particular ingenuity and skill in their manner of killing deer. This has been noticed by all travellers, and is still practised precisely in the same manner.

"We saw an Indian (says La Pérouse) with a stag's head fixed upon his own, walk on all fours, as if he were browsing the grass, and he played this pantomime to such perfection, that all our hunters would have fired at him at thirty paces had they not been prevented: in this manner they approach herds of stags within a very small distance, and kill them with a flight of arrows." The same exhibition was made to Vancouver and Langsdorff. Pérouse further says, " By these means they can, nearly to a certainty, get within two or three yards of the deer, when they take an opportunity of its attention being directed to some other object, and discharge their arrows from their secreted bows, which is done in a very stooping attitude." Captain Beechey says, in addition, that the Indian not only imitates the actions but the voice of the deer, and seldom fails to entice several of the herd within his reach.

Equal ingenuity is shown by them in catching water fowl. The following is the account of this given by Captain Beechey: "They construct large nets with bulrushes, and repair to such rivers as are the resort of their game, where they fix a long pole upright on each bank, with one end of the net attached to the pole on the opposite side of the river to themselves. Several artificial ducks made of rushes are then set afloat upon the water between the poles as a decoy; and the Indians, who have a line fastened to one end of the net, and passed through a hole in the upper end of the pole that is near them, wait the arrival of their game in concealment. When the birds approach, they suddenly extend the net across the river by pulling upon the line, and intercept them in their flight, when they fall stunned into a large purse in the net, and are captured. They also spread nets across their rivers in the evening, in order that the birds may become entangled in them as they fly."*

It is difficult to come at the real religion of the natives, on account of the general ignorance of their language. La Pérouse says they have no knowledge of a god or future state : more recent travellers assert that they are idolators, worshipping the sun and believing in both a good and an evil spirit whom they seek occasionally to propitiate. Father Palou gives a somewhat different account of their religion. "In none of the missions (he says), has there been observed any idolatory whatever; only a mere negative infidelity; neither have they shewn the least difficulty in believing any of our myste-

* Vol. II, p. 75.

ries.   We have only observed amongst them some
superstitions and vain observances; and occasionally, among the old, some pretensions to supernatu-
ral power; as that they had the power to send the
rains, thunder, &c.; that they had dominion over
the whales, &c.   But these pretenders were seldom
credited even by their own tribes, and they were
believed to put forth these pretensions for the purpose of obtaining presents. One superstition however seemed firmly believed by all, viz. that any
sickness with which they were afflicted arose from
the incantations of their enemies."

The Indians seem to have some notion of a future
state.   About San Francisco they burn their dead,
after adorning the corpse with flowers, feathers, &c.
and laying beside it a bow and arrows.   The ceremony is attended with loud shouting and other
savage demonstrations of regret.   More to the
southward they always bury their dead; and Father
Palou says that, in his time, there were near Santa
Barbara, enclosed cemetries for the purpose.

It is but justice to these poor people to state that
their affections seem very strong, as exhibited in
the extreme tenderness and love shewn by the parents to their children and the general care of the
sick and wounded, and also the remarkable strength
of their friendships.   Long after the loss of friends
they shed tears on their being brought to their re-

membrance, and they conceive it to be a great offence for any one to name them in their presence. Pérouse says that although they neither eat their prisoners nor their enemies killed in battle, yet that when they had vanquished and put to death upon the field of battle, chiefs or very courageous men, they will eat some pieces of them, less as a sign of hatred or revenge than as a homage which they pay to their valour, and from the belief, common to them with many other savages, that this food will increase their own courage. The same authority informs us that they scalp their slain enemies, and pluck out their eyes, which they have the art of preserving free from decay and carefully keep as precious signs of their victory.

The Indians in their native state are very healthy, notwithstanding their filthy habits : it is very far otherwise in their domesticated state. Both with the wild and the domesticated tribes the hot air bath or *teméschal* is the sovereign remedy for most of their diseases. This is administered in the following manner. A round hovel or oven of mud, is built for the purpose. It has a small opening in the side to enter by and a smaller one at the top for the escape of the smoke. Several persons enter this at the same time, quite naked, and make a fire close to the door on the inside. They continue to add fresh wood to the fire as long as they can bear the

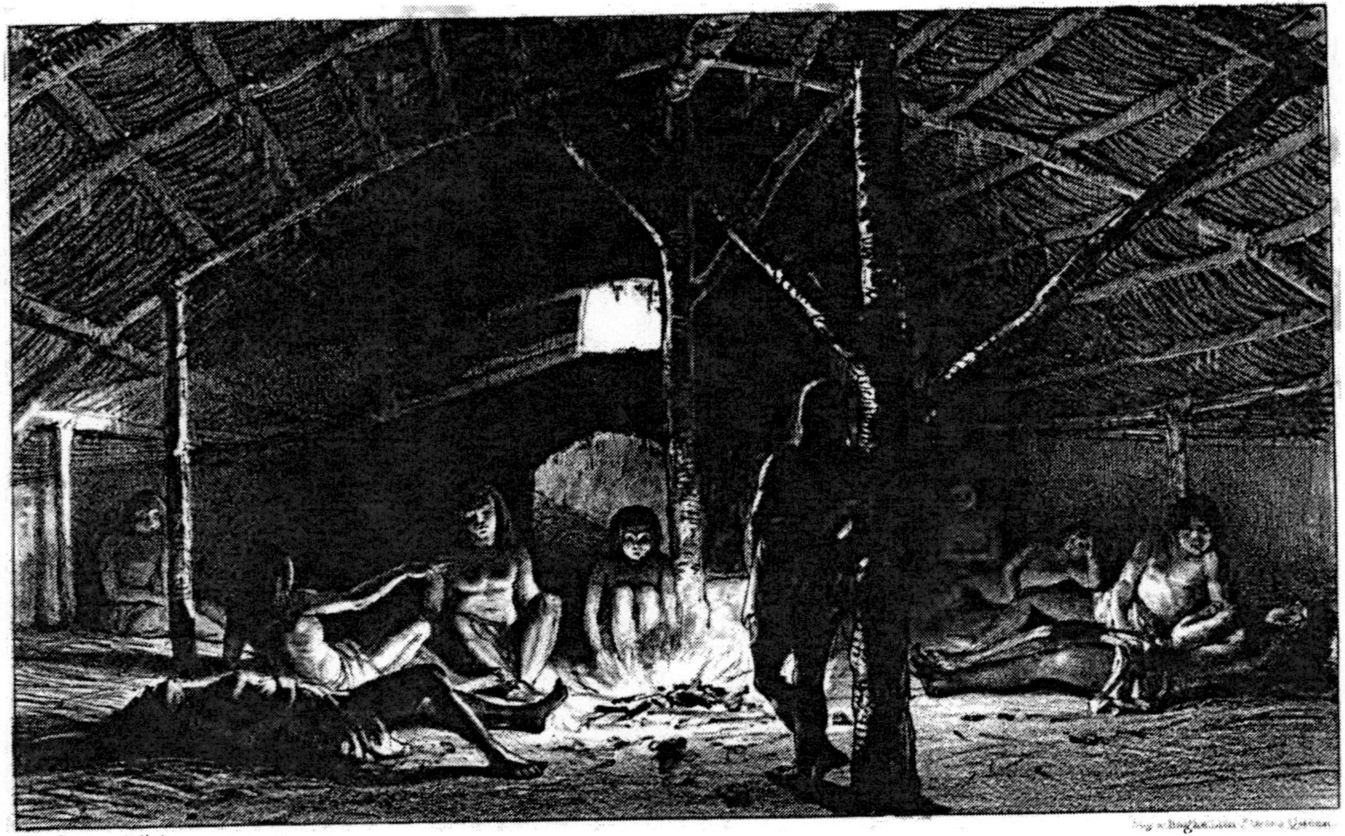

Capt. W. Smyth R.N. del.

heat. This soon throws them into a profuse per-
spiration over their whole frame. "They wring
their hair (says Capt. Beechey) and scrap their skin
with a sharp piece of wood or an iron hoop, in the
same manner as coach horses are sometimes treated
when they come in heated; and then plunge into
a river or pond of cold water, which they always
take care shall be near the teméschal." A variety
of this process—a hot sand bath in place of a hot
air bath—is described by M. Rollin, but it seems
to be more prevalent in the countries further north.
"The manner of preparing the teméschal (he says)
consists in scooping a trench in the sand, two feet
wide, one foot deep, and of a length proportioned
to the size of the patient. A fire is then made
through the whole extent of it, as well as upon the
sand, which was dug out of the hollow. When the
whole is thoroughly heated, the fire is removed,
and the sand stirred about, that the warmth may
be equally diffused. The sick person is then strip-
ped, laid down in the trench, and covered up to his
chin with heated sand. In this position a very profuse sweat soon breaks out, which gradually dimi-
nishes according as the sand cools. The patient
then rises and bathes in the sea or nearest river.
This process is repeated until a complete cure is
obtained."*

* La Pérouse, Vol. III.

It is impossible to form any trust-worthy opinion of the amount of the Indian population in the other parts of California, not in the immediate possession of the missions.

BAY of CARMEL, UPPER CALIFORNIA.

CHAP. V.

ACCOUNT OF THE MISSIONARY ESTABLISHMENTS. — PRESENT STATE OF THE INDIANS IN THEM.—REMARKS ON THE MISSIONARY SYSTEM GENERALLY, AND ON THE CONVERSION OF INFIDELS.

From the feeble and mild physical and moral characters of the aboriginal natives of California, as described in the preceding chapter, the success of the missionaries in subjecting them to their temporal and spiritual dominion, although certainly remarkable, is yet very easily understood. Much credit is unquestionably due to them, and the result exhibits in a striking point of view, the efficacy of the system followed by the Fathers, more especially when compared with that adopted by missionaries in other countries. Still, it will hardly be believed that had the Jesuits of Lower California or the Franciscans of the upper province (and the same may be said of the Jesuits in Paraguay) been set down amid many of the other tribes of the same continent, and yet more, among the fierce races of the islands and continents in the southern hemisphere, they would never have succeeded in civilizing —or to avoid dispute, domesticating them, but would have been destroyed or driven from the country in

a short space of time. Their lot, however, was fortunately different; and assuredly there are few
events in history more remarkable on the whole, or
more interesting, than the transformation, on the
great scale, wrought by the Jesuits and Franciscans
in Paraguay and California,   In the present chapter, I purpose giving an account of the Indians in
their converted or domesticated state; but must
previously detail the progress of the different missionary establishments and their actual condition.

Humboldt says that in 1776 there were eight
villages or missions; and in 1790, eleven; and in
1802, eighteen.   According to La Pérouse (who
visited California in that year) there were ten missions in 1786, and the number of converted or domesticated Indians was 5143.   One of the missions,
Santa Barbara, was only just founded and contained
no converts.   Vancouver visited the coast in 1793,
and found that several new missions had been
founded since the visit of Pérouse; viz. Santa Cruz,
Santa Rosa, and La Soledad.

The following authentic document, supplied by
Humboldt, gives the names of the missions, and
dates of their foundation respectively, and the population in the year 1802, or rather, the number of
the *Converted Indians*—the other classes not being
mentioned.   It is extracted from the Essay on New
Spain :—

Foundation	Missions.	Males.	Females.	Total.
1769 ..	San Diego	.. 737	.. 822 ..	1559
1798 ..	San Luis Rey	.. 256	.. 276 ..	532
1776 ..	San Juan Capistrano	.. 502	.. 511 ..	1013
1771 ..	San Gabriel	.. 532	.. 515 ..	1047
1797 ..	San Fernando	.. 317	.. 297 ..	614
.1782 ..	Santa Buenaventura	.. 436	.. 502 ..	938
1786 ..	Santa Barbara	.. 521	.. 572 .	1093
1787 ..	La Purissima Conception	.. 457	.. 571 ..	1028
1772 ..	San Luis Obispo	.. 374	.. 325 ..	699
1797 ..	San Miguel	.. 309	.. 305 ..	614
1791 ..	La Soledad	.. 296	.. 267 ..	563
1771 ..	San Antonio de Padua	.. 568	.. 484 ..	1052
1770 ..	San Carlos	.. 376	.. 312 ..	688
1797 ..	San Juan Bautista	.. 530	.. 428 ..	958
1794 ..	Santa Cruz	.. 238	.. 199 ..	437
1777 ..	Santa Clara	.. 736	.. 555 ..	1291
1797 ..	San José	.. 327	.. 295 ..	622
1779 ..	San Francisco	.. 433	.. 381 ..	814

	Total 7945	7617	15562

Humboldt informs us that he could not ascertain the numbers of the other classes of the population in 1802 whether whites, mestizos, or mulattoes, either in the presidios or in the service of the fathers; but he believed the whole number did not exceed 1300. This would give the whole population of Upper California, at that time at something less than 17,000 (16,862).

The number of missions founded to the present time is twenty-one: and the total amount of the Indian population in these, in the year 1831, was 18,683. The number of other classes, exclusive of the Indians, that is, of the garrison and free settlers, was 4,342,—making a total of 23,025 for the whole country. The following table gives an accurate state-ment of all classes of the population, and in every lo-cality, in the year just mentioned: the enumeration will hold nearly good for the present time (1835).

Names of the Jurisdictions, Missions, and Towns.	Men.	Women.	Boys.	Girls.	Total
PRESIDIO OF S. FRANCISCO	..124..	85..	89..	73..	371
Town of San José de Guadalupe	..166..	145..	103..	110..	524
Mission of S. Francisco Solano	..285..	242..	88 .	90..	705
id. of S. Rafael	..406..	410..	105..	106..	1027
id. of S. Francisco	..146..	65..	13..	13..	237
id. of Santa Clara	..752..	491..	68..	60..	1371
id. of S. José	..823..	659..	100..	145..	1727
id. of Santa Cruz	..222..	94..	30..	20..	366
PRESIDIO OF MONTEREY	..311..	190..	110..	97..	708
Village of Branciforte	.. 52..	34..	27..	17..	130
Mission of S. Juan Bautista	..480..	351..	85..	71..	987
id. of S. Carlos	..102..	79..	34..	21..	236
id. of Na. Sa. de la Soledad	..210..	81..	23 .	20..	334
id. of S. Antonio	..394..	209..	51..	17..	671
id. of S. Miguel	..349..	292..	46..	61..	748
id. of S. Luis Obispo	..211..	103..	8..	7..	329
PRESIDIO OF STA. BARBARA	..167..	120..	162..	164..	613
Mission of La Purissima	..151..	218..	47..	34..	450
id. of Sta. Ines	..142..	136..	82..	96..	456
id. of Sta. Barbara	..374..	267..	51..	70..	762
id. of Buenaventura	..383..	283..	66..	59..	791
id. of S. Fernando	..249..	226..	177..	181..	833
Town of la Reyna de los Angelos	..552..	421..	213..	202..	1388
PRESIDIO OF S. DIEGO	..295 ⎤				
Mission of S. Gabriel	..574 ⎥ 1911..	683..	621..	5686*	
id. of S. Juan Capistrano	..464 ⎥				
id. of S. Luis Rey	.1138 ⎦				
id. of S. Diego	..750..	520..	162..	146..	1575
Totals 10,272		7632	2623	2498	23,025

* We are unable to give these latter details accurately, the Copy having accidentally caught fire when in the hands of the Printer.

In illustration of the preceding table, as well as
to exhibit the general economy of the missions, it
is necessary to give some account of the various
departments or classes in which the population is
distributed.

PRESIDENCIES OR PRESIDIOS.—Upper California is divided into four military districts, the head
quarters of which are respectively denominated
the *Presidio* of the district or jurisdiction.   At
each of these, troops are stationed under the authority of a military commandant. These presidencies,
as seen in the table, are San Francisco, Monterey,
Santa Barbara and San Diego.   The buildings at
the different stations, are nearly all of the same class
and dimensions; they consist of a square of about
one hundred yards each side, enclosed by a wall of
unburnt bricks called *adobes* of about four yards in
height; within which are the residence of the commandant; lodging for the troops; the church;
warehouses; &c. A short distance from the presidios
are what they choose to call the *castillos* or forts.
That of San Francisco, which is thought to be the
most formidable, is about a mile distant from the
presidio; it is however of little use, both from its
bad construction and too elevated situation.   It is
meant to protect the entrance to the harbour; but
in its present state it can neither protect nor annoy
any thing. That of Monterey, although its situation

is good for commanding the anchorage, yet as it has
no parapet and only a few guns of small calibre,
and in very bad condition, is of no consequence.
At Santa Barbara two old guns lie on an esplanade,
but are quite unserviceable. The castillo of San
Diego is about five miles from the presidio; its locality renders it of no use, but there are good situations in the intricate entrance to the harbour which
could be fortified so as easily to prevent the entrance
of an enemy. Those fortifications resemble the
innumerable others which the Spaniards thought
necessary to erect in all their colonies. A fort was
always thought absolutely necessary at every supposed vulnerable point; but so that a castillo was
once erected, with a few guns generally of heavy
metal—the duty of the government and the commandant for the time being was considered as fulfilled; and the rot and the rust were for ever after
left to their natural province of destruction. It is
nearly a century since any thing has been done for
the castillos of California. A good practical illustration of the strength of these forts was afforded
in the year 1819, when a pirate vessel from Buenos
Ayres landed a few men at Monterey, captured the
fort, destroyed most of its guns and pillaged and
burnt the town.

In each of the presidios there are a certain number of soldiers stationed, who have always been

troops of an inferior description.   Those that went
with the first settlers were a sort of militia raised
on the Indian borders of Sonora and denominated
" *companias de cueros*," literally *Hide companies*,
from their wearing a sort of cuirass of hides (cuero)
in order to defend them from the arrows of the
Indians.   The number of troops assigned to each
presidio was two hundred and fifty, but this number
was never complete : they consisted entirely of horse.
They were always badly clothed and worse paid, so
that their appearance was that of tattered ragamuf-
fins; and from their undisciplined state and idle
habits they were good for nothing except to retake
any of the miserable Indians who might escape from
the missions, which was indeed their chief employment.   The policy of the missionaries always was
to prevent the increase of any considerable population except at their own missions ; and the soldiers
were not allowed to marry except by express permission from the king, and this was of course not
easily obtained ; so that those men lived in a sort
of celibacy which corresponded with the other
monastic establishments.   In the present day things
are somewhat altered, but not much for the better ;
for whatever soldiers are sent to California are the
refuse of the Mexican army, and most frequently
are deserters, mutineers, or men guilty of military
crimes.   Those presidios are also appropriated as

receptacles, for transported felons; so that California is the Botany-bay of Mexico.

RANCHIOS OR NATIONAL FARMS. — In the neighbourhood of each presidios and generally at the distance of four or five leagues, certain farms, called " *Ranchios*," are set apart for the use of the soldiers. These, on their first establishment, were also meant to be depositories of tithes to be collected in cattle and grain by the government; but as the missions have never been liable to tithes, and the other settlements are of small value, this branch of revenue was never of much consequence, and those ranchios only contain a few cattle belonging to the presidios. They are under the direction of the commandants of the respective presidios.

TOWNS OR " PUEBLOS."—There are only three free towns independent of the missions and presidios in all Upper California. These towns owe their origin to the retirement of the old Spanish or Creole soldiers in the service of the missions, who, after a certain length of service, become entitled to exemption from any further military services and have permission either to return to their native land or to settle in the country. Most of these soldiers are married and have families; and when the retirement of the pueblos is preferred, grants of land with some necessary articles are given them to commence their new occupation of husbandry, which, with the aid of the natives, they generally cultivate successfully. The most fertile spots have been generally chosen for the pueblos; and the produce of these not only supports the inhabitants of the place, but supplies the wants of the neighbouring mission and presidio.

The principal pueblo is *Nuestra Senora de los Angelos;* situated about eight miles from the mission of San Gabriel, and about twenty miles from a roadstead on the Pacific called San Pedro. The population of the town is about fifteen hundred. It has an alcalde or mayor, three regidores and a syndico : this composes its *"Ayuntamiento"* or Town Council. The vicinity is occupied by vineyards and maize fields ; and as the lands are level and highly fertile, it is capable of great agricultural improvement. This town has been proposed as the capital of the country ; and as the Spaniards have in their colonies always chosen an inland situation for their capital towns, this scheme might have been adopted if the country had remained in their hands ; but it is to be presumed that Monterey, will, under the present circumstances, be considered as the capital until a population shall arise on the bay of San Francisco, when, from its superiority as a harbour, the capital town will ultimately, no doubt, be fixed there.

The second town is *San José,* situated about a league from the mission of Santa Clara, and twenty leagues from the bay of San Francisco. A small river, or rather large rivulet passes by it, and discharges itself into that bay. The inhabitants amount to about six hundred, and it has its alcalde and council the same as Los Angelos. The inhabitants occupy themselves in the cultivation of wheat and other grain; they have a considerable number of cattle, and trade in the skins and tallow of deer which are found in great numbers in this district. The situation of this town is in a very extensive plain, and in a part of the country highly adapted for the cultivation of wheat; but in some places it is deficient in water, at least for the purpose of irrigation, which in many parts of California is necessary for successful cultivation, owing to the long droughts which are experienced at certain seasons of the year. In this neighbourhood there are still large tracts of fine land unoccupied by the missions.

The third town is called *Branciforte:* it is about a mile distant from the mission of Santa Cruz, a mile and a half from the shore of the bay of Monterey, and eighteen leagues from the Presidio of that name. Its inhabitants do not much exceed a hundred and fifty, and their occupation is rural labour. This town has also its Alcalde, but is dependent on the military commandant of Monterey.

This account of the few free towns or rather, villages, that exist in Upper California, shows how little progress population has made in this country by free settlers. This arises not only from the inaptitude of the Spaniards for colonizing a country of this description, but also from the jealousy of the missionaries, who arrogated to themselves the property of almost the whole of the land, so that settlers could only establish themselves by their toleration. By this means only a select number were admitted, and these firm adherents of the missionaries, who would blindly obey their mandates; which mandates, with the inquisition in their neighbourhood, were not to be trifled with. The whole of the free settlers even at this time do not exceed five thousand. In this number is included the whole population of white and mixed casts who live in the country, in the free villages, and at the missions and presidios, exclusive of the Indians bound to the missions. Of these free settlers many live at the missions and on their lands, and can hardly be said to be independent of them. It is obvious that it is from the free white and creole races and from the introduction of fresh colonists, the future population of California must proceed; for the enslaved Indians are already on the decline, and, on the dissolution of the missionary system, they will dwindle away and soon become almost extinguished.

Nothing can be more remarkable than the physi-

cal difference between the free creole race (including
the mestizos or those of mixed blood) and the enslaved Indians of the missions.   The Creoles are a
remarkably fine set of people, of large stature, and
of as athletic form as perhaps any other in the
world. I have seen natives of Upper California who
might pass for the fabled giants of Patagonia : and
when they go at times to the Mexican coast, the
contrast between them and the emaciated inhabitants of the agueish shores of the more southern
country, is most conspicuous.

THE MISSIONS.— These establishments are all
formed on the same plan and consequently greatly
resemble each other.   They vary, however, according to their extent, standing, and population, and also
according to the individual character of the directing fathers for the time being.   Each mission is
governed by one or more missionaries, all friars of
the order San Francisco.   One of these is styled
Prefect, and not President as was formerly the
case.   Through him is (or was) carried on all the
public correspondence with the government of
Mexico; but he has no power superior to the
others, and each may be said to be absolute in his
own mission.   Each mission has allotted to it, in
the first instance, a tract of land of about fifteen
miles square, which is generally fertile and well
suited for husbandry.   This land is set apart for the

general uses of the mission, part being cultivated, and part left in its natural condition and occupied as grazing ground. The buildings of the mission are, like the Presidio, all on the same general plan, but are varied according to the locality and number of the inhabitants. Most of the missionary villages or residences are surrounded by a high wall enclosing the whole; others have no such protection but consist of open rows of streets of little huts built of bricks: some of these are tiled and whitewashed and look neat and comfortable; others are dirty and in disrepair and in every way uncomfortable. In the mission of Santa Clara, which in several respects excels the others, the houses of the Indians form five rows or streets, which compared with the old straw huts must be considered really comfortable: and this is the greatest improvement that has taken place in the domestic civilization of these people at the missions. The buildings are generally built in the form of a square or part of a square, the church usually forming a portion of the elevation. The apartments of the fathers, which are often spacious, the granaries and work-shops compose the remainder. The Indian population generally live in huts at about two hundred yards distant from the principal edifices; these huts are sometimes made of *adobes*, but the Indians are often left to raise them on their own plan; viz. of rough poles erected into

a conical figure, of about four yards in circumference at the base, covered with dry grass and a
small aperture for the entrance.   When the huts
decay, they set them on fire, and erect new ones;
which is only the work of a day.   In these huts the
married part of the community live, the unmarried
of both sexes being kept, each sex separate, in large
barn-like apartments, where they work under strict
supervision.   The storehouses and workshops, at
some of the larger missions, are of great extent and
variety.   There may be seen a place for melting
tallow, one for making soap, workshops for smiths,
carpenters, &c., storehouses for the articles manufactured, and the produce of the farms; viz. stores
for tallow, soap, butter, salt, wool, hides, wheat,
peas, beans, &c. &c. &c.   Four or five soldiers have
their residence a few yards further off, and are meant
to watch the Indians, and to keep order; but they
are generally lazy, idle fellows; and often give the
missionary more trouble than all his Indians; and
instead of rendering assistance increase his troubles.   But in all Spanish countries, nothing can
possibly be done without soldiers, and the idea of
having any public establishment without a guard of
soldiers would appear quite ridiculous.

The church is, of course, the main object of
attraction at all the missions, and is often gaudily
decorated.   In some of the missions where there is

good building-stone in the vicinity, the external appearance of the sacred building is not unseemly; in other missions the exterior is very rude. In all of them the interior is richer than the outside promises.   In several there are pictures, and the subject of these is generally representations of heaven or hell, glaringly coloured purposely to strike the rude senses of the Indians.   Pérouse says that the picture of hell in the church of San Carlos has, in this way, done incalculable service in promoting conversion; and well remarks that the protestant mode of worship, which forbids images and pompous ceremonies, could not make any progress among these people.   He is of opinion that the picture of paradise in the same church, has exerted comparatively little effect on account of its tameness : but Langsdorff tells of wonders in this way wrought by a figure of the virgin represented as springing from the coronal of leaves of the *Agave Americana*, or great American aloe, instead of the ordinary stem! The priests also take care to be provided with rich dresses for the same purpose of inspiring awe.

The object of the whole of the Californian or missionary system being the conversion of the Indians and the training of them up, in some sort, to a civilized life, the constant care of the fathers is and ever has been directed towards these ends.

The children born in the missions are, of course, devoted to the missionary discipline from their infancy; but the zeal of the fathers is constantly looking out for converts from among the wild tribes on the borders of their territories. Formerly when the missionaries were strangers in the land, and the natives were numerous, and spread around their settlements, there was no lack of materials on which to exercise their converting zeal. But for a good many years the case has been different; the natives have become fewer in number and have been gradually receding from the missionary territory : the very progress of conversion has necessarily occasioned this. New means of obtaining converts have been therefore had recourse to; and there can be no doubt that some of these means go far beyond the bounds of legitimate persuasion. It would be injustice to tax the Fathers with openly sanctioning, much less directing the more severe of these means; yet they cannot be altogether ignorant of them, and must be regarded as encouraging them indirectly. And, indeed, it must be admitted that with their particular views of the efficacy of baptism and ceremonial profession of christianity in saving souls, the conversion of the Indians even by force, can hardly be otherwise regarded by them than as the greatest of benefits conferred on these people and therefore justifying some severity in

effecting it.   No one who has seen or known any
thing of the singular humanity and benevolence of
these good Fathers will for a moment believe that
they could sanction the actual cruelties and blood-
shed occasionally wrought in their name by the military and more zealous converts.   Certain it is, however, that every encouragement is held out to all, who
shall bring in *Gentiles* for conversion.   Converts
that can be depended on are stationed in the vicinity of the haunts occupied by their wild brethren,
whose business it is to represent their own condition
in the most favourable light possible, with the view
of inducing them to join the missionary fold.
Others are permitted to pay visits to their kindred
of more distant tribes, with the same views, and
are almost expected to bring back converts with
them.   " At a particular period of the year also "
we are told by Captain Beechey, " when the Indians
can be spared from the agricultural concerns of the
establishment, many of them are permitted to take
the launch of the mission and make excursions to
the Indian territory.   On these occasions the
padres desire them to induce as many of their unconverted brethren as possible to accompany them
back to the mission, of course implying that this is
to be done only by persuasion ; but the boat being
furnished with a cannon and musketry, and in every
respect equipped for war, it too often happens that

the neophytes and the *gente de razón,* who super-intend the direction of the boat, avail themselves of their superiority, with the desire of ingratiating themselves with their masters and of receiving a reward. There are, besides, repeated acts of ag-gression which it is necessary to punish, all of which furnish proselytes. Women and children are generally the first objects of capture, as their hus-bands and parents sometimes voluntarily follow them into captivity."*

One of these proselytising expeditions into the Indian territory occurred during the period of Cap-tain Beechey's visit in 1826, which ended in a battle with the loss, in the first instance, of thirty-four of the converted, and eventually in the gain (by a second expedition sent to avenge the losses of the first) of forty women and children of the invaded tribes. These were immediately enrolled in the list of the mission, and were nearly as immediately converted into Christians. The process by which this was effected is so graphically described by Cap-tain Beechey that it would be doing him injustice to use any words but his own.

"I happened (he says) to visit the mission about this time and saw these unfortunate beings under tuition, They were clothed in blankets, and ar-ranged in a row before a blind Indian, who under-

* Voyage II, 24.

stood their dialect, and was assisted by an alcalde to keep order. Their tutor began by desiring them to kneel, informing them that he was going to teach them the names of the persons composing the Tri- nity, and that they were to repeat in Spanish what he dictated. The neophytes being thus arranged, the speaker began: "Santissima Trinidada, Dios, Jesu Christo, Espiritu Santo"—pausing between each name, to listen if the simple Indians, who had never spoken a Spanish word before, pronounced it correctly or any thing near the mark. After they had repeated these names satisfactorily, their blind tutor, after a pause added, " Santos"—and reca- pitulated the names of a great many saints which finished the morning's tuition."*

After a few days, no doubt, these promising pupils were christened, and admitted to all the benefits and privileges of Christians and *gente de razon*. Indeed I believe that the act of making the cross and kneeling at proper times and other suchlike mechanical rites, constitute no small part of the re- ligion of these poor people. The rapidity of the conversion is, however, frequently stimulated by practices much in accordance with the primary kidnapping of the subjects. "If, as not unfre- quently happens, any of the captured Indians show a repugnance to conversion, it is the practise to im-

* Ib. p. 30

prison them for a few days, and then to allow them
to breathe a little fresh air in a walk round the mission, to observe the happy mode of life of their
converted countrymen; after which they are again
shut up, and thus continue incarcerated until they
declare their readiness to renounce the religion of
their forefathers."*   As might be believed, the ceremonial exercises of the Roman Catholic religion,
occupy a considerable share of the time of these
people. Mass is performed twice daily, besides high-
days and holidays, when the ceremonies are much
grander and of longer duration; and at all the per-
formances every Indian is obliged to attend under
the penalty of a whipping; and the same method of
enforcing proper discipline as in kneeling at proper
times, keeping silence, &c., is not excluded from the
church service itself.   In the aisles and passages of
the church, zealous beadles of the converted race
are stationed, armed with sundry weapons of potent
influence in effecting silence and attention, and
which are not sparingly used on the refractory or
inattentive.   These consist of sticks and whips, long
goads, &c., and they are not idle in the hands of the
officials that sway them.

The following is the course of proceedings in the
missions, on ordinary occasions; and as there is
little or no variety in their monotonous life, the pic-

* Beechey, Vol. I, 18.

ture may be received as a general one. It was
thus witnessed by Pérouse, and it is equally extant
at the present time. The Indians as well as the
missionaries rise with the sun and go to mass, which
lasts about an hour. While this is in progress the
breakfast is prepared, the favorite *Atole* or pottage,
which consists of barley flour, the grain being
roasted previously to grinding. It is cooked in
large kettles, and is seasoned with neither salt nor
butter. Every cottage or hut sends for the allowance for all its inmates, which is carried home in
one of their bark baskets. Any overplus that
remains, is distributed among the children as a
reward for good behaviour, particularly for good
lessons in the catechism. After breakfast, which
lasts about three quarters of an hour, they proceed
to their labours, either out of doors or within. At
noon the dinner is announced by a bell, and the
Indians quitting their work go and receive their
rations as at breakfast time. The mess now served
is somewhat of the same kind as the former, only
varied by the addition of maize, peas and beans : it
is named *pozzoli*. After dinner they return to their
work, from two to four or five; afterwards they attend evening mass which lasts nearly an hour, and
the day is finished by another supply of *atole*, as at
breakfast. In the intervals of the meals and prayers, the Indians are of course variously employed

according to their trade or occupation, that is to say, either in agricultural labours, according to the season, or in the store-rooms, magazines, and laboratories of the mission. The women are much occupied in spinning, and other little household labours, the men in combing wool, weaving, melting tallow, &c., or as carpenters, shoemakers, bricklayers, blacksmiths, &c. One of the principal occupations of the missions is the manufacturing a coarse sort of cloth from the wool of their own sheep, for the purpose of clothing the Indians. The grinding the corn is left almost entirely to the women, and is still performed by a hand mill. All the girls and widows are kept in separate houses during the day while at work, being only permitted to go out occasionally, like boys at school. The unmarried of both sexes, as well adults as children, are carefully locked up at night in separate houses, the keys being left in the keeping of the Fathers; and when any breach of this rule is detected, the culprits of both sexes are severely punished by whipping, the men in public, the women privately.

It is obvious from all this, that these poor people are in fact slaves under another name; and it is no wonder that Pérouse found the resemblance painfully striking between their condition and that of the negro slaves of the West Indies. Sometimes, although rarely, they attempt to break their bonds

and escape into their original haunts.   But this is
of rare occurrence, as, independently of the difficulty of escaping, they are so simple as to believe
that they have hardly the power to do so, after
being baptised, regarding the ceremony of baptism
as a sort of spell which could not be broken.   Occasionally, however, they overcome all imaginary
and real obstacles and effect their escape.   In
such cases, the runaway is immediately pursued,
and as it is always known to which tribe he belongs,
and as, owing to the enmity subsisting among the
tribes, he will not be received by another, he is
almost always found and surrendered to the pursuers by his pusillanimous countrymen.   When
brought back to the mission he is always first flog-
ged and then has an iron clog attached to one of his
legs, which has the effect of preventing his running
away and marking him out *in terrorem* to others.

Notwithstanding this dark picture of the general
mode of life of the converted Indians, it must not
be imagined that it is one of much real hardship, or
that it is generally thought so by the parties themselves.   On the contrary, it accords too well with
the native indolence of their character and total
defect of all independent spirit.   It is true, that
the system tends most powerfully to keep up and
to aggravate the natural defects in their character,
and to frustrate all prospect of true civilization and

all rational improvement; still it cannot be said that they are discontented ; if they lead the life of grovelling animals, they have at least their negative happiness. If they are cribbed like the stalled ox, they are fed like him, and they have hardly more care or fear for the future than he has.

> The bliss is theirs
> Of that entire dependence that prepares
> Entire submission, let what may befal......
> No forecast, no anxieties have they :
> The Jesuit governs and instructs and guides;
> Food, raiment, shelter, safety he provides :
> Their part it is to honor and obey,
> Like children under wise paternal sway.*

Their labour is very light, and they have much leisure time to waste in their beloved inaction, or in the rude pastimes of their aboriginal state. These last consist chiefly of dances and certain games, and gambling of various kinds. Of two games they are especially fond, and spend much of their time, like boys as they are, in their performance. They are thus described by La Pérouse. " The first, to which they give the name of *takersia*, consists in throwing and rolling a small hoop, of three inches in diameter, in a space of ten square fathoms, cleared of grass. Each of the two players holds a stick, of the size of a common cane and five feet long ; they endeavour to pass this stick into the hoop whilst it is in motion ; if in this they succeed they gain two

* A Tale of Paraguay, Canto IV.—SOUTHEY.

points, and if the hoop, when it stops, simply rests upon their stick, they gain one by it: the game is in three points. This game is a violent exercise, because the hoop or the stick is always in motion.

The other game named *Toussé* is more easy. They play it with four, two on each side ; each in his turn hides a piece of wood in his hands, whilst his partner makes a thousand gestures to take off the attention of the adversaries. It is curious enough to a bystander to see them squatting down opposite to each other, keeping the most profound silence, watching the features and most minute circumstances which may assist them in discovering the hand which conceals the piece of wood ; they gain or lose a point, according to their guessing right or wrong, and those who gain, have a right to hide in their turn. The game is five points and the common stake is beads."*

These and other games of chance, some of them learnt from the Spaniards, as those at cards, are indulged in to a criminal excess; and frequently they lose in this way, all they can call their own, the clothes off their backs, the favours of their wives, and even their wives themselves. This pic-ture is not softened by the addition of intoxication, a vice not unfrequent in the missions.

From the total subjection in which the Indians

* Vol. II, 224.

grow up and live, never being taught or indeed allowed to act and hardly to think for themselves, it could scarcely be expected that they should attain any real knowledge of life or independence of conduct, even if they had been originally of a better stock; as it is, they are, in regard to the capacity and power of acting as members of a civilized community, on a lower scale than even the domesticated negroes of the West Indian colonies: they are reduced to the state of mere automatons, totally subjected to the direction and guidance of others. It has accordingly been invariably found that, when any of them have been set at liberty or placed in a position to act for themselves, by leaving the missions or otherwise, they were utterly incapable of maintaining themselves; nay even so stupid as to be incapable of exercising the office of a beggar, even when their very existence seemed at stake. This seems hardly credible, yet it is a fact.

The extreme state of debasement in which they are held, not only has deprived them of their mental powers, but it has diminished their physical strength; they are not only stupid and pusillanimous but puny and feeble. It is well known that savages are prone to be filthy in their habitations; but in their natural state their living so much in the open air, their exertions in hunting and diversions, counteract this cause of disease ; but at the missions, the Indians being still allowed to live in all their native filthiness, and their lives being now comparatively sedentary, with little corporeal and less mental exercise, they inevitably grow up debilitated in body as well as in mind.   And how could it be otherwise ?

> All thoughts and occupations to commute,
> To change their air, their water, and their food,
> And those old habits suddenly uproot,
> Conform'd to which the vital powers pursued
> Their functions,—such mutation is too rude
> For man's fine frame unshaken to sustain.[*]

Great numbers fall a prey to fevers, dysenteries, and other acute diseases.   Langsdorff tells us that the missionaries informed him that upon the least illness they become wholly cast down and lose all courage and care for recovery, refusing to attend to the diet or any thing else recommended for them. Chronic diseases of various kinds are also prevalent and add to the mortality.   Syphilis prevails to a frightful extent, being indeed almost universal not only among the Indians but the Creoles and Spaniards : it produces frightful ravages among the former, as they refuse all treatment of it even when this is accessible to them, which is not always the case. These circumstances, with the natural tendency which all the Indian race have to diminish in num-

* Southey, ib. c. iv.

Q

bers in a state of civilization, much more in a state of bondage, make the loss of life very great in the missions : and now that fresh recruits can be procured with difficulty, and under recent events probably not at all, and consequently the stock maintained only by the procreation of those already domesticated, it is probable that the whole race will gradually diminish and in a few generations more will become entirely extinct.

In concluding this sketch of the present state of the domesticated Indians of California, which unquestionably betrays a lamentable want of judgment and sound philosophy on the part of the men who have been the original founders and are still the strenuous supporters of the system under which these melancholy results have arisen, it would be extreme injustice not to place in the strongest contrast with their want of judgment, the excellent motives and most benevolent and christian-like intentions by which they have been always influenced. Considering the perfectly absolute and totally irresponsible power possessed by the missionaries over the Indians, their conduct must be allowed to have been invariably marked by a degree of benevolence and humanity and moderation, probably unexampled in any other situation. To each missionary is allotted the entire and exclusive management of his mission. He is the absolute lord and master of all his Indians, and of the soil; he directs without the least interference from others, all the operations and economy of the establishment, agricultural, mechanical, manufacturing, and commercial; and disposes, according to his will and pleasure, of the produce thereof. He allots his lands, orders his seed time and harvest, distributes his cattle; encourages, chastises, and commands all the human beings under his charge; and all this without being accountable to any power on earth; for by a convenient fiction, this property belongs to the Indians, and the Indians are his slaves.   There are, I fear, few examples to be found, where men enjoying such unlimited confidence and power, have not abused them.   And yet I have never heard that the missionaries of California have not acted with the most perfect fidelity, or that they ever betrayed their trust, or exercised inhumanity; and the testimony of all travellers who have visited this country is uniformly to the same effect.   On the contrary, there are recorded instances of the most extraordinary zeal, industry, and philanthropy in the conduct of those men.   Since the country has been more opened, strangers have found at their missions, the most generous and disinterested hospitality, protection, and kindness; and this without one solitary instance to the contrary that I have ever heard of.

I cannot avoid this opportunity of gratifying my

feelings, by noticing in a more especial manner one of those worthy men as affording a recent example of what I have said of their order.

FATHER ANTONIO PEYRI, whose portrait appears in the front of this volume, took possession of the mission of San Luis Rey, in the year 1798. He first built a small thatched cottage, and asked for a few cattle and Indians from the mission. After a constant residence of thirty-four years at this place, he left it stocked with nearly sixty thousand head of domesticated animals of all sorts, and yielding an annual produce of about thirteen thousand bushels of grain, while the population amounted to nearly three thousand Indians! He left also a complete set of buildings; including a church, with inclosures, &c. Yet after these thirty-four years of incessant labor, in which he expended the most valuable part of his life, the worthy Peyri left his mission with only what he judged to be sufficient means to enable him to join his convent in the city of Mexico, where he threw himself upon the charity of his order. The toil of managing such an establishment would be sufficient motive for a man of Father Peyri's age to retire; but the new order of things which has introduced new men and new measures,— when the political power has been entrusted to heads not over-wise, and to hands not over-pure, when the theoretical doctrines of liberty and equality have been preached while oppression and rapine have been practised,—has doubtless accelerated his resignation. Whatever his motives may have been, his voluntary retirement in poverty, to spend his remaining days in pious exercises, must be applauded by the religious; and his noble disinterestedness by all. At his mission, strangers of all countries and modes of faith, as well as his fellow subjects, found always a hearty welcome, and the utmost hospitality. Many of my countrymen and personal friends have related to me, with enthusiasm, the kindness and protection which they have received at his hands, boons which are doubly valuable where places of entertainment do not exist, and where security is not very firmly established.

I had the pleasure of seeing the Father Peyri on his way to Mexico; and although I had heard much of him before, yet his prepossessing appearance, his activity and knowledge of the world, far above what could have been expected under the circumstances, gave me even a higher opinion of his worth than I before entertained. The excellent climate from which he had come, and his constant employment in the open air, made him look like a robust man of fifty years of age, although he was then sixty-seven; and although his general character and manners were, necessarily, very different from what could be expected from a mere cloistered monk, yet in his grey Franciscan habit, which he always wore, with his jolly figure, bald head, and white locks, he looked the very *beau ideal* of a friar of the olden time. This worthy man having now entered the cloisters of a convent, may be considered as dead to the world; but he will live long in the memory of the inhabitants of California; and of those numerous strangers who have been entertained at his hospitable board at San Luis Rey.

The best and most unequivocal proof of the good conduct of these Fathers, is to be found in the unbounded affection and devotion invariably shown towards them by their Indian subjects. They venerate them not merely as friends and fathers but with a degree of devotedness approaching to adoration. On the occasion of the removals that have taken place of late years, from political causes, the distress of the Indians in parting with their pastors, has been extreme. They have entreated to be allowed to follow them in their exile, with tears and lamentions, and with all the demonstrations of true sorrow and unbounded affection, Indeed, if ever there existed an instance of the perfect justice and propriety of the comparison of the priest and his disciples, to a shepherd and his flock, it is in the case of which we are treating. These poor people may indeed be classed with the " silly sheep" more than with any other animal; and I believe they would, in the words of the poet, even "lick the hand" thought it were " raised to shed their blood" —if this were the hand of the friar.

--- --- ---

Before concluding this sketch of missionary and of still Indian life, it may not be inappropriate or useless to consider, in a few words, the actual benefits conferred by the missionary systems of converting savage nations; what is the relative value of those systems; and whether they are the best that could be adopted.

In the first place, what have the natives of California gained by the labours of the Missionaries? What service have those Friars rendered to the Spanish nation, or to the world in general? They have transformed the aborigines of a beautiful country from free savages, into pusillanimous, superstitious slaves, they have taken from them the enjoyment of the natural productions of a delicious country, and ministered to them the bare necessaries of life, and that on the condition of being bondsmen for ever. Is there any one who can suppose, that those men who formerly wandered in their native wilds, " free as the wind on their mountains," were not happier than the wretched herds of human animals which are now penned in the missionary folds? It must be owned, that the arts of agriculture, and the use of the domestic animals are infinitely preferable to the scanty endowments of the hunter or barbarian state : but what share of the blessings resulting from these, do the Indians enjoy ? They are made to assist in the toil which those improvements bring along with them, but for this toil they have no reward : for them there are no hopes ! Can any one of a well constituted mind approve of this transformation, or reflect on it without sorrow ?

Admitting, which I most readily do, that the natives in this part of America were and are very low in the scale of even savage happiness, surely we must allow that their actual condition as domesticated animals—I will not say as civilized men—is a degree even below this, when we look to *the mind*, the only source, seat, and criterion of enjoyment, that deserves the name of human. True it is, as the poet whom we have already several times quoted says of them—

> Their inoffensive lives in pupilage,
> Perpetually but peacefully they lead,
> From all temptation saved and sure of daily bread ;

still, I think, no one with the feelings of a man capable and conscious of independence, will for a moment prefer this happiness of the stalled ox to the enjoyments of the free and robust Californian savages (chequered and embittered as these enjoy-

ments were with many hardships and privations)
when left to subsist on the spontaneous productions
of their woods and fields, tracking the wild deer
on their plains, bringing up fish from their waters;
traversing, without control, their forests and their
mountains, or basking, in dreamy inactivity, on the
banks of their rivers, or on the shores of the ocean.
Does it benefit the world more that twenty thousand Indians should live in aggregated huts on one
side of the mountains, than in scattered tribes on
the other? Does it promote the cause of true religion, that this number of beings should be repeating the offices of Saint Francisco and singing hymns
before the image of the virgin Mary in a church,
more than that an equal number should offer their
orisons under the canopy of heaven to the supreme
being whom they suppose to be represented by the
rising sun? I think not: but it certainly interests
humanity to know, that one of the finest countries
on earth has been doomed to be the abode of men
reclaimed from one state of misery and barbarism
only to be plunged in another sort of barbarism and
an aggravated state of misery; whereas, under other
management, it might now have been the abode
of millions of the human race, enjoying all the advantages and comforts of civilization and opulence,
which some other states of America not so favourably
situated, are so fully possessed of. The mind of man

can hardly conceive a contrast more complete than that between the present state of California, and the united states of America. On the one hand, we see an immense population formed into a community governed by wise laws, and outvieing the old countries of Europe, not only in the arts of life and the various improvements of modern times, but even in numbers; sending out fleets over all the earth, and in constant and intimate connection with the whole world. On the other hand, we see a few helpless slaves engaged in superstitious exercises, immersed in the most complete ignorance, utterly unknowing and unknown to all beyond the precincts of their wretched huts! If north America had been first peopled under the influence of Spanish Friars; if the red men of the north had been enclosed in folds, and taught to sing hallelujahs to the virgin, and repeat the offices of San Francisco; if they had been made nominal owners of the soil to the exclusion of white men, and governed according to the Franciscan system, what would have been the rank of that country at this day among the nations of the earth? Nay had even Mexico, Peru, and the other Spanish colonies been subjected to this system, what figure would they have now made in the new world of republics?

All that we can allow is, that the missionaries are honest men; that they pursue with assiduity

what they believe to be their duty; that they labour
in their vocation with zeal: but we entirely con-
demn their system, and lament its results. In their
view of the subject, the conversion of those infidels
to the Roman Catholic faith is the sole object of
their labours: attention to their temporal comforts
or intellectual cultivation cannot be expected of
teachers, whose tenets are, that to abstain from all
worldly comforts, and to despise all human learning,
is their paramount duty: consequently no instruction has ever been given to their neophytes beyond
learning to repeat in Spanish or Latin the offices of
the church. Those offices, they of course, repeat
by rote without at all knowing their meaning: but
as it is sufficient in the Romish church, that its
members perform the ceremonies, and repeat the
offices in any language, whether understood or not,
the jargon muttered by the Indians is perfectly
orthodox, and intitles them to all the future happiness which this infallible church has to bestow.

What would those respectable and philanthropic
persons think, who are so numerous in England,
and so much interested in the propagation of civilization and religion, if all their labours and immense pecuniary sacrifices ended only in changing
the condition of the wild but free inhabitants of a
fine country into one of slavery and superstition?
Would they consider the religious, moral, or tem-

poral advantages of pusillanimous slaves to be very
superior to the original condition of the wild infidel
hunters? I know there are none of those benevolent persons who would be satisfied with such a
transformation; but I fear some of their own enterprises have not had much better success. It is
true that their agents and missionaries have other
aims than those of the Spanish catholic friars: their
views are to instruct those they convert; and they
are more fastidious in admitting their neophytes to
the rites of baptism and other privileges of christianity. This is, no doubt, as it should be; but it
has the effect of diminishing greatly the number of
proselytes: and experience has shown how infi-
nately more successful the catholic missionaries
have been than the protestant. I do not mention
this with a view to recommend the catholic system;
but I cannot help thinking, that some modification
of the rigid British missionary plan might be
adopted which would be more successful. I even
venture to think, that men might be easier reclaimed from a savage, barbarous, or semibarbarous
state, by other means than by that of religion. I do
not mean that they should be left without religious
instruction; far from it: but I mean to say, that
the first attempt to civilize them might be better
done by teaching them, by degrees, the arts and
comforts of a more advanced state of society by

laymen. How is it to be supposed that a savage could, on the very first contact with a stranger, be made to comprehend a series of mysteries of which he never before dreamed, and which are in exact contradiction to all the knowledge or prejudices of his by-gone life,—to every thing which he had hitherto considered sacred and venerable, and which had been handed down to him, in the ancestral legends, with the character of incontrovertible truths?—those new mysteries, too, being such, that reason alone cannot enable the most powerful mind even of those born under the christian dispensa-tion, to comprehend? It is impossible that savages should be made at once saints or philosophers; but I think a system of progressive instruction by enlightened and prudent teachers, whose duty should be, not to instil literary or religious know-ledge so much as the common arts of life, might be successful in bringing a people living in a state of barbarism and ignorance to adopt great improve-ments in the course of time; and finally accomplish their complete civilization. I do not despair that the time will come when instead of illiterate fana-tics with cargoes of bibles and religious tracts only; prudent men will be sent among the heathens carry-ing with them—bibles and tracts certainly, but also agricultural and manufacturing implements,—use-ful mechanical inventions, furniture and clothing,

with instructions to reclaim the savage, not merely
by the terrors of future punishments, but likewise
by the fascination of a more comfortable worldly
existence.

I much question if ever the task should be undertaken of attempting to instruct the adult savages
in any sort of literary knowledge; and I have some
doubts of the possibility of instilling into their
minds the rudiments even of the christian religion;
but, under a proper system, no difficulty need be
apprehended of the children imbibing as much
literary instruction as should be thought necessary,
and of their learning thoroughly all the tenets of
christianity. I should hope, however, it would in
all cases become consistent with the promotion of
religious instruction to teach it in a milder form
than is usually done by the protestant missionaries
abroad. Can it be supposed that a human being arrived at the use of reason will hear for the first time,
without the most appalling horror, the announcement of a future abode of penal fire into which he
must be cast for ever, if he do not renounce all his
former customs and religion, and conform to certain
conditions which must at first sight appear to him
impossible? In this first encounter is it to be wondered at, that the savage imbibes an unconquerable
aversion to the new creed, or is inspired with a dis-
belief of its truth, never afterwards to be overcome?

Those missionaries, however well meaning they may be, take generally an erroneous view of the means they ought to adopt for the accomplishment of the end they are pursuing.　It also happens but too often that those men, in addition to their profession of religious teachers, assume the character of legislators and governors, for which offices none can generally be more unfit: and when they are so situated that they can, without control, exercise such powers, the greatest disorder and mischief have ensued.　Instead of making good christians, or a moral and industrious people of the natives, they have merely broken up all their old customs and rude rules of morality and order, and converted them into a lawless and profligate rabble. This, according to the report of some of the most respectable voyagers, is the case in many, at least, of the Islands in the South sea, where the missionaries have had the most unlimited opportunity of domineering.

Is there then no possibility of civilizing mankind but by divines？ Would an enlightened layman have no influence over savage people？ Would the announcement of the art of agriculture, of mechanical inventions, of the use of clothing, of good houses and furniture, of the comforts enjoyed by other men, have no charms for people destitute of all these things？ Would the advantages of improved implements and improved accommodation, good clothes and good food have no attractions for them? Would the plain and easily-understood explanation of all these advantages, told by a man of this world, be less attended' to, than the rapsodies of an enthusiast, whose benefits are all in prospect, and the most comprehensible of whose doctrines announces an eternity of horrors in another life?

When religious instruction becomes necessary and practicable, certainly let it be taught; but let it be taught as in every civilized country, under the control of the civil power: experience teaches us, that missionaries—such missionaries as have heretofore been sent to foreign countries, among savage tribes, are not fit to be entrusted with civil power: they have never yet succeeded in governing well,— not even an Island of Madripores inhabited by a few families.

The foregoing observations apply to religious missionaries such as they are at present, or at least, such as they were formerly: and I repeat, that laymen, capable of merely instructing savages in things concerning their temporal weal and comfort, would be infinitely more serviceable to them and to the case of humanity and christianity as primary teachers, than such men can possibly be. I am, however, far from thinking that religious mis-

sionaries might not be so educated as to combine
all the advantages to be found in lay-teachers,
with the capacity and authority to instruct in
religion also.   In regard to such instructors, I
would only say that they should be careful, in com-
bining the spiritual with the temporal information,
not to give too prominent a position to the former,
but rather to insinuate than enforce their severer
precepts, trusting, in the first instance, to the
means already mentioned, as more suited to the
capacities and ignorance of their pupils.   I have
been so long absent from England that I know not
whether there is any special education for those who
are now sent abroad as missionaries; but I am sure
there will be no success in the undertaking until
they are not only instructed in the arts of life most
calculated to attract and benefit the savage, but
taught also (to pious men the severer lesson of the
two) to let the earthly food of temporal knowledge
take the precedence, and even for a time to super-
cede the heavenly manna which it is their more
especial duty to administer.

Although the system of the catholic missionaries
may not much improve the moral or physical state
of their converts yet their success in gaining proselytes must ever be superior to that of the protestant,
particularly the English methodist protestant.   Nothing can be better adapted to captivate the simple

savage, than the gorgeous ceremonies of the catholic service; nor can there be agents more fitting than the persevering and well disciplined Friar, whose whole life and studies have been directed to this end; whose angry passions no injury can rouse; or whose humility and patience no insult or obstacle can overcome. With him, our missionary can bear no comparison; any more than can the attractions of their respective forms of worship. To a savage who must be chiefly taught through the medium of his senses, the catholic service is most fascinating. The whole ceremony of the mass is performed by a sort of dumb shew, accompanied with music and glittering ornaments, which may be said to be just as well understood by a savage of California as by a Hidalgo of Spain; and which will soon become to the one as it is to the other, a duty or a show which he feels himself uneasy at missing. He will also soon be made to believe, that on such easy terms as attending punctually on this pleasing exhibition, he will be entitled to everlasting happiness. By the tenets of the Catholic church this title is not doubtful but *positive*; for its dogmas teach, that the fiat of the priest in this world, is certainly confirmed in heaven, if the exercises prescribed are performed. Not so the doctrine of protestantism, even when administered by the calm and rational minister of an established church; for even then a

doubt hangs over the mind of the most virtuous:
but when the doctrine of a doubtful salvation and
an eternity of punishment is inculcated by a fana-
tical methodist, who not unfrequently may be taken
from the anvil to hammer divinity into the heads of
the heathen, then a truly sledge-hammer method of
conversion is the result, and the astonished convert
cannot but be confounded with horror! This gloomy
doctrine is increased by the nudity and sombre
style of their places of worship; sometimes also by
the austere and forbiding physiognomy of the
preacher, whom the frightened hearer often regards
as directing his eyes and his denunciations to him
individually: under such circumstances there are
not wanting examples of the scared savage fairly
taking to his heels, and fleeing from the preacher
and his doctrines for ever.

When the protestant missionaries have absolute
dominion, as in some of the islands, and among
insulated tribes, they put down all the ancient customs and diversions, however innocent; not solely
by persuasion, but by coercion: and in this way
their gloomy system is carried to its extreme. This
is another of the great causes of their inferiority to
catholic missionaries, in gaining the good will of
savages. The prohibition of sports and diversions
to men bred in a savage state, and comparatively
idle, will be always intolerable. They have much

time which cannot be otherwise filled up; and so strongly will their ancient customs have fixed themselves in their very constitutions, that it will be impossible for them to forego altogether their use; and when it is attempted to deprive them thereof, the loss of their friendship and confidence will inevitably be the consequence. Of the diversions amongst savages, music and dancing form the chief part, and as both these exercises are contrary to the tenets of some of the protestant missionaries, they must be absolutely prohibited; so that on the first encounter the missionary and his convert are at issue. The poor savage finds himself debarred from all his pleasures, and deprived of what he thought a recompence for his toil and his privations; the the white man comes and takes away the few comforts he hitherto enjoyed—and what does he give him in return? Why, he promises him, that if he lays aside the song and the dance, forgoes all pleasure and mirth—puts on a sour instead of a laughing countenance—attends to the rapsody of the preacher—then he promises, that he may *perhaps* escape being damned for ever, and avoid passing his eternity amid fire and brimstone prepared for him in the world to come. This is no encouraging outset for one who was taught to think, that he could dance and sing till the end of his mortal days, and then join his departed friends in the land of spirits beyond the western wave, to spend his eternity in bliss. .It is no wonder if such expounders of the scripture appear to the untutored savage more like the agents of an evil spirit sent on earth, to terrify mankind, than the ministers of a benevolent God who " willeth not the death of a sinner ;" —more like the sowers of the seeds of evil than the cultivators of the vineyard of the Lord of mercy ! There can hardly be a greater contrast than between a jolly, laughing friar, cajoling his converts into his fold by indulging their innocent foibles and propensities, and the spare, sour, ascetic methodist who takes from his followers all their pastimes and pleasures : but it must be admitted that the contrast in the numerical results of their conversions is no less striking.

CHAP. VI.

The lands of California, as we have seen, are
almost exclusively in the hands of the missionaries,
and consequently its agricultural operations are
chiefly carried on by them. This art or science
is well known not to be even now in a very advanced
state in Spain, and could not possibly have been
well understood—even in its then state—by the
monks who first settled in California in the last
century. The actual state of agriculture in this
country—which has not in any degree improved
since its first introduction—may, consequently, easily
be imagined to be most rude and backward. It is
not thought necessary by those primitive farmers
to study the use of fallows or green crops; to
adopt the six or seven *course shift*, or any other
shift whatever; nor to study the alternation of
white and leguminous grains, or any such modes of
improved husbandry: these are refinements they

never heard or dreamed of, and it would be as reasonable to expect, that they should adopt such novelties, as that they would the doctrines of Luther or Calvin. Their only plan of renovating the fertility of an exhausted soil, is to let it rest from culture, and to abandon it to its native weeds until it may again be thought capable of bearing crops of grain. From the superabundance of land in the country, a second cultivation of exhausted ground is not resorted to for many years, and perhaps not at all.

The grains chiefly cultivated are maize or Indian corn; wheat; barley; and a kind of small bean called *frixol:* this bean is in universal use all over Spanish America, and is a most pleasant food. They are cooked, when in a ripe state, fried with lard, and much esteemed by all ranks of people.

Maize is the staple bread corn and is cultivated in rows or drills. The cultivation of this grain is better managed than that of the others, and is certainly superior to what might be expected from such rude farmers and with such implements of husbandry as they possess. The plough used, not only in California, but in all other parts of America inhabited by the Spanish race, is of great antiquity—and is also I believe still used in old Spain. It is composed of two principal pieces, the one which we shall call the main piece, is formed out of a crooked branch of timber cut from the tree, of such a natural shape as to form this main piece, which constitutes of itself the sole and handle or stilt; it has only one handle, and no mould-board or other contrivance for turning over the furrow, and is therefore only capable of making a simple rut equal on both sides : a share is fitted to the point of the sole, but without any feather, and is the only iron in the whole construction of the plough. The other piece is the beam, which is of great length so as to reach the yoke of the oxen by which the plough is drawn; this beam is also formed of a natural piece of wood, cut from a tree of the necessary dimensions, and has no dressing except the taking off the bark : it is inserted into the upper part of the main piece, and connected with it by a small upright piece of wood on which it slides, and is fixed by two wedges: by withdrawing those wedges the beam is elevated or lowered, and by this means the plough is regulated as to depth of furrow, or what ploughmen call, giving more or less earth.

Californian Plough.

The long beam passes between the two oxen like the pole of a carriage or ox-wain, and no chain is

required for drawing the plough: a pin is put
through the point of the beam which passes before
the yoke, and is fixed there by thongs of raw hide.
The ploughman goes at one side of the plough
holding the handle or stilt with his right hand, and
managing the goad with his left. There are never
more then two oxen used in these ploughs, and no
driver is required; the ploughman managing the
plough and directing the oxen himself. The manner of yoking the oxen is not as is done in the
north of Europe, by putting the yoke on the shoulders and fixing it by a wooden collar or bow, round
the neck: the yoke is placed on the top of the head
close behind the horns, tied firmly to their roots and
to the forehead by thongs, so that instead of drawing by the shoulders they draw by the roots of the
horns and forehead. When oxen are so bound up
they have no freedom to move their heads; they go
with their noses turned up, and seem to be under
great pain.

I know not if this was the custom of the ancients;
but I am persuaded that no guide to the ancient
customs of Europe can be sought for in the present
day so safely as amongst the Spaniards, who seem
in few respects to differ from their ancestors of the
earliest ages.   On my asking a native of Spain
what could be the motive for making an ox to draw
by the head, and a horse by the shoulders; he re-

plied, that wise men had found, that particular animals had their strength lodged in particular parts of their body; and it was found that the strength of the ox lay in its horns. I then stated to him that almost all other nations thought otherwise, and yoke their oxen by the shoulders; therefore, the question was, whether the Spaniards or the other nations were in the right; to this he immediately replied in a tone of indignation, " What! can you suppose that Spain which has always been known as the mother of the sciences can be mistaken on that point?" Against this, of course, no further argument could be offered; and in the Americas oxen will continue to draw by the horns perhaps for ages to come, as taught by their scientific mother of Spain. Their carts are drawn by oxen yoked in the same manner; and in this case, they have to bear the weight of the load on the top of their heads, which is certainly the most disadvantageous mechanical point of the whole body: this renders their sufferings more severe than in the plough, and it is truly distressing to see the poor animals writhing under a load which on their backs or shoulders, they could easily support. The form of the ox-cart is as rude as that of the plough; it is composed of a bottom-frame of a most clumsy construction, on which is raised a body of a few bars stuck upright, of a great height, and connected at

the top with other slight bars; this cart is usually
without lining, but when used for carrying maize,
it is lined with canes tied to the upright bars.
The pole is of very large dimensions, and long
enough to be fastened to the yoke in the same
manner as the beam of the plough. This also adds
greatly to the distress of the poor oxen, because,
the pole being tied fast to the yoke which rests on
their heads, they feel every jerk and twist of the
cart in the most sensible manner; and when the
road is full of stones, sloughs, and all manner of
obstructions, as it generally is in America, it appears
as if the animal's head would every moment be
twisted off!

The wheels of the Californian ox-cart, as well as
those of the other Spanish Americas, are of a most
singular construction. They have no spokes, and
are composed of only three pieces of timber. The
middle piece is hewn out of a huge tree, of a sufficient
size to form the nave and middle of the wheel all
in one: this middle piece is made of a length equal
to the diameter of the wheel, and rounded at the
two ends to arcs of the circumference. The other
two pieces are made of timber naturally bent and
joined to the sides of the middle piece by keys or
oblong pieces of wood, groved into the ends of the
pieces which form the wheel: the whole is then
made circular, and resembles the wheels of the

barrows used in the north of Scotland for carrying peat or turf out of the mosses or bogs. There does not enter into the construction of this cart a particle of iron, not even a nail, for the axle is entirely of wood, and the linch-pin of the same material, as well as the pins that fix the cart to the axle.

From the construction of the plough, as already described, it will be perceived, that there being no mould board or feathered shear, the furrow cannot be cut up and turned over as with an English plough, a rut only being made; consequently the soil can only be broken by successively crossing and recrossing the field many times; and it is evident that however often crossed by a machine of this kind, the root weeds of any tenacity can never be cut, so that this mode of ploughing must always be very imperfect; and although four or five crossings are often given, yet the soil is not sufficiently broken or the weeds eradicated.

The necessity of giving so many crossings is a great waste of labour; and as the ploughing is deferred till the commencement of the rains, and very near the time of sowing, an immense number of ploughs must be employed; it is no uncommon thing to see on the large maize estates in some parts of Mexico, upwards of one hundred ploughs at work together! With these ploughs it is not ne-

cessary to divide the field into ridges or brakes.
As they are equal on both sides they have only to
begin at one side of the field and follow one another up and down, as many as can be employed
together without interfering in turning round at
the end, which they do, in succession, like ships
tacking in a line of battle, and so proceed down the
same side as they came up.

A harrow is totally unknown, and where wheat
or barley is sown a bush is generally used to cover
in the seed; but in some places, instead of this, a
long heavy log of wood is drawn over the field
something on the plan of a roller, but dragging
without turning round, so as to carry a portion of
the soil over the seed.

In the cultivation of maize, when the field is sufficiently ploughed or crossed, a rut or furrow is
made by the plough at the distance intended for
the drills, which is generally five or six feet. In
this rut the seed is deposited by hand, the labourers
carrying it in small baskets, out of which they take
a handful and drop from three to five grains at
once, which they slightly cover with their foot from
the loose earth on the side of the rut; and so proceed depositing a like number of seeds at the distance of about three feet. In this state the seed is
left to spring up to a moderate height, and then
the ploughs are again put to turn a furrow on each

side of the rut towards the young plants, thus forming a drill. When the maize grows up to a considerable height, it is commonly cleaned by hand, by pulling up the weeds; the middle between the drills, is again turned up by the plough passing up and down, and the labour is then finished.

The sowing of maize as well as of other grains in Upper California, commences in November, or as near the commencement of the rains as possible, and the harvest is in the months of July and August.

The process of harvesting maize is as follows. The labourer carries with him a large and very deep basket of wicker work, with which he proceeds along the drills and fills it with the heads of maize; when full he carries it on his back to the end of the field where an ox-cart is stationed, and into which he empties his basket; when the cart is full it proceeds to the place of deposit. In this way the stalks are all left; and when all their heads are gathered the cattle are then turned into the field and eat up the leaves and such part of the stalks as are eatable; these are found to be very nutritious; and the cattle get fat at this season more than on the best grass pastures.

The next operation is to separate the maize from the head or husk. This is done by rubbing the full head againt a few empty husks bound together,

and is a very tedious operation. Maize in warm
countries is very liable to spoil, and to be infested
by an insect called in Spanish *gorgoja*; and as it is
found that maize keeps longer in the husk, it is
sometimes left so till it is required for use; but
although it may be kept somewhat longer in this
state than when separated, yet it is also soon subject
to the attack of this insect. On the coast of the
tropical country of Mexico, it is difficult to keep
maize above six or eight months, but in California
it can be kept for a much longer time. Perhaps by
kiln-drying and other methods, maize might be
preserved even in tropical climates for a great length
of time; but I have seen no attempt at any plan of
this kind, although it would be, if successful,
attended with immense benefit to the growers of
this grain in the populous parts of Mexico; particularly on the coast, where the prices vary so much
in different years, and even at different seasons of
the same year.

The produce of maize, in proportion to the seed,
is perhaps more than that of any other grain whatever; but this doubtless chiefly arises from its being
always planted in drills, and I am not certain if
wheat and other grains might not give equal returns
if planted or dibbled in the same way. The return
from maize in good land is often as high as a hundred
and fifty fold, and even higher, and if it is much un-

der a hundred it is thought to be an inferior crop.
The calculation however of the produce of grain by
returns from the seed, is founded on an erroneous
principle; but in South America it is always so calculated, as they have no fixed land measure, so that
it is difficult to ascertain what any certain quantity of
land actually produces. This has led to very mistaken
notions respecting the fertility of those countries.
When I first arrived in Chili I was told that wheat
seldom or never yielded less than fifty returns, and
that it sometimes gave one hundred and fifty, but
could not reconcile this with the appearance of
the crops I saw in the fields, which certainly
never surpassed the appearance of a good crop in
England. I could only suppose that it was to be
accounted for by thin sowing, which I afterwards
found to be the fact. Perhaps on measuring an
acre of land in any part of the world, the produce
in any kind of grain will not greatly exceed that of
the best crops of wheat produced in the north of
Europe. I measured a small piece of ground in
Mexico sown with barley, and the seed used was
about the third part of what is ordinarily used in
England, but I had not an opportunity of ascertain-
ing its produce: it must have produced three times
as much from the seed as the ordinary returns in
England, to have given an equal quantity per acre
as in that country. One thing, however, may be

allowed which is, that grain raised by irrigation in hot countries must produce more than by any other mode of cultivation ; and as much of the wheat in South America is cultivated in that way, the produce in such circumstances may be more than in Europe : but I have never seen even by irrigation any thing which could promise a very superior return per acre to a heavy crop in England.

Wheat is sown " in broad-cast" on land prepared as for maize. In the south of California, owing to the length of the dry season, it is cultivated by irrigation ; but in the north, and particularly round the bay of San Francisco, as formerly stated, the rains and dews are sufficient, and irrigation is not necessary. From the lands being new, and naturally fertile, the produce of wheat ought to be very great; and from the excellence of the climate the quality of the grain should be very fine. Samples of wheat from the Cape of Good Hope were exhibited many years ago in London as a curiosity for their superior fineness, and sold at an exorbitant price for seed. California corresponds in situation to the Cape of Good Hope ; and if the culture and quality of the seed were attended to, wheat of equal fineness must be produced. At present from the unskilfullness of the culture, and the inattention to procure good seed, neither the quantity nor quality is equal to what they ought to be. The cultivation of wheat is at present but very limited, although from the excellence of the soil and climate, and the abundance of land fit for the production of this grain, Upper California ought to be—and one day must be—the granary of all South America.

Barley is cultivated but in small quantities, no use being made of it except to feed horses; they make no malt liquor or spirits from this grain. The kind cultivated both in California and Mexico, is what is called " bigg" in Scotland, being the old variety with six rows: it produces a very small grain.—What will my northern friends think when they are informed, that oats are not known in any part of the Spanish Americas! They not only do not raise this species of grain for their own use, but not even for the use of their horses. All kinds of grain in California are threshed out at once, without stacking or housing any part of it with the straw.

In the neighbourhood of the mines and large towns in Mexico, wheat and barley straw is used as fodder for the working horses and mules, and from its dry and brittle state in those warm countries, it is, in the act of threshing, reduced to a state which more resembles chaff than straw; it is in fact like straw cut by machinery in England, and is carried to market on mules' backs, enclosed in large net bags, one on each side. Hundreds of mules are to be seen daily entering Guanajuato and other large mining towns, with these immense globes of cut straw at their sides more resembling balloons than any thing else. In California, however, as the pastures are so abundant, and few mules or horses worked, little use is made of the straw.

The following table gives the whole produce in grain of Upper California, in the year 1831, calculated according to the localities, and in *Fanegas*:

GRAIN.

Names of the Jurisdictions, Missions and Towns.	Wheat.	Maize or Indian corn.	Frizol or Small Beans.	Barley.	Beans, Garvanzos, and Peas.	Total Fanegas.
Jurisdiction of S. Francisco.						
Presidio of S. Francisco ..233	..	70..	40..	,, ..	,, ..	343
Town of San José de Guadalupe..1657	..1560..	191..		,, ..	,, ..	3408
Mission of S. Francisco Solano ..1171..	200..	24..	241..	24..	1660
id. of S. Rafael	.. 774..	130..	15..	388..	20..1327
id. of S. Francisco	.. 670..	15..	9..	340..	58..1092
id. of Santa Clara	.2400..	60..	25..	,, ..200..2685
id. of S. José	..4000..1000..123..1100..418..6641
id. of Santa Cruz	.. 160..	300..	10..	386..	20.. 876
Jurisdiction of Monterey.						
Presidio of Monterey	.. 490..	332..	131..	,, ..	,, ..	953
Village of Branciforte	.. 103..	160..	80..	,, ..	,, ..343
Mission of S. Juan Bautista	.. 840..	170..	40..	255..	6..1311
id. of S. Carlos	.. 200..	,, ..	,, ..	215..	62.. 477
id. of Na. Sa. de la Soledad..538..	50..	,, ..	243..	62.. 893
id. of S. Antonio	.. 955..	115..	40..	568..	23..1701
id. of S. Miguel	.. 599..	36..	9..	57..	33.. 734
id. of S. Luis Obispo	.. 350..	60..	20..	20..	,, .. 450

Names of the Jurisdictions, Missions, and Towns.	Wheat.	Maize or Indian Corn.	Frixol or Small Beans.	Barley.	BeansGarvanzos, and Peas.	Total Fanegas.
Jurisdiction of Sta. Barbara.						
PRESIDIO OF STA. BARBARA ..	„ ..	300..	90..	„ ..	„ ..	390
Mission of La Purissima ..	700..	100..	20..	56 ..	17..	893
id. of Sta Ines ..	800..	400..	20..	„ ..	„ ..	1220
id. of Sta Barbara ..	730..	90..	50..	336..	30..	1236
id. of Buenaventura ..	700..	200..	160..	800..	„ ..	1860
id. of S. Fernando ..	200..	250..	40..	„ ..	65..	555
Town of la Reyna de los Angelos..	138..	1758..	179..	„ ..	„ ..	2075
Jurisdiction of S. Diego.						
PRESIDIO OF S. DIEGO ..	140..	125..	5..	„ ..	„ ..	270
Mission of S. Gabriel ..	1400..	400..	13..	„ ..	25..	1838
id. of S. Juan Capistrano ..	450..	625..	30..	„ ..	5..	1110
id. of S. Luis Rey ..	1800..	2000..	200..	1200..	15..	5215
id. of S. Diego ..	2946..	420..	80..	1200..	„ ..	4646
Total Fanegas	25,144	10,926	1,644	7,405	1,083	46,202

Taking the Fanega at 2½ English bushels, the harvest in 1831 will be as follows :—

	Quarters.
Wheat	7857½
Maiz..	3414½
Frixol	514
Barley	2314
Beans, Garvanzos, and Pease.................	338
Total Quarters	14438

Now, reckoning the following as the average price of grain in California at the present time, viz. wheat and barley 2 dollars the fanega, or £1. 5s. the English quarter, and maize at 1½ dollars, or £1. per quarter, the following will be the value of the produce in English money :—

	£.	s.	d.
Wheat	.9822	17	6
Maize	.4268	0	0
Barley	.2314	0	0
Pease and Beans reckoned as Barley	852...	0	0

Total, £17256 17 6

The quantity of wheat produced, it will be perceived, is much greater than any of the other sorts of grain, which is the reverse of what takes place in the other Mexican states, wheat bearing a small proportion to maize, which latter is the staple bread corn.

The mills for grinding flour in Upper California are but few, and of the most primitive construction; but none better are to be found in the other parts of Spanish America, not even in Chili where wheat abounds. These mills consist of an upright axle, to the lower end of which is fixed a horizontal water-wheel placed under the building, and to the upper end the mill-stone; and as there is no intermediate machinery to increase the velocity, it is evident, that the mill-stone can make only the same number of revolutions as the water-wheel; this makes it necessary that the wheel should be of very small diameter, otherwise no power of water thrown upon it could make it go at a rate sufficient to give the mill-stone the requisite velocity. It is therefore made of very small dimensions and con-

structed in the following manner. A set of what
is called cucharas (spoons) are stuck into the peri-
phery of the wheel, which serve in place of float
boards ; they are made of pieces of timber in something of the shape of spoons, the handles being
inserted into mortices on the edge of the wheel,
and the bowls of the spoons made to receive the
water, which spouts on them laterly and forces
round the small wheel with nearly the whole velocity of the water which impinges upon it. I never
knew of the existence of a mill of this construction
till I saw one in South America, but I since find
that Sir Walter Scott in his Pirate describes a similar one as having been in use in the Shetland Islands.
This mill is erected at very small expense, but it is
no small boast for a mission in California to have
one of them, and I believe there are only three in
all the country.

That most useful plant, the potatoe, thrives well
in California, but the people in this as in every other
Spanish country, do not make this root a staple
article of subsistence, nor is it used as a substitute
for bread. When potatoes are brought to the table
in Spanish countries they are made up into a dish
to be eaten alone: they are however now much
more cultivated than before the introduction of
strangers, who use them as in Europe, and who will,
in time, shew the inhabitants their value.

Of green vegetables for the table, the peasantry

and all those who live in the country, make little or no use. It is a remarkable fact, that in all parts of Spanish America no such things are to be seen in the gardens of the peasants, nor even in those of the proprietors of estates, as cabbages or greens of any kind: only in the vicinity of large towns are to be found cabbage gardens. In California it may be said that before the admission of foreign setlers, neither the potatoe nor green vegetables were cultivated as articles of food.

No such thing as the cultivation of turnips in the large way, or for the food of cattle, is at all known. They have a small white kind for the table, but its flavour is insipid, and as well as other green vegetables is but little used.

The cultivation of hemp was formerly carried to some considerable extent, and furnished a supply of this article to the arsenal of San Blas : its produce was abundant and of very excellent quality. Its cultivation, however, was discontinued soon after the withdrawing of the Spanish squadron from San Blas, and has not again been renewed; but in the hands of industrious settlers this undoubtedly would be a source of great profit.

Flax has also been tried, and proves congenial to the soil and climate; but from the total want of machinery for dressing it, and industry to manufacture it, nothing has been done except merely by way of trial.

The vine thrives in California in an extraordinary degree. It is cultivated already to a very considerable degree, and might be extended almost without limits : wine is now made of tolerably good quality, and some even very excellent. Nothing is wanting but intelligent persons, to make wine of superior quality, and which would find a ready market in Mexico and the neighbouring countries where the vine does not grow.

The quantity of wine and brandy consumed in those countries is immense; all of which could be supplied from California at a price infinitely less than what is now paid for that brought from Europe. Raisins also, the produce of the vine, are articles of considerable consumption, so that this branch of industry would be a source of great riches to an interprising and industrious people, but at present, instead of exporting either wine or brandy, they have to purchase them for their own use.

The olive is also produced in very great perfection ; and when well prepared is not inferior to that of France ; and the oil would be equally good if expressed and preserved with care. These are articles of great consumption among a Spanish population, and would be of much importance as exports to the neighbouring republics.

Pasturage, however, is the principal object pursued in California as well as in all the Spanish settlements of America. The immense tracts of country possessed by them in proportion to the population, added to the indolent and unenterprising habits of this race of men, renders the pastoral state the most congenial to their situation and disposition. Few men and little labour are required to take care of herds of cattle, which naturally increase rapidly in the vast plains abounding with rich pastures ; whereas, to raise grain, great labour and a numerous population are required. The pastures of Upper California are most abundant, and the domestic animals have increased amazingly.

The following table gives the total number of cattle, of all descriptions, in the year 1831.

DOMESTIC CATTLE.

Names of the Jurisdictions, Missions, and Towns.	Black Cattle.	Horses.	Mules.	Asses.	Sheep.	Goats.	Swine.
Jurisdiction of S. Francisco.							
PRESIDIO OF S. FRANCISCO	5610.	470.	40.	„	„	„	„
Town of San José de Guadalupe.	4443.	2386.	134.	„	„	„	„
Mission of S. Francisco Solano	2500.	725.	4.	„	6000.	„	50
id. of S. Rafael	1200.	450.	1.	„	2000.	„	17
id. of S. Francisco	4200.	1239.	18.	„	3000.	„	„
id. of Santa Clara	9000.	780.	38.	„	7000.	„	„
id. of S. José	12000.	1300.	40.	„	13000.	„	40
id. of Santa Cruz	3500.	940.	82.	„	5403.	„	„
Jurisdiction of Monterey.							
PRESIDIO OF MONTEREY	5641.	3310.	70.	„	„	„	„
Village of Branciforte	1000.	1000.	3.	„	„	„	„

Names of the Jurisdictions, Missions, and Towns.	Black Cattle.	Horses.	Mules.	Asses.	Sheep.	Goats.	Swine.
Mission of S. Juan Bautista	. 7070.	401.	6.	1.	7017.	,,	. 17
id. of S. Carlos	. 2050.	470.	8.	,, .	4400.	55.	,,
id. of Na. Sa. de la Soledad	. 6599.	1070.	50.	1.	6358.	,,	. ,,
id. of S. Antonio	. 5000.	1060.	80.	2	10000.	55.	60
id. of S. Miguel	. 3762.	950.	106.	28.	8999.	15.	60
id. of S. Luis Obispo	. 2000.	800.	200.	50.	1200.	,,	. 24
Jurisdiction of Sta. Barbara.							
PRESIDIO OF STA. BARBARA	. 7900.	1300.	220.	,, .	,,	. ,,	. ,,
Mission of La Purissima	. 10500.	1000.	160.	4.	7000.	30.	62
id. of Sta. Ines	. 7300.	320.	112.	,, .	2200.	,,	. 50
id. of Sta. Barbara	. 2600.	511.	150.	2.	3300.	37.	63
id. of Buenaventura	. 4000.	300.	60.	,, .	3100.	30.	8
id. of S. Fernando	. 6000.	300.	60.	3.	3000.	,,	. ,,
Town of la Reyna de los Angelos	. 38624.	5208.	520.	,, .	,,	. ,,	. ,,
Jurisdiction of S. Diego.							
PRESIDIO OF S. DIEGO	. 608.	625.	150.	58.	,,	. ,,	. ,,
Mission of S. Gabriel	. 20500.	1700.	120.	4.	13554.	76.	98
id. of S. Juan Capistrano	. 10900.	290.	30.	5.	4800.	50.	40
id. of S. Luis Rey	. 26000.	2100.	250.	5.	25500.	1200.	250
id. of S. Diego	. 6220.	1196.	132	14.	17624.	325.	,,
Total	216727	32201	2844	177	153455	1873	839

In addition to the above there are a great number running wild, particularly mares, which they hunt and kill in order to prevent their eating up the pasture from the useful cattle.

From this immense number of domestic animals little advantage is obtained beyond the value of the hides and fat. The management of the dairy is totally unknown. There is hardly any such thing in use as butter or cheese, and what little is made is of the very worst description. It will no doubt appear strange when I assert, that the art of making butter and cheese, is unknown in all the Americas inhabited by the Spaniards and their descendents, yet as far as my own experience goes, as well as my information, this is in reality the case; for although something under the name of butter and cheese is generally to be found, yet they are made in a way entirely different from that practised in the north of Europe, and certainly have but little resemblance to those so much esteemed aliments as there prepared. Both the butter and cheese, particularly the former, are execrable compounds of sour coagulated milk and its cream mixed together, the butter being made of the cream or top of the milk mixed with a large proportion of the sour coagulated part, and beat up together by the hand, and without a churn, till something of the consistency of butter is produced: it is of a dirty grey colour and of a very disagreeable flavour, which in a short time is rendered still worse by it tendency to get rancid, in which state it is almost always found before it arrives at the place of sale, and is of course intolerable to palates used to that of a better sort. The cheese is made of the remainder of the sour milk, or sometimes of the whole milk and cream; in either case it is made up in small moulds containing about half a pound, and undergoes no pressure except by the hand; it is always mixed with a large proportion of salt, and is of a soft crumbling consistency.

There is another sort of cheese or something resembling it, made of sweet milk coagulated with rennet: it is made in thin cakes which they form by pressing the curds between the hands till they are freed of the whey, and then left to dry: this is called *panela* and is much better than the sour composition: it is used as a luxury and sent about as presents.

In some parts of Lower California situated on the gulf, and in the northern parts of Sonora and New Mexico, real cheese is made and some of it of very good quality. This, however, is only an exception to the general observation, and proves that there is nothing to prevent good cheese from being made in those countries. How this art has been introduced into such remote corners of the Spanish possessions as lower California and New Spain, whilst unknown in the others, I am unable to ascertain.*

It is truly incredible that from such an immense number of cows as is contained in Upper California

* Good butter has also been made and continues to be so, though in small quantities (and I believe confined to one dairy) in the neighbourhood of the city of Mexico. This practice was introduced by a stranger since the revolution—but I understand the consumption is chiefly confined to foreigners, and the price very high.

no attempt should be made to reap advantage from their milk. The produce of the dairy has always been an object of consideration and profit in all ages and in all countries.   It seems however, that even in old Spain at the present day, this branch of husbandry is much neglected, and it is well known that Cadiz and other maritime towns have always been supplied with butter and cheese from Holland and Ireland. A Mexican gentleman who was lately at Madrid informs me, that no butter is used in that city except as a rarity, and that if it be wanted it must be ordered before-hand and paid for at a high rate.

It is doubted whether the ancients knew the art of making butter and cheese, such as are used in our time.   Articles of food under these names were known, but authors doubt if they were at all of the same   character as our modern aliments of the same name.   I am strongly inclined to favour those who argue against true butter and cheese being known in antiquity, and this solely from the example of the Spaniards; for, as I have before said, they must be taken as great authorities in whatever relates to ancient customs. They have preserved them not in books, but in practice, in much greater purity than any other of the European nations. The Hebrew word which is taken to mean butter, I find is interpreted by some to signify

sour thick milk; this is exactly the Spanish butter.
Sour thick milk covered by its own cream, is what
they make their butter of—and sour thick milk with
or without the cream, constitutes the material for
their cheese. The Greek word, I am told, is said to
mean a mixture of butter and cheese; and the
Spanish butter is a mixture of butter and cheese,
and their cheese, a mixture of cheese and butter.
Be this as it may, a prejudice undoubtedly exists
amongst the natives of Spain, and their American
progeny, against the aliment of the dairy.   Butter
is never used in cooking or in sauces, and the physicians strictly prohibit in all cases of illness not only
butter and cheese, but every sort of milk diet, and
it is never recommended and often prohibited even
in health.

It is at all events certain, that the dairy in Upper
California is entirely neglected, and in consequence
a source of great agricultural riches lost.

The supercargo of a British ship from India,
bound for the coast of Mexico, informed me, that
on making the coast of California they touched at
the Russian settlement, called La Bodega, and which
borders on the Spanish territory — or rather of
right belongs to it, and although the part which the
Russians possess is steril in comparison to the fine
plains occupied by the Spaniards, yet they found
immediately on their arrival a present sent on board

by the Russian Governor, of most excellent butter,
cheese, fat mutton, and good vegetables; all things
most desirable to people arriving from a long voyage.   They soon after proceeded to Monterey, the
capital of Spanish California, where they could find
nothing but bull beef!   Neither bread, butter,
cheese, nor vegetables were to be procured,   This
was in the beginning of the year 1822; and immediately before the revolution ; and I am assured by
a Mexican officer lately arrived from Monterey,
that the strangers who comprise a considerable
proportion of the inhabitants of that town, are at
this time (1834) actually furnished with butter and
cheese from the Russian settlement of La Bodega.

The Spanish mode of managing cattle is in many
other respects peculiarly their own; they leave
their oxen uncastrated till they are three or four
years old.   The operation of castration they have
no idea of performing on calves, so that in a large
herd of cattle we find a great proportion of them
are bulls, roaring and goading each other at a fear-
ful rate.   The greater part of the beef consumed
in the city of Mexico is of bulls.   It is no uncommon thing to see a drove of them without the
admixture of a single ox, wending their way to the
shambles of Mexico from the very remote parts of
the Republic.   Some estates on the shores of the
Pacific were formerly accustomed to send a thou-

sand bulls at a time to the city of Mexico. This custom exists to the present time, but the *Haciendas* or estates having been much ruined by the revolutionary wars, the numbers are not now so great as formerly, but considerable droves at certain seasons of the year still pass on as heretofore. I never could find any reasonable motive alleged for this custom : the true one, doubtless, is their having inherited it from their forefathers; and I have no doubt it has descended to them uninterruptedly from the ancient Lusitanians; this custom is strictly preserved in California, and thousands and tens of thousands of bulls now roar, in all their native virtue and vigour, on its wide-extended plains.

Owing to this practice, and from the circumstance of the cattle being seldom folded, they are very shy, and in a half wild state, for which reason it is necessary in catching them to use the *Laso*. This has been so often described that it is perhaps unnecessary to do so here; yet it is so wonderfully managed by the South Americans, that it can never be seen practised without admiration; and, like a horse race, or fox chase, attracts every one within its reach to witness it. For although it is in general a useful and necessary occupation to secure the cattle in this way, yet it is by the lookers-on, and even by those engaged in it, considered as an amusement, and to which they are passionately

CALIFORNIAN MODE OF CATCHING CATTLE.

attached.   There is in all the cattle estates in
Spanish America a time set apart, at certain seasons
of the year, for the purpose of collecting the cattle
in order to overlook and count them, and to brand
the young ones with the mark of the estate, and
perform certain other operations, as well as to accus-
tom them to take the fold, and prevent them from
running wild. This is called a *rodea* and is a holiday-
time to all the inhabitants of the estate and its
vicinity.   Numbers come from great distances to
assist gratuitously at the féte. On this occasion the
cattle are driven into a large ring fold at a wide
opening on one side : this is afterwards all closed up
except a small door left for the cattle to be forced
out at.   Those that are to be operated upon are
made to escape at this door singly; and when a bull
finds himself in the open field, he makes off with
the utmost speed, pursued by a space of horsemen
swinging their lasos in the air; and while in full
chase and when they get within point blank, those
foremost throw their lasos, some round the horns,
others round the neck; some entrap a hind leg,
others a fore one : they then stop short their well-
trained horses, and the bull falls as if shot, tumbling
heels over head.   In a moment he is secured by
tying the lasos round his legs, and by some of the
people lying down on his head.   In this state the
wildest bull lies perfectly motionless, and suffers

T

whatever operation has to be performed, almost without making an effort at resistance.

Although I have so often seen the feat of the Laso, I never was tired of looking on and wondering at the dexterity with which it is performed; nor could I ever comprehend exactly, by what art a man at full gallop could throw a noose so as to catch a bull by the hind leg while he was flying from his pursuers at all his speed. The noose must necessarily go under the foot, be drawn up, and run tight on the leg, which appears to be a slight of hand almost impossible. Early and constant practice can only enable one to acquire such dexterity; and, indeed, the practice of the *Lasores* begins from their earliest infancy. The first thing you see in a little urchin's hand is a laso of thread or twine with which he essays to ensnare his mother's kittens and chickens, and perhaps from those elemental essays the theory of the aso can only be comprehended: for the rapidity and magical-like effect with which the real laso is thrown, leaves no time or opportunity to see how it acts. It appears that to secure the hind leg, the large noose of the laso,—which, by swinging it round the head, is formed into a circle,—is thrown so as to pass under the leg at the very moment when this is elevated in making the spring, while the bull is galloping , and placed exactly where the leg must fall on coming to the ground : when the laso is thus thrown, and the leg placed within the circle of its noose, the thrower instantly checks his horse, and gives his laso a jerk in the very instant of time when the bull's foot touches the ground, and thus draws the noose up and tight round the leg. All this must be done in a moment of time, and although it appears almost impracticable, yet I think this is the mode of operating. To catch the animal by the horns or neck is easily understood, and does not require so much skill; yet even to do this with certainty to a bull at full speed, and on a horse in chase, requires much practice and dexterity. The saddles used are well fitted to the exercise : they rise high before and behind, and have a knob on the fore part on which the riders can lay hold to secure themselves, and on which they can make fast or wind up the laso, the end of which however is not tied to this knob, but to a ring in the girth of the saddle. The horses are so taught as to lean over when checked, against the direction in which the bull draws, and thereby secure themselves from falling down under the sudden tug occasioned by the impetus of the animal when it is brought up by the laso. This, as well as the whole proceeding is admirably shown in Captain Smyth's drawing, from which the Plate is taken. The bridle used is equally well adapted to the purpose, being most powerful in its structure and calculated

for suddenly checking a horse. It is a single curb of
a peculiar construction, having the bit doubled up
high in the mouth without a joint; and instead of
a curb chain, it has a solid ring of iron which passes
through the upper part of the doubled-up bit within
the mouth, and then passes behind the lower jaw,
thus forming a most tremendous lever sufficient to
break the horse's jaw if powerfully applied. The
use of this makes the horse's mouth so sensible, and
gives the rider such complete power over him, that
he is checked at full speed in the most instantane-
ous manner. It is a common practice in some parts
of Spanish America for the people in exercising
their horses to ride up full speed at a wall, and
when the horse's head is within a few inches of it
to check them all at once: this masterly mode of
management of their horses can alone enable them
to use the laso with such dexterity as they do.

I have before said that little milk is used by the
Spanish race in America, and when they do use it
they have a very awkward way of taking it from
the cow. They think it is absolutely necessary to
use the calf to induce the cow to give her milk;
for this reason, they first let the calf suck for some
time alone, and then lay hold of one of the
teats while the calf is still sucking the others, and
so by a kind of stealth procure a portion only of
the milk. They have no idea that a cow would

give milk at all if the calf was altogether taken away from her; so that when cows are kept for their milk, the calves must be kept along with them, and as they get the best share, a great number of cows and calves must be kept to produce a small quantity of milk.

It will be seen from the table given at page 266, that the number of sheep in all Upper California is only one hundred and fifty three thousand odd, which might be increased almost without limits; but as their wool is of a quality unfit for exportation, and mutton little used for food, there is no encouragement at present for any attention being paid to their propagation. The sheep in California as well as in all the other parts of Spanish America are of a bad breed, and their wool of the very coarsest quality: the whole seem to be exactly of the same kind. It is strange, that while in Spain the finest-wooled sheep in the world—the merinos— have so long existed, an inferior breed, producing the coarsest wool, should have been carried to their colonies. Perhaps the propagation of the merinos, like the grape, was discouraged or prohibited in the Americas, in order, as was the policy of the mother country, to give the monopoly to the flocks of Estremadura, as well as to the vineyards of Catalonia. It is extraordinary, however, that some one should not have introduced into any of those vast countries a

better breed, even in the time of the Spanish government; and still more extraordinary, that, since the
revolutions which have removed all obstacles, no amelioration of this breed has taken place.   There are
large flocks of sheep in Chili; immense numbers
on the table lands of Mexico which abundantly
supply the capital with mutton; and myriads scattered over the middle or southern republics, all of
which, as well as those of California, are of the
same breed, and their wool invariably exceedingly
coarse.   It might be thought that in the tropical
climates, the temperature and other circumstances
may have changed the quality of the fleeces; but
in Upper California the latitude nearly corresponds
with that of Estremadura, and in some parts exactly so; yet the quality of the wool is equally bad
there as in the equatorial latitudes of Peru and
Columbia.   The British settlements of New Holland and Van Dieman's Land correspond with the
latitudes of Chili and California; and we see what
a fine quality of wool is produced there, equalling
that of Spain, and already forming an important
article of exportation from those colonies.

It is impossible to conceive a country more
adapted to the breeding of sheep than Upper
California; and if a good kind were introduced
by intelligent breeders the benefit would be incalculable.   The same plan is followed with the sheep

as with the black catttle in respect to castration ;
and the flocks consist only of rams and ewes without any wethers, which are the most valuable stock.
The mutton, like the beef, is therefore bad ; droves
of rams as well as bulls are seen daily entering the
city of Mexico and other places of consumption all
over the Spanish Americas.

Swine do not seem to be very much attended to
in California, but in other parts of Mexico they are
bred in great numbers. They are reared and fed
chiefly for their lard, and are of a very good kind
derived from the Chinese breed. They are fed in
a manner so as to produce as much fat and as little
flesh as possible They are allowed to grow to
a certain age in a lean state, subsisting chiefly
on such roots and herbs as they can procure
at large in the woods and fields, and when they
arrive at the proper age and size for killing they
are then shut up, or at least kept at home, and as
much maize given them as they can eat ; this being
administered to them in moderate quantities, at a
time, so as not to surfeit them. By this means
they soon get enormously fat, and when slaughtered
they are found to be almost all lard to the very bones.
This lard they peel off as blubber is peeled off from
a whale, the whole being entirely separated from
every part of the flesh and entrails, leaving an aston-
ishingly small proportion of flesh. They are often

so highly fed as to be unable to move. I have seen some unable to get farther up than on their haunches, just far enough to reach their food, and when satiated tumble down again and grunt themselves to sleep. In the sale and purchase of these animals their weight of flesh is never taken into account; the calculation is how many pounds of lard they will produce. Lard with all ranks is a necessary of life. Perhaps in the whole range of their cookery— which is sufficiently ample—no dish is done without hog's lard : from the *sopa* to the *frixoles* all have a large proportion of it in their composition ; even their bread, to eat with the indispensable *Chocolate*, has its proportion of lard; and although they delight in seeing every dish swimming in this their favourite fat, yet butter in any dish, or used in any way as sauce, is abhorred as much by a Spanish American, as by an Englishman is the train oil of a Russian boor.

The following may be taken as about the average price of cattle in Upper California at the present time :—

Fat Ox..... 5 dollars..	£1	Mare...... 5 dollars..	£1
Cow........ 5 dollars..	1	Sheep ..... 2 dollars..	0 8s
Horse (sadle) 10 dollars..	2	Mule......10 dollars..	2

CHAP. VII.

Commerce of Upper California.—Navigation,—Revenues.

In the time of the Spanish government, California had no foreign commerce; and as its almost insular situation cut it off from any frequent intercourse with Mexico by land, it was considered more in the light of a colony of that country than as an integral part: there was little or no commerce or communication carried on between them except by the transmission from San Blas of the annual supplies to the missions. The greatest impulse which the intercourse between Mexico and California ever had, was about the years 1792 and 1793 when a Spanish squadron was stationed at San Blas for the purpose of settling the dispute with England about Nootka Sound. This squadron on their passage between San Blas and Nootka, called at Monterey and other places in Upper California to take in provisions, wood and water; but on the retiring of the squadron the intercourse reverted to its former state, and continued so till the breaking out of the revolution in 1821. Soon after this event, the foreign merchants established in Chili and Peru, as well as those in Mexico, directed their attention to California as a place where some commerce might be carried on, particularly in hides and tallow. With this view an English mercantile house in Lima formed an establishment at Monterey; and several vessels soon after went for the purpose of trading. The North-American traders, who are always the first to take advantage of new and remote markets, also turned their attention to California, and several vessels of that nation soon resorted there from the ports of South America, as well as from China and the Sandwich Islands. By this means some impulse was given to this trade and which was expected to increase, but as the articles have been chiefly confined to hides and tallow, and the consumption of goods small, it has not risen to much importance.

The amount of the annual exports in the first few years after the opening of the ports to foreign vessels, was estimated to be about thirty thousand hides, and about seven thousand quintals of tallow, with a few small cargoes of wheat which the Russians required for their settlements on the N. West coast of America: this, with trifling quantities of wine, raisins, and olives, carried to San Blas, constituted the whole of the exports. Those exports were paid for in barter, chiefly in coarse manufactured cottons, together with a few other articles of small value necessary to a community who had but few artizans, but whose wants were very limited. Taking the the value of the hides at two dollars each, and the tallow at eight dollars per quintal, and reckoning the value of the wheat and other articles at fourteen thousand dollars, the whole amount of exports would have been one hundred and thirty thousand dollars, or about twenty-six thousand pounds sterling.   Since this period, however, the trade has increased considerably, particu-larly in the last year 1834, owing, it is said, to the missionary friars, in anticipation of being displaced, having slaughtered a very large number of cattle— some say to the amount of one hundred thousand. Even if this be true, the number of black cattle stated in the table for 1831 need not be lessened : it is said that the missionaries who published those tables always gave an account of fewer cattle than they actually possessed, so that I presume the amount stated in the table is not more than what actually exists at the present time, but is more likely to be under the real number.

There has been considerable intercourse of late between California and the Sandwich Islands, to which live cattle have been carried. This trade, which is almost entirely in the hands of the Ameri-cans, is not yet of much importance, but will increase as the two countries proceed in civilization. There has also been lately some demand for wheat and provisions for the establishment of the English Hudson's Bay company on the river Columbia.

The trade in furs, particularly that of the sea otter, formerly so considerable and once so promising, has dwindled into insignificance. This is so much the case that otter-skins are now occasionally imported from the Russian settlements to the north, and at an extravagant price, although the animal, as we have seen, is so abundant in their own waters. When Pérouse visited California in 1786, he found at Monterey a Spanish commissary appointed by government to collect all the skins of the other missions, as a perquisite of the government: they amounted then to 20,000 and might have been increased to 30,000. Perouse himself says in his official letter to the Minister of Marine, that 50,000 could easily be procured annually. When it is considered how great the demand for this article is in China, and that this demand is not always satisfied but at an extravagant price, the great potential if not the actual value of this article of commerce to California, will be admitted.

The imports are such as will be easily understood from the account which we have given of the inhabitants and of their habits and wants : they consist of cloth, wearing apparel, articles of furniture, agricultural implements, deals, salt, silks, candles, fire-works, &c.

The internal commerce of California is of very little consequence.   There are, as we have seen, no large towns, and the inhabitants of the country have not advanced to a state which requires the division of labour which is the basis of internal commerce.   Where all are cultivators of the soil, and at the same time artificers and manufacturers, each for his own necessities, there can be few interchanges.   Before the revolution, a circulating medium—that great engine of commerce—was scarcely known, and little esteemed; for when nothing was to be bought, money was of no value; and when the strangers arrived first on the coast they found no coin, barter being the only thing understood; this however was advantageous for the first adventurers, who sold their goods at the exorbitant prices which were established by the Spanish merchants for articles which had formerly to be conducted from Vera Cruz or Panama, passing through many hands before they got to California, and surcharged with duties and old fashioned profits without number; yet goods at those enormous prices were more acceptable to the missionaries than money, they having their numerous Indians to cloathe and a superabundance of cattle to slaughter. This state of things, however, has now consider-

ably altered;—the success of the first adventurers drew others after them, and the missionaries
having been well supplied with goods, and finding
the avidity with which the traders demanded their
hides and tallow, began to know better the relative
value of the articles dealt in, and more equitable
prices were fixed.   There is yet very little currency
in California; and as the small population and little
industry of the inhabitants do not give room for
much consumption, the advancement of commerce
has not been rapid, and it is but yet of very little
consideration.

The whole coast of the Pacific ocean, from Bal-
divia in latitude 40° South to the extremity of
California in 42 degrees North, was in the exclusive
possession of the Spanish nation for three centu-
ries; this line of coast bounded countries the most
fertile in every production the earth affords; the
abundance of the precious metals was infinitely
superior to that contained in all the world besides;
in this immense space is to be found all the varieties
of climate, and consequently all the exchangeable
commodities which stimulate commerce: all this
gave an inexhaustible field for traffic, which ought
to have exalted that part of the world above all
others in the scale of commercial opulence.   The
British possessions either in the East or West Indies, cannot be compared in extent or variety of

productions to the immense continuous territories of the Spaniards in America; nor can the navigation of the seas which surround or border on the British Colonies—which have their hurricanes, their shoals and currents—be compared to the mild Pacific coast of America, which is entirely free of all sort of dangers: no hurricane, shoal, nor dangerous current is to be found in all the extensive coast from the southern to the northern boundary of the Spanish possessions on the Pacific; no line of coast is so perfectly safe to navigate; it is literally without danger of any description whatever, and more resembles a lake-navigation than that of an immense ocean.

The Pacific coast of Spanish America is, in uninterrupted extent, equal to the whole coast of the old world from the Naze of Norway to the Cape de Verd in Africa. What reflections must this give rise to when we consider, that this line of coast comprehends Denmark, Germany, Holland, the Netherlands, Great Britain, France, Portugal, Spain, Italy, the countries round the Mediterranean and part of Africa? And, certainly, the American shores are bounded by countries naturally more rich than all those ancient and powerful countries united. The whole of this American coast was inhabited before its discovery by the Spaniards, and many parts of it possessed by a people far advanced in civilization; yet this immense coast, possessing all the natural productions on the terrestrial globe, and enjoying every conceivable advantage for trade, had over its whole extent—after being three hundred years in the possession of Spain—not more than about thirty vessels exclusive of launches !

Had this coast and the adjacent countries fallen to the lot of England, or any other commercial and enterprising nation, what would have been their state at this day? Would they not have rivalled Asia? Would they not have been even superior in riches and commerce to that celebrated continent? The American countries so situated are in fact naturally richer than India, and offer more objects of commerce if they were well peopled by an enterprising race: the productions of the soil are more varied, owing to the greater variation of climate; their mineral riches are beyond comparison greater ; and the useful domestic animals abound in much greater perfection, and in greater numbers ; while the whole of the valuable tropical fruits of Asia either are produced there or might be so, if cultivated. All those immense advantages, however, had not the power to rouse the dormant energies of the Spaniard. It appeared as if those extraordinary bounties of nature had the effect of lulling them into apathy; but whatever the cause might have been, certain it is, that until the time that those magnificent countries were wrested from the

Spanish nation by her own sons, the whole, or almost the whole of so many sources of commercial wealth, were entirely neglected. The coasts were without commerce or navigation; a death-like tranquillity reigned in all the provinces, the inhabitants of one being scarcely known to the other. Indeed it may be questioned if the people of Mexico at that time know much more of Chili or Buenos Ayres, than the inhabitants of Labrador know of Patagonia at the present day.

The Spanish system of exclusion and restrictions on all foreign trade with their possessions in America, is well known, but it is remarkable that the duties and restrictions on their own coasting trade were also most oppressive. The reason for this is quite incomprehensible, as it bore only on the subjects of Spain and could hardly be supposed to promote their leading principle, viz. to favour the trade of the mother country. The produce of one district could not be imported into another without paying a heavy duty under the name of Alcavala, neither could it be removed from one place of sale to another in the same district, without paying over again the same Alcavala; so that every time goods were moved from one town to another an additional duty was to be paid, and this duty has been justly styled the *never-ending Alcavala*. The multiplicity of laws and regulations by which Spain fettered every sort of commerce in the American colonies, the vexatious and capricious conduct of the military and custom-house officers, so notorious in those countries, also tended greatly to discourage coasting navigation; and so little practised, and so ignorant of their profession were the navigators on the Pacific coast, that it was considered a greater adventure for a coasting vessel to go from one province to another, than it would be by others to make a voyage round the world.   There were in Lima two or three large vessels for the purpose of bringing wheat from Chili.   Those vessels belonged to the bakers and made one voyage during the year: they had their stated seasons at which they sailed, and their departure was fixed to a day; they had also their fixed tract from which they never deviated. The voyage from Lima to Valparaiso is only about four hundred leagues, but took usually about three months to perform it in.   A story is told of one of these vessels having got to Chili in fifty days, and the captain was put into the inquisition on the suspicion of his having had to do with the devil. The voyage back to Lima being by a favourable wind was performed in much less time.   This voyage is now performed outwards in about twenty days, and back in about ten.   The same practice was observed in the navigation of the other parts of the coast; that from San Blas to Monterey in California required from two to three months, but is now performed in about twenty days. In all the coasting trade of America, as well as in the foreign voyages of the Spaniards, a fixed tract was laid down and never on any account deviated from. The orders of the government often pointed out the day of sailing at certain seasons of the year, and the route pursued; and a law was in force regulating the day on which vessels and fleets should depart from the different ports of America to Spain, Manilla, &c. which neither the captain, agents nor owner durst disobey. When a Spanish merchant vessel arrived in any of the American ports, the captain was obliged immediately to wait on the commandant and to deliver up to him the ship's papers: from that moment the vessel and captain were entirely under the orders of the commandant. Under the Spanish law all merchant seamen and officers are subject to the marine law; they are liable to be tried for all offences, and have the privilege to be sued for civil debt only, before the marine military tribunal; so that the captain and crews of merchant ships were always under martial law, and subject to the immediate orders of the naval officers commanding at the ports where they might arrive. All merchant vessels before their sailing had also to be examined by the orders of the commandant, and must be pronounced by him as fit for performing their voyage in respect to the sufficiency of the hull, tackle, provisions, officers, and men; and receive a certificate to this effect. This, as may be supposed, led to the most scandalous abuses; and in the state of corruption at which Spanish agents had arrived in the Americas, this certificate was not often to be obtained without fees and bribes proportionate to the ability of the giver, or the rapacity of the receiver: no redress was left to the unhappy captain or supercargo of a vessel who fell into the hands of a rapacious commandant, or one whom he might have offended; for a Spanish Employé never failed to fortify himself with such an overwhelming multitude of legal documents, signed and countersigned by judges and notaries, and approved by all the cautious checks which the Spanish government in its wisdom had invented to prevent fraud in their American officers! The civil institutions of the Spaniards were, in this respect, much in the style of their religious discipline. If an officer took care to make out the whole of the complicated written documents required by the regulations, if he had the number of prescribed signatures, the approbation and attestation of the various officers appointed to check and countercheck his accounts, he might rob and oppress as much as he pleased; all his documents being correct no charge could be made against him; just as a good Spanish catholic may commit all the sins in the decalogue, yet if he conform to the ceremonies prescribed by the church, he is a good catholic still, and the inquisition itself could not meddle with him.

It would be curious to collect some of the voyages performed by the Spaniards, not only on the American coasts, but from Manilla and other parts of Asia, as well as from Europe; and to compare them with the improved navigation of the present day. I shall only here give a brief account of one of the voyages, from Manilla to America, as related to me by an officer of the vessel which performed it.

The ship Philipina, of seven hundred tons burden, in the service of the Spanish Philipine company, commanded by Don Juan Yvergoytie a captain in the Spanish royal navy, officered by lieutenants and midshipmen also of the navy, and manned with a crew of a hundred and forty men, sailed from Manilla in 1799, with a cargo of bale goods, bound to Lima. On leaving Manilla it was the captain's intention to keep to the southward by a track which had been recommended to him, and which was sanctioned by the royal authorities; but in attempting this new route they encountered nothing but contrary winds, and were obliged after being some time at sea, to put first into the island of Mindonao, and afterwards into the Pellew Islands, in order to procure a fresh stock of water and to recover their crew, many of whom were already affected with scurvy.   The captain then gave up his plan of pursuing this route, and proceeded by the usual course to the northward.   After a long passage they made the coast of California and put into Monterey, where they laid in a fresh stock of water and provisions and refreshed their crew; they then left that port and proceeded to San Blas. The whole time occupied in the voyage from Manilla to San Blas was eleven months; but as a great proportion of the voyage to Lima was still to be performed, and as there were rumours of English vessels being in the Pacific, the captain petitioned the viceroy of Mexico to be allowed to discharge his cargo at San Blas, which was granted, and a termination put to this eventful voyage.   At the present time a voyage from Manilla to San Blas is performed in about seventy days, and from Manilla to Lima in three months.   If the good ship Philipina had proceeded to Lima her ultimate destination, her voyage could not have been shorter than fourteen or fifteen months.   This vessel remained a year at San Blas, where her expenses amounted to 72,000 Spanish dollars, and then returned to Manilla.

A friend of mine has often told me that he was the first who owned a square rigged Mexican vessel on the Pacific.   He arrived at San Blas in 1802, in in a vessel belonging to the Philipine company, and having obtained liberty to remain in the country, set about constructing a vessel at that port, for the purpose of trading on the coast.   After an infinity of difficulties he succeeded in launching and rigging his vessel, which he called the Guadalupe in honour of the Patron Saint of Mexico.   This vessel was of the burden of 26 tons and brig-rigged.   The owner was not a little proud of his enterprise and of his vessel, with which he proceeded to trade in the gulf of California.   He had also the honour to be the first who entered the port of Guaymas with a sailing vessel, although it is now so much frequented by vessels of all descriptions.   On approaching this fine harbour he had his doubts if there was suffi- cient water to admit the Guadalupe, for she drew no less than four feet and a half; but by keeping the lead constantly going, and approaching under easy sail he anchored in safety, and found that a 74 gun ship might have done so along side of him. This vessel being the first of that class which was ever seen on that part of the coast, created great curiosity and wonder; and on the report of her arrival reaching the interior, the country people flocked to see her, the most respectable families coming from a great distance to Guaymas for that purpose.

Although what has been said may in some measure account for the backwardness and want of enterprise which was so remarkable in all the Spanish colonies of America, yet another great cause sprung from the immense field which every one found unoccupied in his immediate neighbourhood, and which presented at home more objects than his industry or his capital could embrace, and prevented him from embarking in maritime enterprises to distant parts, with which he had few or no commercial relations, and of which he had little geographical knowledge. A Spanish creole of Peru had much more knowledge of the land of Canaan or Palestine, than of Mexico or California.

The separation however of the colonies from the mother country, and consequently from the Spanish monopoly, opened a wide field to all sort of enterprise; but the native inhabitants were without knowledge or means to profit by the circumstance, in as far as regarded the navigation and commercial facilities of these coasts. The want was at first almost entirely supplied by strangers who resorted to these countries on the opening of the ports, and by them the coasting trade was at first exclusively carried on. The vessels were owned by strangers, and the crews consisted of foreign seamen. This however was soon looked on with jealousy by the new republics, although some of the more enlightened saw that the only way to create a marine was to admit foreign sailors, foreign vessels, and foreign capital, in order to breed up their own people to a seafaring life, and to give time for native artizans and native capital to grow up, so as to enable them to have ships and a coasting trade by degrees. Chili seemed to adopt this principle, as it has done every other liberal one, in a much greater degree than any of the other states; but Mexico, which is the least maritime of all the others and ought to admit foreign seamen with most freedom, has adopted the old-fashioned and exclusive measures, as if it were a first rate maritime nation of the old school; decreeing that all Mexican vessels shall be commanded and officered by Mexicans, and that two thirds of their crews shall be native seamen. This wise decree was made when there was not one Mexican captain, officer, or seaman, on the whole Pacific coast of the Mexican republic! Mexico, in this as well as in all other matters of commercial regulation, has adhered more than any of her sister republics to the old Spanish regimen; and like her maternal prototype has succeeded in putting herself almost out of the list of commercial countries. While the government is continually talking of the country's regeneration and of its determination to adopt a liberal system, and particularly to protect the coasting trade, it is daily issuing some absurd law founded on the jealousy of strangers interfering; by which it manages to put the country almost on the same footing as it was in the time of the Spanish monopoly. If the laws now in existence on paper were rigidly enforced, there would not at this moment be a single coasting vessel on all the Mexican coast of the Pacific. There is not a single vessel at this moment commanded by a Mexican, nor are there any officered or manned by natives; yet decrees are thundered out against abuses and contraband and infractions of laws, as bulls are from the Vatican, and are as much attended to. The miserable and antiquated commercial policy of Mexico has rendered the merchants in her dominions a set of smugglers; her custom-house officers their abettors; and has reduced her trade and the revenues from her custom-houses to a point almost of insignificance.

From what has been said it will not appear strange that the intercourse between California and Mexico has never been very active : it has not improved much since the separation of the countries from Spain. The communication between the two is still very infrequent, and the commercial transactions of no importance whatever. California holds hardly the relation of even a colony to Mexico : Mexico has more intercourse with China than with California. Even at the time I am writing, advices are not received in Mexico from Monterey above once or twice in a year. The last deputy elected by California to the Mexican congress informed me that during the two years he served, he only re- ceived two letters from California, while in Mexico. It remains to be seen whether the new order of things in this country will lead to more enlightened views, and greater commercial enterprize. The new project, also, of a line of communication by steamers along the whole coast of the Pacific, if ever carried into effect, will doubtless modify consi- derably the present state of things; but nothing can permanently benefit California until she pos- sesses inhabitants of more enlightened views, and consents to remodel her internal economy, civil and political.

Although no further connected with the subject of the present chapter, than in having reference to navigation, I cannot help mentioning in this place two circumstances of recent occurrence, which have come to my notice, and which may by some be considered as illustrating the very difficult and long-contested question of the first peopling of America.

The British brig, Forester, bound from London to the river Columbia, and commanded by Mr. John Jennings, fell in with, in the year 1813, a Ja- panese junk of about 700 tons burden, one hundred and fifty miles off the north west coast of America, and abreast of Queen Charlotte's Island, about 49° of N. latitude. There were only three persons alive on board, one of whom was the captain. By the best accounts captain Jennings could get from them, they had been tossing about at sea for nearly eighteen months: they had been twice in sight of of the land of America and driven off. Some beans still remained on which they had been maintaining themselves, and they had caught rain water for their drink. This vessel had left the northern coast of Japan, loaded with timber for some of the islands to the southward, and had been blown off the coast by gales of wind. She had no masts standing, but was in other respects not much injured. Captain Jennings took the survivers on board of his vessel, and delivered them at the Russian settlement of Norfolk Sound; the governor of which, owing to the friendship existing between Russia and the Japanese, sent a vessel on purpose with them to their own country. In the course of ages many such circumstances might happen; and if a vessel in a like situation having some women on board should have been driven on shore on the American coast, the origin of a race would have been the result. And considering the high antiquity of the Japan empire, and the number of ages which navigation has been known to them, it is quite probable that many such contingencies should have happened; particularly when it is considered that in these latitudes the prevailing winds blow from the westward, and consequently directly from the coast of Japan to that of America.

The other circumstance is the recent arrival of a Japanese junk at the Sandwich Islands, and of which I have received the following account. " On the first of January, 1833, a Japanese junk appeared off those islands, and anchored on the west side of Waohoo, when a native of China living on the island went on board and found four men alive, but only one able to walk. The account they gave was, that they had left Japan about eleven months before, with a crew of eight people; that they were driven off the coast; that they had been living on salt fish and rain water; and that the other four men had died of starvation. This vessel was only of about 80 tons burden, and was lost in attempting to get her into a harbour in Waohoo." This is a proof that the islands in the Pacific might have been, at least, peopled from the same quarter; although the arrival of vessels from Japan at these islands must have been more rare than on the north coast of America,—because they are situated more southerly, and not in the tract of the prevailing westerly winds, but on the contrary within the easterly trade winds. The present circumstance, however, removes all doubt of the possibility of such arrivals, and is the more remarkable, as the Sandwich Islands are amongst the most easterly, and consequently most distant from the Asiatic continent, so that the arrival of vessels at the other less remote islands is still more probable.

REVENUE.—From what has been stated, in this and the preceding chapter, of the agriculture and and commere of California, its revenue cannot be supposed to be of much consequence.   It may be said, indeed, that before the revolution it produced no national revenue whatever.   The tithes which belonged to the government were collected from the free settlers, but as the missions were exempted, their value was a mere trifle.   On the opening of the ports in 1821, and for some years after, the collectors of the customs were officers appointed by the different presidios to receive such duties as might be obtained from any vessels arriving in their respective districts; and although a commissioner was sent from Mexico in 1825 little was done by him.   The same practice continued till 1828, when Don José Maria Echandia was named commandant general, who appointed a collector and comptroller of the custom-house to reside at San Diego, and to have subordinate officers at Monterey. Since that time some order has been introduced in the collection of the duties.   About this time it was conceded by the Mexican government, that owing to the poverty of California, and to encourage its settlement, two-fifths of the duties established by the general Mexican Tariff should be deducted on all goods landed in both Californias; but on being re-exported to the other Mexican states these two-fifths should be exacted on the goods so re-exported : this regulation still exists. The Mexican duties are charged by a Tariff which fixes the rates on every different article. This Tariff was promulgated in 1828, and discovers the utter incapacity of its framers for such a task. The whole of the imports are fixed at a most exorbitantly high rate, which causes a duty of not less, in most cases, than from a hundred and fifty to two hundred per cent on the first cost. But ridiculous distinctions are formed in order to protect the imaginary interests of their native manufactures, and fruits of their soil, as well as many prohibitions with the same object. The modern governments of the world are at last discovering their errors and striving to explode the old fashioned and ruinously illiberal system of protecting duties and national preference to manufactures and arts not adapted to their soil or circumstances, and which has contributed so much to the alienation of one people from another ; as if they had distinct interests, and as if they ought to contribute to the discomfort of their neighbours for the purpose of securing some imaginary advantage to themselves.

The Mexicans, however, still see nothing but wisdom and the sources of political prosperity in all the antiquated prohibitions, protections, and exorbitant duties, of the most barbarous age of commerce! This outrageous system, so contrary to sound policy, and so opposite to the modern and enlightened doctrines of political economy, has reduced the revenue from her custom-houses to a trifle, and her treasury to bankruptcy. The old colonial system, however much decried by the new republics, seems so rooted in their natures, that nothing but what savours of its ancient principles seems good policy. The same organization of the custom-houses, the same divisions of duties under different denominations and per-centages which create an interminable set of accounts and documents, the same number of officers,—in short, the same confusion and facilities for contraband, still exist in their revenue department in all the perfection of the olden time. These and their necessary appendages of Alcavalas and custom-houses in every inland town, which rendered the fiscal laws and practices of Spain and her colonies so intolerable, still flourish in all their vigour and place the new republics almost out of the pale of enlightened commercial communities, and at the same time make them so remarkable for their bad financial credit. The whole of the new republics which have arisen out of the old Spanish colonies, have strictly imitated their parent, in putting their finances in a state of bankruptcy; in which under their present systems they are likely to remain.

I should be exceedingly sorry by the foregoing general observations, to inculpate the whole of the statesmen in those new countries now erected into republics; I know that many of them are of the most liberal and enlightened views and capable of governing their country on better principles; and I also know that supposed circumstances of necessity oblige a great proportion of their best informed citizens to yield to the policy which they know to be mischievous, in the hope that in better times wiser measures may be adopted. But it unfortunately has happened, particularly with Mexico, of which country I am now speaking, that its government has been hitherto controuled by persons who have not put in practice not even the rudiments of an enlightened policy in its commercial laws, nor made one step to the reform of its ruined and bankrupt finances. Unfortunately, the great bulk of the people think, that instead of reducing the duties, abating the eternal custom-houses, and simplifying the absurd classifications of duties at the maritime custom-houses, in order to augment their prosperity and better their revenue; they have only to impose higher duties, multiply officers of the customs, pass restrictive measures for the encouragement of native manufactures which do not exist, and to fulminate decrees and issue moral precepts against unfaithful employés, and smuggling citizens, and foreigners. In this manner the Mexican government has gone on through all its changes in the steady course of heaping duties upon duties, multiplying restriction and augmenting offices, till its mercantile system has become a monstrosity not to be paralleled in any corner of the world.

The general Mexican tariff applies equally to California as to the other parts of the republic, except the abatement of two-fifths already mentioned ; but as this is only a temporary measure it is liable to be recalled at any time the government may think fit.   Many of the regulations and prohibitions of this tariff are quite absurd as applied to California, for its productions are entirely different from those of the tropical climates of Mexico for which it is adapted : but nothing has been attempted to modify its provisions so as to fit it to the peculiar circumstances of that country.

The following account of the financial state of Upper California in 1831 may be depended on: it was furnished to me by a friend well acquainted with the subject.

The expense of the presidial companies—according to the late regulationsis estimated at ninety-one thousand dollars per annum, to which must be added the pay of the commandant general, sub-inspector, auxiliary troops of the squadron of Mazatlan, maintenance of the convicts, and other various charges; which altogether may be reckoned at forty thousand dollars, This will make the whole charges borne by the general Mexican government amount to one hundred and thirty-one thousand dollars. The nett amount of the revenue does not exceed thirty-two thousand dollars, thus making a deficiency of about one hundred thousand dollars annually to be borne by the Mexican treasury, over the revenue produced in the territory of Upper California.

This is the state of the revenue of Upper California, to which Mexico would have, if it paid its debts and its soldiers, to remit one hundred thousand dollars annually; but as the Mexican treasury is not in the habit of satisfying very punctually the demands against it, and as it has quite as urgent claims from other quarters of the republic nearer home, California is left to bear the deficiency the best way it can. Instead of money, military officers and placemen are sent, with reams of laws and orders to repair the system, and to apply the current nostrums of the day to heal all maladies

—leaving as heretofore the soldiers in rags and the employés without pay : the result of the whole is, that all parties have to recur to the missions and the friars for their daily maintenance to prevent them from starvation. The debt owing by the government to the missions for such supplies, amounted in 1831 to four hundred and fifty thousand dollars.*

* No alterations have been made in this chapter since it was first written : it must, consequently, be understood to refer to the state of things previously to the late revolution.—ED.

CHAP. VIII.

———————

IT would not be supposed *a priori*, that men would select for their abode either the extreme northern regions, where the fruits of the earth are scarce, and the labour required to produce them great, and where all manner of privations are excessive ; or the burning climes of the tropics, where dangers and discomforts of a very different kind, but equally great, abound : and, yet, however inexplicable it may be, we find human beings who seem to prefer for their habitations the frozen regions of the higher latitudes, and the scorching plains of the torrid zone. We find people clinging to a soil which does not yield them sufficient subsistence, and to a climate which threatens to freeze them to death : we find human beings in Patagonia, who have to support life by eating raw fish taken from the sea, or the flesh of wild animals, whose skins serve to preserve them from perishing of cold. We

also find near the opposite pole beings equally
wretched, and refusing to remove from their native
snows. We find on the other hand, men inhabiting
the most pestiferous situations, under the very line,
in the midst of forests and marshes, whose exhala-
tions communicate to the air they breathe pestilence
and death, and whose whole lives are passed in
defending themselves from noxious animals and
poisonous reptiles. Is it not astonishing that the
frozen and unhabitable shores of Patagonia, Hudson's Bay, the pestiferous marshes of the tropical coast
of America, and the burning sands of Africa, should
be filled with people, whilst such delightful countries as California are so devoid of inhabitants ?
Again, we find in Europe a superabundant and
daily increasing population, the utmost exertions of
a great part of whom, cannot procure them bread.
In Great Britain and Ireland, there are millions of
human beings of superior intellects, and varied ac-
quirements, who find it utterly impossible to get
employment or food ; and yet countries exist, in
which the choicest fruits of nature are left to waste
for want of hands to gather them, and where labour
is hardly necessary to enable every one to live in
plenty. While in Europe lands can only be acquired by the rich and the powerful, in some of the
finest countries of the earth luxuriant soils are lying
waste without proprietors, and without cultivators.

Taking every circumstance into account, perhaps no country whatever can excel or hardly vie with California in natural advantages. Its geographical situation is such as one would point out if he was desired to select the most favoured situation in the world. Its topographical relations are also most favourable : it stretches along the shores of the Pacific ocean, without extending much inland, and thereby enjoys all the manifold advantages of a maritime country.* By its great extension from north to south settlers have also the option of selecting a climate suited to their health or views. Other countries there are, of course, which have the same relative situation on the globe ; but I think it may safely be asserted, that there is no other of the same extent, which possesses so many natural and local advantages. Some countries although they are placed in the same geographical relation, are sandy deserts or inundated marshes; others are uninhabitable mountains, or impervious forests; some are destitute of ports, and rivers ; while others are surrounded or possessed by savages, or bordered by shoals and unapproachable shores. California, on the contrary, enjoys natural and local advantages equal to its geographical situation. Its soil is of the most fertile description, capable of producing the

* I speak of that part inhabited by the Spaniards, for, taken in its whole extent, California reaches far inland.

choicest fruits and grains in the greatest perfection
and abundance ; its coasts are bold, and free of
danger, washed by the placid Pacific ocean, and
possessed of ports of the first order.   It is also
watered by abundant rivers ; and there is nothing
in the configuration of the surface of the country
to forbid the eternal spring which its situation promises.   There is found a temperature equally removed from extreme heat or cold : and the range
of hills which bound the maritime portion of California to the north-east shelter it from the only winds
which might be apprehended seriously to injure the
fruits of its soil, or to incommode its inhabitants.

The situation of California for intercourse with
other countries and its capacity for commerce—
should it ever be possessed by a numerous and industrious population—is most favourable.   Its western shores on the Pacific, as has been already
shown, possess capacious ports.   The port of San
Francisco for size and safety is hardly surpassed by
any in the world ; it is so situated as to be made
the centre of the commercial relations which may
take place between Asia and the western coasts of
America.   The route by which the voyage from
India, China, Manilla, and other Asiatic countries
is performed to the American coast, particularly
to that of Mexico, Guatemala, &c., obliges vessels
to pass very near the coast of California ; because

in order to avoid the easterly trade winds, it is necessary to stand to the northward to get into the
variable and prevailing westerly winds, just as
vessels must do when bound from the West Indies
to Europe. The vessels of the Spanish Philipine
company on their passage from Manilla to San Blas
and Acapulo generally called at Monterey for re-
freshments and orders. Thus it appears as if California was designed by nature to be the medium of
connecting, commercially, Asia with America, and
as the depôt of the trade between those two vast
continents, which possess the elements of unbounded
commercial interchange; the one overflowing with
all the rich and luxurious commodities, always characteristic of the east, the other possessing a superabundance of the precious metals and other valuable
productions to give in exchange.

California is also admirably calculated for carrying on a trade with all the new republics bordering
on the Pacific; and as its productions are of a different description from those of the countries chiefly
situated within the tropics, it is capable of furnishing
them with articles of indispensible necessity, which
hitherto they have been obliged to procure from
Europe, at an enormous expence, and often, from
the length of the voyage, rendered useless by the
damaged state in which they arrived. California
could furnish abundantly all those countries with

flour, potatoes, salted provisions, hides, tallow, butter, cheese, wine, brandy, oil, olives, raisins, apples, and other fruits; as also with hemp or cordage, flax, wood, pitch, tar, &c. all of which would arrive by a short voyage, and in perfect condition, and be furnished at reasonable prices.

Another commercial field offers to be gradually opened in the numerous islands scattered over the Pacific ocean, with some of which, particularly with the Sandwich Islands, considerable dealings are already carried on by foreign vessels and also by those under the Sandwich Island flag. These carry live stock to those islands, which have benefitted amazingly by the introduction of black cattle and horses, of which they now possess large numbers.

The foregoing is a brief view of what commercial consequence California might soon arrive at, if peopled by an active and enterprizing race of men; but under the present system, and while the population retain their present character of indolence and total want of enterprize, it must stand still.   If, on the contrary, this country was under an enlightened and liberal government, which knew how to promote its colonization, and to encourage the resort of industrious settlers from whatever quarter they might come, it could not fail to become known and selected as a refuge by the innumerable starving population of the old world; and would soon be one of the most interesting and prosperous spots on the earth. It is true that its distance from Europe is great, but it is not much greater than that to New Holland or Van Dieman's Land, which so many emigrants now reach at a moderate expence.

The great number of vessels proceeding to fish for whales in the Pacific might, also, perhaps, be made the means of conveying emigrants to California, so as to be advantageous both to the owners of the vessels and the passengers. This fishery has, of late years, been most successful on the coast of Japan; and to vessels passing to that coast round Cape Horn, California would not be much out of the way. They would there be able to refresh their crews, and lay in a fresh stock of provisions and water for their ultimate destination. These vessels carry out empty casks for the purpose of holding their oil: these would serve for carrying water for the passengers, so that except in the article of provisions, scarcely any additional expense would be incurred.

Should the projects now much talked of, of forming a railroad across the Isthmus of Panama, and of establishing a line of steamers along the western coast of South America, be ever carried into effect, the means of transport of individuals to California, would be extremely easy, and in less than half the time required for a voyage to Austra-

lia.   The probability of the commercial advantages
of such projects forms quite a separate subject of
inquiry.

The opening of a passage from the Atlantic to the
Pacific, across the Isthmus of Panama, or at some
more favourable point in that neighbourhood by
means of a canal, has long occupied the attention
of the nautical and scientific world ; and if this enterprize should ever be carried into effect, a voyage
from Europe to California would be comparatively
short, and emigrants could be carried there with
little more expence than to Canada.   If ever this
route shall be opened, California will then be one
of the most interesting commercial situations in the
world ; it would in that case be the point of rendez-
vous for all vessels engaged in the trade between
Europe and Asia by that route : it is nearly midvoy-
age between those two countries, and would furnish
provisions and all naval supplies in the most ample
abundance; and most probably would become a mart
for the intercharge of the commodities of the three
continents.   No other station in the course of this
route would be in any way equal to California. The
parts of America through which the supposed canal
must pass, must be low and in a tropical climate,
consequently unhealthy ; they are also unproductive
of provisions and naval stores ; whereas California
presents a healthy climate, good harbours, provisions,
and naval stores of all descriptions.

The opening of this passage may perhaps be considered as a remote contingency : but when we reflect on what has been achieved within the last fifty years ; what has been the progress of the world in that time ; and look at what is in progress ; is it too much to indulge in a hope that this enterprize so manifestly useful, and on all hands allowed to be practicable, may at no very distant period be accomplished ? If California and the country through which the proposed canal has to pass, had appertained to England for three hundred years, as they have done to Spain, would not at this day such a canal have been the thoroughfare for the trade to Asia ? Nay, would not the people of England have opened this communication for the sole purpose of settling such a country as California, if no other object had been taken into account ?

I shall here presume to give my opinion, that all attempts to make a passage between the two oceans will be abortive, unless the territory through which the canal passes shall be ceded in sovereignty to some powerful European state, or put under the guaranty of a convention of European states ; because the new republics into which the late Spanish colonies have been divided, have not the stability, nor have they adopted that liberal policy, which is necessary to ensure a free transit, indispensible for the good success of such an undertaking. The security of those who had to expend such large sums of money, and the protection of the extensive commerce which would have to pass through such territory, are alike indispensible. Another consideration in my opinion is also indispensible to the success and utility of this undertaking, viz. that the canal should be made of a capacity sufficient to admit merchant vessels to pass through without discharging their cargoes. To make a canal for boats, or on any other scale than to permit vessels to pass on to the ulterior destination of the goods, would be entirely nugatory; the expence and delay of transporting the cargoes by boats in such a country as that through which the canal passes, would be very great, and the loss by periodical rains, robbery by an ill-regulated population, and a thousand causes, would counterbalance all other advantages; but the principal difficulty and expence would be to procure vessels in the Pacific, to prosecute the remaining part of the voyage. On this ocean, at present, the freights paid for vessels are most exorbitant, and from the nature of the coasts in the neighbourhood of the canal, which are all unhealthy, and unfit for the creation or maintenance of a marine, no improvement of consequence is to be expected. It would result in the case supposed of a mere boat canal, that after a cargo had been forwarded to the eastern entrance of the canal, and transmitted to the Pacific by boats, the time that might elapse before a vessel could be procured to proceed with this cargo to China or other destination, would be more and the expence greater, than if the original vessel had proceeded directly round the Cape of Good Hope.   It has been lately much recommended to make a railroad from Portobello to Panama, or somewhere in that vicinity; but the foregoing objections exist to this in all their force, as to a canal for boats, and I should consider such an undertaking utterly useless, in a commercial point of view.   If, on the contrary, the canal was made capable of admitting vessels to pass through with their cargos, the delay would be very small, and the expence trifling; Asia would be thereby brought by one-half nearer to Europe, and the passage to all the west coast of America and the Pacific islands shortened in a still greater degree.   This revolution in the commerce with Asia and the Pacific ocean, if it were to happen, would aggrandize the country of which we have been treating in an extraordinary manner : and however distant this era may be, it is not to be supposed that in the present state of the world, when such rapid progress is making in every thing that is useful, this gigantic improvement will be indefinitely delayed; and particularly when it would appear, that the means are but trifling in comparison to the end

proposed.   When we look at what has already been
done in North America, England, Holland, France
and other countries, the undertaking alluded to does
not appear to be formidable.   Perhaps the Caledo-
nian canal which passes through Scotland, and
unites the North Sea with the Atlantic, is not a
much inferior undertaking to the one proposed ; and
the plan on which it has been constructed, ought
to be adopted.   This canal is capable of admitting
the largest loaded merchant vessels to pass through
it without discharging ; and one of the same capacity between the Atlantic and Pacific, would effect
all the vast advantages which I have mentioned—
and indeed many more.

In the present unsettled and uncertain state of
Upper California, in its internal and external political relations, and more particularly in the state of
anarchy which has resulted from the changes that
have taken place since the preceding chapters of
the present work were written, it would be absurd
to recommend it as a field for emigration at this
moment.   As, however, this state of things cannot
be expected to be permanent ; and as it is to be
hoped that whether the country re-unites itself with
Mexico or achieves permanent independence, more
liberal and enlightened principles of government
and state polity will prevail ; there appears much
probability that the views that have heretofore been

entertained respecting the colonization of the country by foreigners, will be greatly modified, and that encouragement will be given to the only proceeding calculated to effect the permanent prosperity of the country. Should such be the case, I know of no place, as I have already stated, better calculated for receiving and cherishing the superfluous population of Great Britain. Hitherto nothing could have been less encouraging to the settlement of strangers than the proceedings of the sucessive governments of republican Mexico. For although the different parties who have ruled the country have, in many public acts, held forth their great desire to encourage emigration to all parts of the country, all their laws, devised with this object, have been dictated too much in the old Spanish spirit to be really practically useful. By the multiplication of regulations and restrictions they contrived to envelope their meaning and provisions in such uncertainty that they could scarcely be understood, while most of them embraced some antiquated prohibitive principle which rendered the whole nugatory. In all of the acts relating to emigration, for instance, there have been such absurd clauses as that the emigrant must profess the catholic religion, that he shall have a certain capital, a trade or profession, that he shall appear before the authority, shall have a regular passport, &c.

As yet few strangers have established themselves

in Upper California. Such as have done so, have
proceeded thither, as it were casually, in vessels trading to the coast, and are, consequently, chiefly seafaring men ; but several mechanics and others have also
established themselves, and all have been received
with the utmost kindness by the natives, and the
greater part of them have intermarried with them.
The native inhabitants are indeed remarkable for
their peaceable inoffensive character ; and on their
part no opposition is to be apprehended. It might be
presumed that the chief opposition to the admission
of strangers was to be expected from the missionaries : it would be supposed that from their education, and from the fear of losing the influence they
possess, none could view the entrance of strangers
with so much jealousy as they ; but it is a curious
fact, that from the first establishment of these
missions to the present day, as well in the time of
the Spanish government as under the republican
system, the reception of strangers has always been
much more cordial by the missionaries than by the
government officers ! The different navigators who
have touched on the coast of California since its first
settlement, have unanimously borne testimony to
this fact ; and since the country has been opened
to strangers indiscriminately, the hospitably and
kindness of the missionaries have been the praise of
every one who has been there. Foreign mechanics

have been employed at almost all the missions, and the most cordial reception experienced by all of them. As, however, the greatest part of the lands to the southward of Monterey, and along the coast, are in the hands of the Missions, it is not to be expected that they could view with satisfaction any large number of emigrants landing in their territories, and which might require the cession of land, or interfere to disturb their peculiar system.

But, indeed, whenever circumstances permit foreign emigrants to establish themselves in Upper California, they ought to settle to the northward and eastward of the bay of San Francisco, and on the lands around that bay, and on the banks of the river Sacramento, and other streams which fall into it. These are the best lands, and in the best climate for settlers from the north of Europe. They are peculiarly favourable for the raising of wheat and other grain, and for the rearing of cattle. The immense tracts of fertile land not incumbered by forests, the facility of water intercourse by the country being intersected by the creeks on the Bay of San Francisco, and the various branches of the rivers which fall into it, render this situation highly advantageous; and its northerly situation, and the general distribution of the rains throughout the year, make it fitter for agricultural pursuits than the more southerly districts. It has also the ad-

Y 2

vantage of being but little inhabited, and is unconnected with the possessions of the missionaries.

It ought also to be a fundamental principle in any plan of emigration to this country, that a sufficient number should go together, in order that they might form at first a society by themselves. Their lands should be selected as distinct from those of the missions and the present free towns as possible, so that no dispute as to territory or on any other account could ensue: for this reason, the lands on the bay of San Francisco, as before recommended, are the most proper. In the course of time the emigrants and the native settlers would become acquainted and approximate; their union would be the consequence, and this would tend to promote their mutual happiness and prosperity. But all this pre-supposes great reform to be made in the character of the Mexican goverment and its agents; for it must be admitted that, at present, British emigrants would not find themselves much at ease under the controul of the local authorities in any district of the republic. Nothing can be more different from the non-interference with private eniterprize, and private conduct, which characterises the British policy, than the meddling and vexatious nterference of the military and civil authorities, which mixes in all the business of life in the present Spanish American countries, and which is thought necessary to enforce the infinity of laws and regulations enacted for the guidance of the citizens in their most minute affairs. This is a never failing source of annoyance and disgust, and gives perpetual opportunities for injustice and oppression. The prisons in all parts of the republic are more full than they ever were in the time of the Spaniards, and the most slight pretext is quite sufficient to justify an alcade or a military officer in sending any one to prison, and keeping him there during his will and pleasure.

APPENDIX.

I.

REMARKS ON THE HARBOURS OF CALIFORNIA, WITH DIRECTIONS FOR NAVIGATING THEM. BY CAPT. JOHN HALL. (EXTRACT OF A LETTER TO THE EDITOR.)

* * * * * The following particulars are extracted from my journal of a voyage made to the coasts of California, in the year 1822. I give them literally as set down in my log-book at the time.

LA BODEGA.—On the 8th of June we entered the port of this the most southern settlement of the Russians on the west coast of California. It lies in lat. 38° 19′ North, and is only about 58 miles N.W. of San Francisco—the most northern of the Spanish missions on that coast. On the following day we were visited by the Russian Governor, who came from the town, which is situated about 30 miles north, on the coast. He brought with him two fine fat sheep, a large tub of butter and some milk, which were very acceptable after a long voyage, and gave us proof, at once, of his hospitality and of the abundance and cheapness of provisions. The price of a bullock at this time was only twelve dollars, and of a fine sheep two dollars. Vegetables were also plentiful in their proper season.

To sail into this port, when the winds are from the N.W. (and these are the prevailing winds throughout nearly the

whole year, with the exception of the winter months), a
vessel coming from the Northward should pass between
the point and the rock; as a dangerous shoal lies immediately off the south end of the rock. We anchored with
the rock bearing W. by S. distant three-quarters of a mile.
The bottom is good holding ground all throughout, being
a mixture of clay and sand. In port, a vessel is sheltered
from all winds but the South and S.W. The watering
place is situated in the small bay where the Russian storehouse stands, and the water is good and easy of access.

On the 14th of June we sailed from La Bodega, proceeding southward for the adjoining Mexican port of San
Francisco, which we entered on the 17th, having been
detained on account of the thick foggy weather and light
winds which caused us to anchor frequently.

San Francisco.—In entering this port, which is one of
the best and most interesting, from its security and magnitude, in the world, great attention must be paid to the
tides, which, during the full and change of the moon, run
very rapid, and, I should think, in mid-channel, at the rate
of six miles per hour. A vessel going in, would do well to
keep in the middle of the stream, as on both sides there
are very strong eddies in which you are apt to lose the
command of the helm, and consequently are obliged to
anchor. After getting within the heads, keep *Fort Blanco*
about a point on the starboard bow. Passing the fort, the
anchorage is situated in a small bay, immediately abreast
of the *Presidio*, where a vessel will find good holding
ground in five fathoms, about a cable's length from the beach.
Provisions are cheap; a bullock costs only six dollars, and
eggs are two dollars per hundred: the harbour also abounds

with fish, which can be procured with a net in great quantities.

MONTEREY.—On the 20th, we weighed for Monterey, where we came-to on the 24th, saluting the fort with five guns, which were returned by the same number. As a harbour, Monterey is extremely inferior to San Francisco; however, it is quite protected from the South and S.W. winds; and by anchoring well under the point, a vessel may also be protected from the N.W., although the N.W. winds send in a very heavy swell. Fish here also is plentiful, as are likewise provisions generally, including *good bread*.

On the 27th of the same month, we took our departure for Santa Barbara, where we came to an anchor on the 29th.

SANTA BARBARA.—This bay is only sheltered from the N.W. winds, being exposed to the South and S.W. The anchorage is not very good, being hard sand, and overgrown with sea-weed. We had such a quantity of this on our anchor, when we hove it up, that it entirely impeded the ship's progress until we got it clear. We found no tide nor currents; but there appeared to be a rise and fall, in-shore, of about two feet. All kinds of provisions are cheap here, as also fruits, viz. grapes, pears, apples and plums, in their season.

SAN PEDRO.—We sailed from Santa Barbara on the 6th of July, and anchored in the bay of San Pedro, on the 8th, in the evening. We found the anchorage good, and a safe landing place, about three-quarters of a mile South of the small Rock or Island, marked in the chart. The mission of San Gabriel, is about ten leagues distant from the landing place, which latter is called San Pedro. This name can be only applicable to the *anchorage*, as the shore at the time we visited it had no houses erected upon it, nor were there any cultivated grounds adjoining.

SAN JUAN.—On the 13th we sailed for San Juan, where we anchored on the following day (it being distant only about 30 miles) in five fathom water. In coming into this bay, from the North, care must be taken to give the bluff Point a wide berth, as some dangerous rocks lie off it, distant about a mile or more. Here, provisions, fruits, vegetables and fish are plentiful. Good wine can also be procured from the Friars, both white wine and red; the latter being of a peculiarly fine flavour.

SAN DIEGO.—On the 18th we got under weigh again, for the neighbouring port of San Diego, where we arrived on the following day, anchoring in ten fathoms, about a mile wide of the point. We found the tide setting out at the rate of one and a half mile per hour. A vessel should always keep the North shore aboard, as we found the deepest water there. Grapes here are in great abundance and good wine is produced from them.

The ports of *La Bodega, San Francisco, Monterey, Santa Barbara, San Pedro* and *San Diego* are so accurately delineated in the chart, by Mr. Arrowsmith, now before me,* that any further remarks would be superfluous; and it is needless to dilate upon the minor ports both of Upper and Lower California, which, although the seats of *missions,* are yet of little mercantile importance; always, however, excepting the port of San Quintin, lat. 30° 23′ N.

When we arrived on the coast, the country had only a few

* The map attached to this volume.—ED.

weeks before declared itself independent of Spain; we were consequently received on our entrance to every new port in a hostile manner, or with great suspicion, until they satisfied themselves that we were not a Spanish cruizer.

We were surprised to find a *Russian establishment* so far South as La Bodega, but the inhabitants all along the coast considered it as an intrusive settlement within the boundaries of Mexico, and threatened to drive them (the Russians) out whenever they should have sufficient force. By the latest accounts the Russians are still there, and increasing.

In conclusion I would remark that California viewed as a maritime station is unrivalled by any other section of the western coast of America. The ports of San Francisco, San Diego and San Quintin, afford the most secure anchorage for numerous fleets, with facilities for establishing wharfs, docks and arsenals of all descriptions. The climate is one of the best and most healthy I have ever visited, and the country is one of the most fertile. Exclusive of Lower California, this country contains upwards of 430,000 square miles, and, allowing only fifty inhabitants to each, is capable of supporting a population of twenty-one millions of people. From its geographical position it possesses very great advantages on account of the expeditious and easy intercourse which it can maintain with Japan, China, the Phillipine Islands, India, Australia, and all the Islands in the Pacific. In the above computation of space and population that small part of territory occupied by the Russians is included, as I believe, neither by treaty nor by conquest, can they allege any right to its possession.

I am, Sir, your obedient Servant,

JOHN HALL.

Home Cottage, Blackheath, Dec. 15, 1838.

II.

London, Dec. 20, 1838.

I have taken some pains to make myself acquainted with the grounds on which the " Pacific Steam Navigation Company" is founded, with its proceedings as far as they have gone, and its prospects as far as I can comprehend them. Of this you may rest assured that it has already received the patronage of the leading merchants trading to the Pacific, several of them having subscribed, with the expressed object of forwarding an undertaking fraught with so many *public* benefits, while others have entered more largely into it, with the view of participating in the great profit which it promises as an investment. The *general result* given in the 34th page of Mr. Wheelwright's pamphlet, shewing 466,950 dollars as the amount of annual receipts on four steamers, costing from 400,000 to 450,000 dollars, and against the same only 236,630 dollars of annual expenditure, whereby the company will realize an annual profit of 230,320 dollars or (at 48d. exchange) £46,064, is so extraordinarily large that my first impression was to look upon the project, as one hatched by parties connected with our Stock Exchange; but on turning to schedules A. and C., I not only found that the above results were verified by a committee of British merchants residing in Lima, and presided over by Her Majesty's Consul General for Peru, but that a note was added, giving reason to hope for still larger profits, under economical arrangements, in the management of the items of expenditure.

It appears that this plan, speculative though it seems, dates its rise from the circular officially issued by Her Majesty's Consul General for Peru, dated Lima, 18th June, 1826, directed to British merchants and residents generally, requesting their attention to despatches from Her Majesty's Government promising facilities to carry it into effect, and requesting their active co-operation. No undertaking, therefore, could originate under more respectable auspices, and from inquiries I have made I have no hesitation in stating that the gentlemen who have taken it up in London are of the utmost respectability and influenced by the most honourable motives.

The *Author* of "California" has not expressed himself in favor of the extension of this proposed line, from Panama to the Northern Pacific, further than as the reader may construe his remarks in pages 315 to 320. But I feel confident, after viewing the success of steam in the Arabian Gulph and Red Sea, in the Mediterranean, and backwards and forwards to England, at all seasons of the year; and, above all, in so many safe and expeditious voyages across the Atlantic, that the day is not far distant when either the directors of the present Pacific Steam Navigation Company, or some new Company will take up the *Northern line.* The numerous population along the Western coasts of Central America and Mexico, and the rich products of the adjoining provinces in gold, silver, pearls, cochineal, and indigo, ought to afford profitable employment for steamers as far up as the Gulph of California at least; and were emigration ever turning its tide to California, in the way suggested by the author, from page 320 to the end, whether under the direction of Her Majesty's Government, or of a public company, the aid of steam could not fail to be required.

Under the strongest presentiment that these ideas will not lie many years inoperative, I have made calculations of the distances from Panama to the principal northern ports which I here subjoin, as not without importance in the present inquiry. These calculations do not pretend to be exact to a mile, or to an hour, but they are sufficiently so for our purpose; nine miles are allowed per hour.

The distances from Panama to San Diego, Monterey, San Francisco, Bodega and Columbia river are given in two ways; first by the line of coast, *via* Mazatlan, and second from Panama direct.

Table of Distances and Hours Steaming from *Panama* to the following Ports, viz :—

	MILES.	HOURS.
From Panama to the Gulph of Nicoya	435	48
.. .. the Gulph of Papagayo	590	65.30
.. .. Realejo	680	75.30

			MILES.		HOURS.
From Panama to		Sonsonate	847	..	94
..	..	Yztapa	937	..	104
..	..	Socunusco	1095	.	121.30
..	..	Tehuantepec	1210	..	134.30
..	..	Acapulco	1495	..	166
..	..	Navidad	1810	..	201
..	..	San Blas	1962	..	218
..	..	Mazatlan	2091	..	232
..	..	Guaymas	2448	..	272
..	..	Rio Gila, where it joins the Colorado	2793	..	310
..	..	San Diego, { via Mazatlan	3016	..	335
		{ direct from Panama	2760	..	306.30
..	..	Monterey, { via Mazatlan	3376	..	375
		{ direct	3120	..	346.30
..	..	San Francisco, { via Mazatlan	3456	..	384
		{ direct	3200	..	355.30
..	..	Russian settlement { via Mazatlan	3514	..	390.30
		at Port Bodega { direct	3258	..	362
..	..	the British settlement at Colum- { via Mazatlan	4034	..	448
		bia River..... { direct	3570	..	385.30
..	..	Behring's Straits, via Columbia River	5970	..	663
..	..	Woahoo, Sandwich Islands	4620	..	513
..	..	St. Peter and Paul, Kamschatka via Woahoo	7380	..	820
..	..	Jedo, in Japan, via Woahoo	7950	..	883
..	..	Canton, via Woahoo	9540	..	1060

In the above table the distance to Behring's Straits and the ports that follow, is given to satisfy the reader's curiosity, and not with a view to any practical utility, in the way of Steam Navigation, unless greatly improved and cheapened. It is not impossible that chemists may discover some new power, equal to steam, and producible at less expence, or that our engineers may invent some mechanical mode of propulsion for vessels, rendering the Isthmus of Panama the most direct and expeditious route, not only to these ports, but to *Manila* and the whole Eastern Archipelago.

It will be seen from this Table that the British settlement* on the Columbia river might be reached from Panama, by steam, in nineteen days, or say about forty days from England. By the same route, the important port of San Francisco might be reached in sixteen days, from Panama, or thirty-six, from England; and the Russian settlement of La Bodega, in about six hours longer time. What a change, in our communications, when the nearest Russian settlement on the west coast of America, will be brought within thirty-six days and six hours steaming, from our own shores; when even St. Peter and St. Paul, in Kamtchatka, will be will be within fifty days steaming; Jedo, within fifty-seven; Canton, within sixty-four, and Woahoo, in the Sandwich Islands, within forty-two days! Such are the wonderful results, that sooner or later, may be expected from the mere power of steam (improved and cheapened, as it may be, by fresh discoveries) and the resumption of the *old* line of communication between Europe and the Pacific, via, Chagres and Panama.

I here use the word *resumption* deliberately; for, from the era of Columbus (1502) down to 1824, that line was the high road, between Spain and her Colonies, along the West coast, not only for Spanish settlers and merchants, but for whole cargoes of goods, and regiments of soldiers. The famous Vasco Nunes de Balbao, so early as 1513, crossed the isthmus, with troops, from his settlement of Santa Maria del Darien, to the gulf of San Miguel S.E. of Panama; and the

* I call it *British*, believing we have not yet relinquished its *Northern Bank.*

latter, eleven years afterwards, viz. in 1524, had already become a city of sufficient importance, to have a Governor, and
to furnish to Francisco Pizarro, Diego Almagro and Fernando Luque, the men, arms and ships, with which they proceeded to the Conquest of Peru.   Soon afterwards, it became
the seat of a Royal " Audiencia," and, until the suppression
of the Spanish galleons, and the opening of the free trade,
was the grand emporium of all the merchandize from Spain,
destined for the southern coast of New Granada and Peru,
and the northern ports of Guatemala.   During the late war
of Independence, in Peru, several regiments from Spain,
were sent up the Chagres, to Panama, and from thence, by
transports, to Peru; and it was by the same course that
Cruz Mourgeon—the last Vice-king appointed by Spain for
New Granada—passed, with his forces, in 1822.   The history
of the Buccaneers proves that, as early as the days of Queen
Elizabeth, our own Piratical countrymen, and other lawless
inhabitants of the West Indies, were quite familiar with this
route, which they passed and repassed at pleasure ; and until
the trade with the Pacific, by Cape Horn, became open to
our own merchants, they supplied the wants of the Spanish
Colonists, on the Pacific coasts through Jamaica, by the same
channel.   It is therefore clear, that in *resuming* that old
line of communication, without either the aid of Rail Road
or Canal, (though doubtless either of these would greatly
facilitate the transport of passengers and goods) the Pacific
steam navigation company makes no new nor dangerous experiment.   A British merchant, then sailing on board the
vessel whose course is given in the map attached to the present work, so recently as 1824, took on board in Panama
and carried to San Blas, a thousand bales of goods, bought

z

and packed in Jamaica, and which had been conveyed, across the isthmus, by the way indicated. The expenses on each bale placed in Panama were seven dollars three rials, and consisted of the following items, viz.

	Dol.	Rial.
Freight on each bale from Jamaica to Chagres ..	2	0
Agency at Chagres	0 .	4 .
Freight per canoe from Chagres to Cruces	1	5
Duty of Deposit, in Cruces	0	4 .
Agency	0	2
Mule-hire from Cruces to Panama (7 leagues) ..	2	4 .
in all	7	3 .

on each bale of about 150lb. weight. The canoes on the Chagres are large enough to take eighty of these bales at once; have "Toldos" (a kind of awning, made of cane and palm leaves, impervious to the sun and rain), are quite safe, and managed, with great adroitness, by negro watermen remarkable for their size and strength.

It would require some nicety of calculation to enable me to institute an exact comparison, between these charges, and those on the same goods, carried round by Cape Horn; I am inclined to think that on goods outwards, the latter would be the cheapest route; but, on lace, fine linens, silks and jewellery, the additional expence could not be sensibly felt; and where the object is to be *first* in a market; in the time of war, to save risk; and at all times, to save interest of money, the Panama and Chagres route—even as it was in 1824, and is now—must be the preferable one, both as regards the above description of goods outwards, and bullion, specie, cochineal and indigo homewards.

Besides the seven dollars three rials, above mentioned, I may state that, in 1824, the transit duties levied in Panama, were three dollars two rials, on each bale; but by a late decree of the government of New Granada, all the transit duties have been abolished, so that, perhaps, at this moment, the whole charges may not exceed six dollars per bale, from Jamaica to Panama. I lately conversed with an intelligent Havana merchant, D. R. Clarke, Esq., now in London, who has been six voyages with goods from Jamaica (backwards and forwards) to Panama : he never incurred the smallest loss or risk either from the river, the road, the natives or the climate; but to avoid delay, he thinks that a tram railroad,* either from the junction of the Trinidad with the Chagres to Panama, or from Portobello to Panama, would be of great use, easily made, and cheaply supported. Perhaps the former would be preferable on account of the dangerous fevers which prevail in Portobello but not on the Chagres.

The above remarks are made, assuming that Her Majesty's government establishes a line of Steamers through the West Indies as far as to Chagres, and that the Pacific Steam Navigation Company take the passengers and goods up at Panama, in the Pacific, carrying them, thence, on their way South and North without delay ; for, if the reader will refer to the map, he will find that the vessel whose course is there traced (a fast sailing Schooner of the class known under the designation of "Clipper") took thirty-two days in *sailing* from Panama to San Blas, a voyage which by a Steamer, proceeding direct, might be accomplished, in nine days. A dull sailing vessel would have taken perhaps sixty

---

* I mean a road with rails, where the carriages and waggons are dragged by horses and mules, both of which abound and are cheap in the Isthmus.

z 2

days, or more, to perform the same voyage, from the extreme difficulty of sailing out to the westward from Panama Bay, in consequence of calms, alternating with Squalls from all directions, and the struggle she would have to maintain, in proceeding along the coasts of Central America and Mexico, against opposing winds and currents. The same "Clipper" (though to go eleven and eleven and a half knots per hour, was not unusual with her) took twelve days on her voyage from Valparaiso, in sailing from the Equator to Panama. I mention these apparently uninteresting minutiæ, to establish the important fact, that even were such a Canal made as the Author of "California" recommends (page 319), without Steamers ready at Panama (as the Pacific steam navigation company proposes to have them) to carry on, at once, goods and passengers, northwards and southwards, little advantage would be gained, as regards ports to the southward of Payta, or northward of Manzanillo, on the coast of Mexico. The saving of time would not be very great, and the expence, *allowing for tolls on the canal*, would, I fear, not be much less, than by the voyage round Cape Horn.

I do not think that steamers from Panama northwards, would pay the owners farther than San Blas or Mazatlan : were, indeed, the tide of Emigration setting strongly to California or the settlements on the Columbia River, occasional trips *might* be made *so far*, profitably; but as for Wohaoo, Jedo, Canton and other places named in the calculations above given, steamers from Panama to *them*, will never pay, until in the progress of discovery. the expenses of steamers are brought down more nearly to a level with those of sailing vessels. If ever this desirable event be realized, the ideas here thrown out will assume a practical importance; and it will behove Great Britain, as queen of the sea, to maintain by *Steam*, the same naval character which she has earned by canvas. The isthmus of Panama, will then become a point of very great importance.

The Author of California (page 317) hints the possibility that the Isthmus might be ceded to some European state : if it ever should be so ceded, the nation holding it will acquire an immense influence and power over the communications of the world (supposing the above improvements in steam), with a territory well-wooded, well-watered, fertile in the extreme, rich in gold and pearl fisheries, capable of supporting a numerous population, and not, by any means, *generally* unhealthy; while the inhabitants will acquire that wealth and prosperity, which the advantages of their situation secure to them. But even allowing—as is most probable—that New Granada will continue to retain its sovereignty over the Isthmus, there is nothing in the history or character of that republic which can justify our fears that it will not religiously maintain its stipulations in favour of the route across to Panama. Of all the South American Republics, New Granada has shewn the greatest respect to public faith, and the Hurtados, the Arossamenas, the Gomezes, the Quezadas, the Paredeses and other respectable inhabitants of Panama, are too much alive to the continuance and improvement of the *old overland intercourse*, whereby their city has flourished, not to protest against any injurious imposts, or prejudicial interference. I believe that hitherto no passenger, nor merchant travelling across to Panama, can justly complain of any outrage, either to his person or property, from either the local authorities, or from individuals. They are all aware that nothing short of the resumption of the old line of communication between Europe and the Pacific, can restore their former prosperity, and develope the latent resources of their beautiful country; and they are prepared to make every exertion to secure so desirable an object.

Had the line of steamers above suggested been now in operation, it is obvious that the present French blockade of the Atlantic ports of Mexico could have been counteracted, by sending the cargoes of vessels warned off, to Chagres, across to Panama, and thence to the Mexican ports of the Pacific.

In conclusion, I may state that I understand proposals for steam navigation on the Atlantic ports have been submitted to the Mexican government by a firm of great standing in that country and in London, and that a favourable answer is expected by the first packet.

III.

EXTRACTS.

I.

PANAMA AND THE PACIFIC. A MEMORANDUM SENT TO THE FOREIGN OFFICE, ON THE ADVANTAGE OF USING THE ISTHMUS OF PANAMA AS A MORE RAPID MEANS OF COMMUNICATION BETWEEN EUROPE AND THE PORTS OF THE PACIFIC OCEAN. BY THE HON. P. CAMPBELL SCARLETT.

In passing within the last few months down the coast of South America, on the Pacific side, from Valparaiso, through Lima to Payta, in the neighbourhood of Guayaquil, and to Panama, and from thence to the Atlantic Ocean across the Isthmus of Darien, I had occasion to observe the truth of representations frequently made to me, by British merchants in those settlements; how much shorter, and more certain might be the communication of intelligence from those places to England by that route, than by the passage round Cape Horn. That passage in merchant vessels to and from England direct, averages

DAYS.

For Valparaiso 100
.. Lima 110
.. Guayaquil 120

a length of time, which is not only inconvenient for commercial objects, but which in some degree, cuts off the British settler from correspondence with his friends and family, and unnecessarily pro-

longs the period of receiving such intelligence as the British consuls
in those quarters, may find it expedient to convey to the government. Whereas the passage by Panama might, with ease, be effected
in the following periods :

	DAYS.
From Valparaiso	62
.. Lima	51
.. Guayaquil	46

as the following details will show :

	DAYS.
From Valparaiso to Lima	11
.. Lima to Payta or Guayaquil	5
.. Payta to Panama	10
Across the Isthmus	1
Thence to England, touching at one of the Windward Islands	35
Making in the whole	62*

Taking Lima as a central position, by this calculation, it appears
that the difference of time in conveying correspondence from the
western coast of South America to England. may be thus stated :

	DAYS.
From Lima by Cape Horn	110
.. .. Panama	51
Difference of time in favour of the route by the West Indies	59

The passage from Panama to Chagres is perfectly easy, being
only twenty-one miles by land, and the remainder by a river, safe
and navigable for boats and canoes. This was the route by which
the several towns and provinces on the Pacific Ocean made their
communications with Europe, before the separation of the Colonies
from Spain ; but the frequent revolutions which have taken place in
South America, and the consequent poverty and want of enterprise
in the Spanish part of the population, seem to have put a stop to the
regular and periodical communications between these places, which
were formerly established by public authority.

* This is unnecessarily long. The journey, by way of the isthmus has
been accomplished from Lima to Liverpool in 46 days.

This communication might be very easily effected by the addition of a few small fast-sailing vessels of war, or steamers, which should make periodical visits to the towns I have mentioned.

The advantage of a direct communication between Panama and the West Indies, has already been felt and obtained by the practice of the admiral on the West India station, who is accustomed to despatch a sailing vessel of war, at stated periods, to Chagres, in order to bring official and other correspondence, as well as specie, from the Pacific coast of South America.

I am the more induced to make these representations from a conversation I had with Commodore Mason, in which he expressed his concern, that he had not adequate force under his control, to give protection to British commerce on the South American shore of the Pacific, and his confidence in the opinion, which has been much confirmed by my own observation, as well as by the report of others, more competent than myself, that such commerce has a tendency to increase if duly protected ; and that if vessels of war were more frequently enabled to visit the various ports on the coast from Valparaiso to Panama, better security would be afforded to the British merchants against the revolutions, to which the property of all persons resident on those shores is so often exposed, from the feebleness of the governments and the successive changes, which are the consequence of that weakness.

The establishment of steam-boats would render the return of correspondence, against the prevailing southerly winds, of equal rapidity. The trade-winds are not violent in that sea, and men-of-war, in particular, have generally made passages down the coast with great despatch ; however, the introduction of steam navigation in the West Indies, having already shown that merchant sailing vessels are disposed to carry sufficient coal in ballast, for the supply of fuel ; it is equally obvious that the same facilities might be afforded to carry out coal to the Pacific coast, until such time as, from its raised value and the increased demand for it, the inhabitants of those regions may think it worth their while to work the veins of coal, which are well known to exist at various places on the western coast.*

London, Sept. 6, 1835.

---

* South America and Pacific. Lond. 1838. Vol. 11 p. 281.

II.   .

THE establishment of steam navigation along the shores of the
Pacific Ocean, in connexion with the passage of the Isthmus of Panama to the Atlantic, has long excited much interest, and this has
been more strongly manifested as the commerce and intercourse with
those countries have increased.

In consequence of instructions from the British Government, ad-
dressed to the British Consuls General in Chile and Peru, directing
them to inquire into the best means of establising a communication
between Great Britain and the Western Coasts of South America,
by way of the Isthmus, public meetings of the British and Foreign
merchants were convened for this object. At these meetings in
Chile and Peru, the Consuls General presided, and committees were
appointed to examine my plans and statements, which, after the
fullest investigation, were unanimously approved of, and sanctioned
at subsequent general meetings.

The subject of steam navigation in the Pacific, has occupied my
attention for the last four years ; and that I have carefully con-
considered it, the extent and minuteness of my calculations will I
trust prove. The feasibility of the proposed plan, and the authenticity of the facts upon which I have based my expectations of suc-
ess, have been established by the reports of the committees appointed to inquire into them ; and, large as the anticipated profits of
this undertaking may appear to those not intimately acquainted
with the local peculiarities of the Pacific States, I will nevertheless
assume that the correctness of my statements will be generally admitted, supported as they are by the evidence of disinterested parties
whose probity, as well as practical knowledge of the subjcet, is the
best assurance that my data have been fully and fairly examined.

Her Majesty's Government considering the advantages that
must accrue to the trade of this country with the Pacific, and to
commerce in general, by the establishment of a more prompt communication, has deemed the undertaking entitled to its support, and
conferred on the Pacific Steam Navigation Company a Royal

·Charter : and as these advantages will be common to all nations, it is only reasonable to look for the friendly disposition of other Governments.

The Governments of the Pacific States equally impressed with the benefits that must result from the Establishment of a rapid communication along their shores, as tending to increase their commerce and improve the political and moral condition of society, have materially assisted in furthering this object, by granting to the undertaking for a term of years, exclusive and valuable privileges for the navigation of their coasts.

It will be seen by the Prospectus, that Her Majesty's Government has determined on the early establishment of steam-packets to the West Indies, which, with the co-operation of steam navigation in the Pacific, will reduce the communication between Great Britain and the coasts of Peru and Chile, from a period of four months, to one of thirty or forty days.

This accelerated and easy communication must naturally tend to an increased intercourse, and a more extended trade with the west coast of South America. The uncertainty and fluctuations which at present attend all mercantile operations with those now distant markets, will in a great degree be obviated by the means of transmitting frequent and regular advice ; while the returns for shipments will be available three or four months earlier than they are under present circumstances

Specie and bullion are constantly remitted, and that with ease and security by the Isthmus of Panama ; the means of transporting goods are likewise abundant, and the whole have been exempted from transit duty by a late decree of the Congress of New Grenada. The Directors, being satisfied that whatever tends to facilitate the commerce of the west coast must materially benefit the Company, have in contemplation a plan for insuring all property shipped in their vessels, if it be desired ; by which means bills of lading will at once become available and transferable documents. Thus the proposed undertaking is of the greatest importance to the merchant and manufacturer whose commercial operations are directed to the Pacific ; their property will be placed more within their own control, and on a footing of greater security ; while the facilities extended to trade cannot fail to give it a new impulse, to increase its importance and eventually to produce a greater demand for British manufactures.

The local trade, also, would derive great advantages from an accelerated communication between the several ports in the Pacific.
Owing to the present irregularity of advices, vessels are often indefinitely detained at the different ports of the Coast; and from the
same cause no changes in markets can be beneficially and mutually
acted upon.   By steam, a regular interchange of advices would be
established every fifteen days, and many voyages would be performed in forty or fifty hours, which now occupy twenty or twenty-
five days.

There are other interests in South America, of too important a
character to be lost sight of, and which must reap the benefit of any
measure that tends to the development and improvement of the resources of that country.   To the different States, loans to the amount
of millions of British capital have been made, for which no return
has been received ; nor, till an amelioration of their domestic and
international affairs be brought about, can any such be expected.
One great cause of the political instability of the South American
governments, is the absence of prompt communication, by which the
efforts of the executive to suppress rebellion are constantly frustrated.
The difficulties of journeys by land, and the uncertainty of voyages
by sailing-vessels, impede that regular and rapid intercourse which
steam navigation alone can supply,—an intercourse essential to the
well-being and advancement of those countries.   The effect of it
would be, to strengthen the executive authorities, to promote the
industry of the people, and to contribute to an improved state of
public and private credit.

The accompanying letter of Captain Fitz Roy, of Her Majesty's
Navy, corroborates also a very important fact, as regards the accelerated and easy communication which can be effected between the
Pacific coast, Australia, New Zealand, and the various islands in
that ocean.   By traversing the Isthmus of Darien, the long and
turbulent passage round Cape Horn would be avoided, and the
period of four months, now occupied in performing the voyage from
Europe to those distant parts of the world, would be reduced to
about sixty or seventy days.   This is an interesting point as relates
to the civilization of the inhabitants of the numerous islands of the
Pacific, to which the Missionary Societies have, for a considerable
time past, been directing much of their attention.   A tedious and
painful voyage will be exchanged for one of comparative ease; and

the difficulty of access, which now so much obstructs their labours, will be greatly diminished.

While the important and interesting colony of Australia will be so greatly benefitted by the establishment of steam navigation in the Pacific, its influence over the immediate as well as the more remote sections of the British empire must not be overlooked. The island of Jamaica will once more become an entrepôt of supplies for the northern ports of the Pacific, and, to a great extent, be enabled to resume that lucrative trade by which her prosperity was formerly so much promoted.

There is no difficulty in crossing the Isthmus of Panama. The journey from the Pacific to the Atlantic, is easily effected in eighteen hours, while the return occupies two days. By the proposed line of road, from Panama to the junction of the rivers Trinidad and Chagrès, to which point steamers of from four to five hundred tons may navigate without difficulty, the whole journey across could be accomplished in eight or ten hours.

Having in the course of the preceding observations endeavoured to prove the great benefits which must accrue from the establishment of steam navigation on the waters of the Pacific, I have now to show that the means and facilities for carrying it into operation are amply sufficient.

Coal exists in Chile in great abundance, and is obtainable at a very cheap rate; it may also be had from England at a moderate price; while the nature of the trade between the west coast and Australia, would ensure an abundant and cheap supply from that colony in case of need.

The increasing trade of England with the west coast, is the best proof of the security which is there afforded to commerce. If the merchant and manufacturer whose goods are often deposited for lengthened periods in the public custom-houses, and frequently sent to the interior on long credits, enjoy a security which enables them to repeat and gradually to increase their shipments, how much greater security will be afforded to the company, whose vessels will sail under the British flag, be under the protection of a British squadron, and possess the special guarantee of the separate local governments.

The means of repairing vessels are abundant. Guayaquil is an excellent arsenal, and particularly favourable for the repair of steam-vessels; while some of the ports of Chile offer in this respect almost equal advantages.

In conclusion I may be allowed to state, that a broader or more promising field for steam operations than that which the Pacific affords, does not exist in any part of the world. The prevailing south winds, the calms, and the currents of that ocean render navigation by sailing-vessels tedious and uncertain in the extreme; while the nature of the whole country, from Valparaiso to Guayaquil —presenting a succession of mountains and deep ravines, intersected by sandy deserts—offers every imaginable obstacle to land travelling: and yet there are four millions of inhabitants, within the proposed line of intercourse, ready to participate, to a greater or less degree, in the benefits to arise from the proposed undertaking.

Nature thus seems to have intended for steam navigation that great line of coast, the physical difficulties of which oppose an almost insurmountable barrier to any other mode of prompt communication.

WILLIAM WHEELWRIGHT.

London, Oct. 22, 1838.

Letter from Captain Fitz Roy, referred to in the preceeding observations.

31, CHESTER STREET, OCT. 1, 1838.

Dear Sir,—In answer to the questions contained in your letter of the 25th of September, I send the following brief remarks:

With respect to the general project, I have no doubt whatever of its utility, or of the facility with which it may be carried into execution.

The principal advantages which it holds out to the public, are a very important saving of time in communicating with Peru and Chile, together with a regularity of intercourse which cannot fail to cause a vast augmentation of trade, as well as a material improvement in the state of those countries.

Among the facilities offered for its successful accomplishment are, a sufficient supply of fuel, smooth sea, a regular trade wind, and a great number of safe ports extremely easy of access.

So far as I am competent to give an opinion of your statements relative to the intercourse which might be effected between Great Britain and Australia by a western route, I agree fully to what you have stated ; indeed I cannot help expressing my admiration of the patience and candour by which you seem to have been actuated during the four years you have devoted to the preparations for this great undertaking.

In my own mind, there is no doubt whatever of the existence of coal in abundance at various places on the western coasts of South America ; and that its quality is sufficiently good to make it available for steam-vessels.

I have the honour to be,

Dear Sir,

Your obedient Servant,

ROBERT FITZ ROY.

WILLIAM WHEELWRIGHT, ESQ., London.

III.

EXTRACT FROM THE PROSPECTUS OF THE "PACIFIC STEAM NAVIGATION COMPANY," TO BE INCORPORATED BY ROYAL CHARTER. CAPITAL £250,000 IN 5000 SHARES OF £50 EACH. ISSUED NOV. 5TH, 1838.

The object of this company is to establish Steam Navigation along the shores of the Pacific, from Valparaiso to Panama, embracing all the principal ports in Chile, Bolivia, Peru, Ecuador, and the West Coast of New Grenada ; and, in conjunction with Her Majesty's packets in the Atlantic, to promote a more rapid and regular communication with Europe by the Isthmus of Darien.

The undertaking was projected by Mr. Wheelwright, and sanctioned at public meetings of the British and Foreign merchants in Chile and Peru, convened and presided over by Her Majesty's Consuls General, at the express desire of Her Majesty's Government, to consider the best means of establishing a direct communication between England and the Pacific. The statements and calculations of Mr. Wheelwright, exhibiting the most satisfactory pecuniary results, underwent a most minute and searching investigation by committees appointed for the purpose; and, at a subsequent general meeting, they were unanimously approved of.　Mr. Wheelwright has obtained decrees from the Governments of Chile, Bolivia and Peru, securing to him and his assigns the exclusive navigation of the coasts by steam, with all necessary immunities and privileges (including an exemption from port-dues), for the period of ten years. These decrees, and the powers conferred thereby, have become the property of the company.　Her Majesty's Government also, actuated by a sense of the benefits which will be conferred by this undertaking upon British commerce, has consented to grant the company a Royal Charter, by which alone the important objects of the company can be effectually attained.

Although the nominal capital for this undertaking is stated at £250,000, it is calculated that less than one-half of this amount will be sufficient to carry into full effect the operations of the company.

Mr. Wheelwright, now in this country, will return to South America as soon as the necessary arrangements are completed, for the purpose of superintending the company's concerns, in conjunction with such mercantile firms as may be appointed to act under the control of the directors.

W. P. ROBERTSON, Secretary.

London.

Chichester : Printed by William Hayley Mason.

LaVergne, TN USA
01 October 2009
159558LV00002B/14/A